The Foundation of Rome

In affectionate memory of François Jacques,
who might have smiled as he read these pages.

The Foundation of Rome

Augusto Fraschetti

Translated from the Italian by
Marian Hill and Kevin Windle

Edinburgh University Press

© 2002, Gius. Laterza & Figli S.p.a., Roma-Bari. English language edition
published by arrangement with Eulama Literary Agency, Rome. First published
in Italy as *Romolo Il Fondatore*.

© English translation 2005 Marian Hill and Kevin Windle.

Edinburgh University Press Ltd
22 George Square, Edinburgh

Typeset in Stempel Garamond
by Servis Filmsetting Ltd, and
printed and bound in Great Britain by
Antony Rowe Ltd, Chippenham, Wilts

A CIP record for this book is available from the British Library

ISBN 0 7486 2120 2 (hardback)
ISBN 0 7486 2121 0 (paperback)

Contents

Translators' Note

The translation is based on the Laterza edition of *Romolo il Fondatore*, published in 2002. For the English edition, however, the author has replaced the original Epilogue with a completely new version.

Where the author cites classical authors, we have generally used the English translations – and where necessary the Latin or Greek text – given in the well-known Loeb dual-language series.

The translators wish to record their debt to the kindness of Morrell Aston, Roberta Bonalume, Francesca Foppoli, and Margaret Travers, who helped us in many ways. Robert Barnes gave unstintingly of his immense knowledge of ancient history and read our draft in its entirety, contributing many useful suggestions and corrections. He has our deepest gratitude.

Marian Hill, Kevin Windle
Canberra

Abbreviations

AION ArchStAnt	*Annali dell'Istituto Universitario Orientale di Napoli. Dipartimento di Studi del mondo classico e del Mediterraneo antico. Sezione di archeologia e storia antica.*
AJA	*American Journal of Archeology*
AJPh	*American Journal of Philology*
AncSoc	*Ancient Society*
AnnInst	*Annali dell'Istituto di Corrispondenza archeologica. Roma.*
ANRW	*Aufstieg und Niedergang der römischen Welt*
AntClass	*L'antiquité classique*
ArcClass	*Archeologia classica*
ARID	*Analecta Romana Instituti Danici*
ASNP	*Annali della Scuola Normale di Pisa*
BA	*Bollettino d'Archeologia*
BCAR	*Bollettino della Commissione archeologica comunale in Roma*
BdA	*Bollettino d'Arte del Ministerio dei Beni culturali e ambientali*
CIL	*Corpus Inscriptionum Latinarum*
ContrIstStAnt	*Contributi dell'Istituto di storia antica*
CQ	*Classical Quarterly*
CRAI	*Comptes rendus de l'Académie des Inscriptions et Belles-Lettres*
CTh	*Codex Theodosianus*
DAGR	*Dictionnaire des Antiquités grecques et romaines*
DBI	*Dizionario Biografico degli Italiani*

DdA	Dialoghi d'archeologia
EAA	Enciclopedia dell'arte antica
EMC	Échos du monde classique
FGrHist	Die Fragmente der griechischen Historiker
FIRA	Fontes iuris Romani antejustiniani
G&R	Greece and Rome
HGF	Historicorum Graecorum fragmenta
HRR	Historicorum Romanorum reliquiae
HSCPh	Harvard Studies in Classical Philology
HThR	Harvard Theological Review
I.It	Inscriptiones Italiae
IL	L'information littéraire
ILS	Inscriptiones Latinae selectae
JRS	Journal of Roman Studies
LCM	Liverpool Classical Monthly
LIMC	Lexicon iconographicum mythologiae classicae
LTUR	Lexicon topographicum urbis Romae
MAL	Memorie della classe di scienze morali e storiche dell'Accademia dei Lincei
MDAI(RA)	Mitteilungen des Deutschen Archäologischen Instituts (Röm. Abt.)
MEFR(A)	Mélanges de l'École française de Rome (Antiquité)
MGH	Monumenta Germaniae Historica
MH	Museum Helveticum
NSA	Notizie degli scavi di antichità
OGR	Origo gentis Romanae
OpRom	Opuscula Romana
PdP	La Parola del Passato
PLRE	The Prosopography of the Later Roman Empire, vol. I, ed. by A. H. M. Jones, J. R. Martindale, J. Morris, Cambridge 1971; vol. II, ed. by J. R. Martindale, Cambridge 1972.
ProcCambPhilolSoc	Proceedings of the Cambridge Philological Society
RA	Revue archéologique

RAL	*Rendiconti della classe di scienze morali, storiche e filologiche dell'Accademia dei Lincei*
RBPhH	*Revue belge de philologie et d'histoire*
RE	*Paulys Realencyclopädie der classischen Altertumswissenschaft*
REA	*Revue des études anciennes*
REL	*Revue des études latines*
RFIC	*Rivista di filologia e di istruzione classica*
RG	*Res Gestae*
RhM	*Rheinisches Museum*
RHR	*Revue de l'histoire des religions*
RIASA	*Rivista dell'Istituto Nazionale di archeologia e storia dell'arte*
RIC	*Roman Imperial Coinage*, H. Mattingly, E. A. Sydenham et al. (1923–67)
RIDA	*Revue internationale des droits de l'Antiquité*
RIL	*Rendiconti dell'Istituto Lombardo, Classe di Lettere, Scienze morali e storiche*
RPAA	*Rendiconti della Pontificia Accademia di Archeologia*
RPh	*Revue de philologie, de littérature et d'histoire anciennes*
SCO	*Studi classici e orientali*
SDHI	*Studia et documenta historiae et iuris*
SE	*Studi etruschi*
SMSR	*Studi e materiali di storia delle religioni*
StMisc	*Studi miscellanei*
StRom	*Studi romani*
StStor	*Studi storici*
TAPhA	*Transactions and Proceedings of the American Philological Association*
ThLL	*Thesaurus linguae Latinae*

Preface

This book is not a work of ancient history. Instead it aims to deal with the historical anthropology of the ancient world. As will be seen, the writer is not greatly concerned with the question of whether a figure named Romulus really existed or founded a city called Rome in the mid-eighth century BC. The problem is different and more complex. It lies essentially in the way the Romans of the historical period represented their founder, his miraculous birth, with his twin, the founding of the city, his joint reign with the Sabine Titus Tatius, his mode of government and his wars, right up to his disappearance, whether by ascent into heaven as a god, or by macabre dismemberment by the senators, after being transformed from good king into 'tyrant'.

Plutarch, in the introduction to his *Life of Theseus* (1.2–3), and later the *Life of Romulus*, had already sounded a warning:

> Now that I have traversed those periods of time which are accessible to probable reasoning and which afford basis for a history dealing with facts, I might well say of the earlier periods: 'What lies beyond is full of marvels and unreality, a land of poets and fabulists, where there is neither credibility nor certainty.'

And yet, if Plutarch's stated aim was 'credibility' and 'certainty', my aim here is clearly and necessarily different. It is to review the various stages of the life of Romulus, with emphasis on their 'function' in the story of the founding of Rome; to try and understand the representation of Romulus 'the founder' in the context of varied and stratified traditions, his representation as founder not only of the city and its institutions in the archaic period, but also, in longer perspective, of some of the most important institutions of the republican period, such as the management of the auspices.

For this reason I have tried to follow the 'segments' of the founder's life – notwithstanding the normal division of the book into chapters – in a coherent way, and not, as has often happened, in a 'fragmented' way, so that through it one may see the unmistakable individuality that the Romans of the following epoch projected onto Romulus, a character who was at least ambiguous, frequently accused of the hideous crime of fratricide, but who was, at the same time, a true 'civilising hero'. In his 'civilising hero' characteristics, which arise from a world in the state 'of nature', lie all the ambiguities of this character, who was destined to become, according to Ennius, the one who led the Romans into the 'territories of light'.

The research set forth in this volume was presented for the first time in the academic year 1999–2000, when, as 'professeur associé', I gave four seminars on this subject in Group V of the École pratique des Hautes Études. I am delighted to thank first of all John Scheid, not only for that invitation but also for his frequently illuminating contributions following my presentations. My friends A. Giardina, D. Palombi, Y. Thomas, and F. Zevi have read this book and given me valuable suggestions: to them I am grateful.

CHAPTER I

The twins

I. THE VESTAL AND THE SHE-WOLF

Since at least the last decades of the third century BC (from the time of the chronicler Fabius Pictor, who seems, however, to follow earlier accounts) the sole common component in the legends about the birth of the twins Romulus and Remus is that they were sons of a Vestal Virgin called Rhea Silvia.[1] These legends were not confined to the Romans, but were also widespread in the Greek world. However, many other stories were in circulation. Some of the earliest had maintained that Romulus and Remus were sons of Aeneas or of a daughter of Aeneas. But since according to legend several centuries separated Aeneas' arrival in Italy after the destruction of Troy (about 1184 to 1183 BC according to the accepted version) and the canonical date of the foundation of Rome (754 to 753 BC, according to the chronology established by Varro, though with some significant variations in the view of other historians), this version was quickly abandoned. The important exception was Sallust, who in the second half of the first century BC still held that Aeneas was the founder of the city. Earlier the historian Callias of Syracuse, in about the middle of the fourth century BC, had told how Rhome, a Trojan woman who had come to Italy, had married the king of the Latins and borne him three sons: Rhomos, Romulus and Telegonus. Others said that Romulus was the son – apparently the only son – of Aemilia, the daughter of Aeneas and Lavinia. This daughter of the hero of Troy had married Mars.[2]

Leaving aside other more obscure genealogies, the tradition which came to be unanimously accepted held that when the perfidious Amulius had seized the throne of Alba Longa from his good brother Numitor he had not only had Numitor's only son killed in a simulated hunting accident, but had also consigned his only daughter Rhea to the Vestal order, so that her virginity should be preserved as that order required, and she should bear no sons.[3] At this point the accounts begin to diverge. In one legend – the most widespread – Rhea Silvia once went to the sacred grove of Mars to fetch water for purposes related to the cult of her goddess. The god Mars appeared unexpectedly before her and violated her, promising that in return she would bear two sons who would become – as the Greek historian Dionysius of Halicarnassus wrote in the time of Augustus – 'by far the greatest of men in their valour and achievements'.[4] According to a much less widespread tradition, the twins were the product of a female slave of Tarchetius, king of the Albans, and a male organ which miraculously appeared in the hearth of her house. When Tarchetius sought the advice of an oracle in Etruria, he received the reply that if a virgin coupled with this phallus a child would result who would be distinguished by his strength and bravery. On learning this, the king wanted his daughter to undergo this copulation, but the girl was frightened and sent a slave girl to take her place, and the girl bore the twins.

It was not difficult to show that this story of the conception of Romulus and Remus by a slave girl and a male organ which had miraculously materialised in the hearth of King Tarchetius of Alba was modelled on a legend concerning the birth of the good king Servius Tullius, the sixth successor of Romulus, conceived according to legend in very similar manner in the house of the king Tarquinius Priscus.[5] However, to return to the tradition which is almost equally well known, when Amulius learned that the girl was pregnant, he put her under strict supervision and when the twins were born he had her locked up in a dark dungeon and ordered some of his shepherds to throw the twins into the Tiber to drown.[6]

However, when the king's shepherds reached the Tiber they found it in flood and could not reach the bank, so they laid the basket with the babies in it in a pool at the edge of the river, confident that the infants would still drown. The spot where they laid the basket was close to the place where in the historical period an ancient fig-tree, the Ficus Ruminalis, stood, on the slopes of the Palatine Hill. Here in 296 BC the plebeian aediles Gnaeus and

Quintus Ogulnius dedicated in the Comitium of the Forum a statue commemorating the event, showing a she-wolf suckling them on its teats (*rumae*).[7] It was a she-wolf coming down from the surrounding hills to seek water that noticed their cries and approached the basket. Miraculously it did not harm the children but carried them into a cave to feed them. The cave later received the name of 'Lupercal'. While feeding them the wolf was seen by one of the king's herdsmen, whose name was Faustulus, who took the twins to his hut where his wife Acca Larentia could suckle them. She was very glad to be able to care for them, as she had only just lost her own new-born baby. According to a rationalist interpretation, however, the 'wolf' was actually Acca Larentia herself (Latin *lupa* having the meaning 'prostitute'), as she was in the habit of selling her body to the shepherds of the district.[8]

In his *Parallel Lives* Plutarch added a *Life of Theseus* to his *Life of Romulus*. While Romulus had founded Rome, Theseus, who had overcome the Minotaur and freed Athens from the burden of sending its young men and girls as tribute to Crete, had also brought about the unification of Attica and Athens by collecting all the inhabitants in a single city, Athens. Like Romulus, Theseus has the salient features of a 'founding hero': he not only fights brigands and marauders, he also establishes political institutions, cults and religious ceremonies and feast-days. Like Romulus, to the end of his days Theseus maintains privileged relations with the world of young men, beginning with those whose company he kept on his way to Crete.[9]

And yet, in the matter of babies exposed in wild and inaccessible places, the most striking comparison with the legend of the Roman twins is perhaps the story of another abandoned 'founding hero', in this case not the founder of a city but of an empire, Cyrus the Great of Persia. His grandfather Astyages, king of Media, had a daughter called Mandane. After having a dream about his daughter's offspring, who, according to the interpretation he was given, would present a danger to his throne, he gave her in marriage not to a Median but to a Persian, when the Persians were under the domination of the Medes. Troubled by another dream about his daughter's offspring, Astyages ordered his daughter to come to him when she was about to give birth, and when the child was born instructed his kinsman Harpagus to kill the child.

Harpagus, however, did not readily take orders from anyone and entrusted the child to his herdsman Mitradates, who, as Harpagus knew, according to Herodotus, 'grazed his flocks on the hills . . . where there were many wild animals'. Returning home with the child, the herdsman found his wife deep in sorrow (her name was the Persian equivalent of 'Bitch'): like Acca Larentia, she had just lost her own new-born child. She begged her husband not to expose Cyrus, and said she herself would raise him and care for him. In his place, in the mountains, they laid out their own son, dressed in Cyrus' clothes. A few days later Mitradates returned to Harpagus in the city and assured him that he had carried out his orders, and Harpagus ordered his most trusted guards to verify that the baby was indeed dead. The guards saw the body of the son of 'Bitch', dressed like Cyrus, and committed the body to burial. When Cyrus grew up he learned at last, after many adventures, that he was not the child of the herdsman's son and of 'Bitch', but of Mandane, the daughter of Astyages, the grandfather who had ordered that he be put to death. Thereupon, with all the Persian people behind him, he made war on Astyages, defeated him, subjugated the Medes and established the empire of the Persians in Asia.[10]

Beginning with the story of Moses, legends of 'founding heroes' abandoned and miraculously rescued are very common. The story of Cyrus, however, may well be compared with the legend of the Roman twins, on the basis of two narrative components: the child being suckled by a woman named 'Bitch' (according to the historian Pompeius Trogus, Cyrus was suckled not by a woman with this name but by a real bitch), and the defeat of a kinsman who is then stripped of his throne (Astyages in the case of the infant grandchild; Amulius in the case of Romulus and Remus, who restored the crown usurped from their grandfather Numitor). To the Persians the bitch was a sacred animal which played an important role in the Mithraic cult. The same may be said of the wolf, male or female, in ancient Italy, beginning with the Hirpi Sorani on Mount Soracte near Rome. We may add that in the historical era wolves always seem to have been animals particularly close to Mars, probably because of the suckling of his twin sons by a wolf.[11]

Yet if Theseus and Cyrus could be seen as 'founding heroes', neither of them has a twin brother. We are dealing here with a

4

defining characteristic of the Roman legend, and a broad range of explanations has been posited to account for the phenomenon of twinship. Of late Timothy Peter Wiseman has had no difficulty in criticising in turn the notion of twins as primordial creators of cosmic order; the 'Indo-European' idea, stemming primarily from the work of Georges Dumézil, of 'heavenly twins'; and hypotheses more loosely connected with comparative cultural studies. Wiseman himself has energetically emphasised the highly specific nature of the Roman legend.[12] As for the political interpretations – above all that of Barthold Georg Niebuhr, who favoured a binary structure as the basis of the Roman state from its very beginnings (Latin and Sabine, patrician and plebeian); or that of Theodor Mommsen, who saw the twins as the archetype of the collegiality of magistrates in the republican period; or that of Jérôme Carcopino, in whose view the twins symbolised the alliance between Rome and Capua from 328 BC – one fundamental and inescapable difficulty stands out. The tragic death of Remus at the moment of the foundation of Rome, by the hand of Romulus or a servant of his named Celer, casts much doubt on a pacific or 'irenic' interpretation of their 'twinship' (such as must have been present, if only implicitly, in the views of Mommsen and Carcopino), since one of the brothers dominated the other to the extent that he killed him or caused his death. As for Niebuhr's theory of an originally binary structure of the Roman state, although this has been taken up lately in various ways in connection with the final phase of the struggle between the patrician and plebeian orders, primarily over the plebeians' access to the priesthood, it seems unlikely that the legend of the murder of one of the twins could have been modelled or remodelled on the existing dichotomy between the patricians and the plebeians (in this case, by people of the patrician milieu). One has only to think of the wretched death of Remus, which is certainly not compatible with the triumph of complete access to the magistracy and priesthood for the plebeians and their ultimate admission in 300 BC to the pontificate and the college of augurs.[13]

This simple statement will shape the present study, replacing a purely political line of investigation with one of political anthropology, which may be more complex, but also potentially more fruitful. We presuppose that the more important and unusual elements of the legend which became the canonical one of the foundation of Rome, from the birth of the twins to the disappearance of Romulus, had their own value in the cultural memory of the Roman people. Indeed, to use the terminology employed by Jan Assmann in another context, Romulus and Remus must be regarded, to all intents and purposes, as 'figures of memory' (*Erinnerungsfiguren*) through whom Romans of a later era contrived to establish a definite interpretation and a consistent representation of their past, in this case of their most distant past.[14] Replacing the concept of tradition or traditions, at least in certain circumstances, with that of cultural memory will also allow us to evade a danger which would otherwise be difficult to escape: the danger of having another discussion about the date of origin of the legend of the twins, a date which we have seen fluctuate wildly between the archaic age and the end of the fourth century BC. As has recently been argued, 'the Roman foundation legend provides evidence, first and foremost, of how the Romans of later times chose to see themselves, and how they wished to be seen by others'.[15] In other words it offers vital indications about the cast of mind which governed its development, with the obvious caveat that the literary tradition, like a monument, also has its own stratification, sometimes just as complicated or even more so. Thus it should not surprise us if the *lupa* or she-wolf, totem animal and sacred to Mars, which nourished the twins, is later replaced in rationalist thinking (as we have seen) by a human *lupa*, prosaically interpreted as 'prostitute'.

In a legend of this kind, however, we are dealing with the transmission of a shared patrimony of knowledge, which, in order to be handed down from one generation to the next, needed the means and instruments which would enable it in oral form to bridge the span of time between the moment of its creation – clearly much earlier – and that moment when it was set down in a historical context in the last decades of the third century BC.[16] Regarding the oral transmission of the story of the Roman twins, besides the *carmina convivalia* (the songs which Roman noblemen sang at their banquets, first referred to by Barthold Georg Niebuhr),[17] much attention has quite properly been devoted to the *ludi scaenici*, the performances accompanying the most important Roman festivals (in particular the Liberalia in March, the Cerealia in April, the *ludi Romani* in September, and the *ludi plebei* in November), as occasions when the life of the twins might have been acted out.[18] It is highly unlikely, however, as we shall see, that the conflict between Romulus and Remus over the auspices of the founding should be traced back solely to the years of the plebeian struggle for admission to the pontificate and college of augurs before 300 BC, just as it can be no more than a hypothesis that the death of Remus might have been 'invented' by the patricians after that date during the *ludi Romani*, since if a twin existed he had to be eliminated, and eliminated in a sort of 'founding sacrifice'. A hypothesis such as this – besides presupposing a rather too 'mechanical' connection between the public and the 'commissioning' of art-works – would also restrict the birth of this legend to a very limited time-span, placing its origin entirely in the last decade of the fourth century BC.[19]

If we now turn to some aspects of these problems (above all the need to examine the story of the twins in its entirety, not by isolating segments of it but rather placing them in relation to the whole, from the twins' birth to the death of Remus, at least), we can see how the legend of the wolf suckling the babies in a cave (apparently the Lupercal) was not only known in Rome but had moved beyond Rome to other localities in Latium. In order to gauge the means and range of transmission of this typically Roman legend, we need to consider the figures depicted on a mirror of Praenestine origin discovered in Bolsena and dated to about 340 BC. On this mirror a she-wolf is feeding two babies in a cave. Above them, beside a tree, a woman can be seen, fully dressed, and a young man reclining, naked except for a distinctive wide-brimmed hat. Higher up, in the branches of the tree, are a woodpecker and an owl. On the left is a naked man carrying a stick and with an animal skin hung loosely over his shoulders, and on the right is a man wearing a tunic with a lance in his hand. Beneath this scene is what seems from all appearances to be a lion.

It may or may not surprise us that there is a woodpecker taking care of the children in addition to the she-wolf, but as to the identification of the other figures various suggestions have been put forward. The naked man in the hat has been variously identified as a protective spirit, Mercury or Faustulus;[20] the woman as Rhea

Silvia, Carmenta, Acca Larentia, or even Lara-Tacita, the mother of the Lares;[21] the naked man carrying the stick as Faunus, a *lupercus*, or Pan;[22] the bearer of the lance as Faustulus, Tiberinus or the god Quirinus.[23] Of course, if the proposed equation of the twins with the Lares is accepted (in particular the Lares Praestites),[24] this will reinforce the equation of the woman with Lara, as she was the mother of the Lares. This suggestion, however, significant and innovative though it may be, must unfortunately be dismissed. According to Ovid's account in the Augustan period, the ravishing of Lara by Mercury in the depths of a wood – Jupiter had charged him with escorting the nymph Lara to the *manes*, gods noted for their silence, and Lara had told Juno of Jupiter's infatuation with Juturna – resulted not in the birth of the Lares Praestites but of the Lares Compitales. These watched over the crossroads of Rome and would become in the Augustan era the Lares Augusti, the Lares of the emperor and his family.[25] In reality the apparently calm woman, fully dressed, veiled and with a fan in her hand, cannot easily be identified with the nymph who was perhaps too talkative but who nonetheless received severe punishment: Jupiter is said to have pulled out her tongue and Mercury to have violated her. As for the presence of the god Quirinus, this too is simply impossible since Quirinus could have been venerated, and therefore could have 'existed' as a god in Rome, as we shall see, but only after the miraculous ascension of Romulus from Goat's Marsh into heaven and his subsequent identification with that particular deity; or in any case after the arrival in Rome of the Sabine king Titus Tatius, who had an altar built to Quirinus.[26]

For our part, keeping things simpler, we shall identify the woman with Rhea Silvia and the man in the hat may perhaps be identified with the 'demon' (in this case a demon of the forest) who, according to the historian Dionysius of Halicarnassus in the Augustan age, 'joining now with human beings and now with gods, gave rise, it is said, to the fabled race of heroes'. Here it seems that we are at a stage in the life of the legend in which the god Mars was not yet intervening in any direct way.[27] The naked man with the stick has much in common with later representations of the god Pan, and his presence in a wood conforms well to the characteristics of this particular deity. In addition, he was the god to whom was dedicated the wood where the cave lay in which the she-wolf fed the twins, according to Dionysius of Halicarnassus.[28] The man pointing to the babies being suckled by the wolf may, in spite of his lance, be compatible with the figure of Faustulus, looking on in amazement at the scene.

However, over and above all the problems of precise identification, the composition of the picture with its balance of 'nature' and 'culture' – as Claude Lévi-Strauss would certainly have noted – is striking: beneath the woodpecker and the owl in the branches of the tree, a fully dressed woman is contrasted with a naked man in a hat; a naked shepherd with a stick is placed in front of a fully dressed man with a lance; the children being suckled by the wolf are naturally also naked. The Praenestine mirror also captures very well the interstitial nature of the Roman twins, poised delicately (as we shall have occasion to emphasise again and again) between 'nature' and 'culture'. The sons born to a Vestal who has been violated by a god or a 'demon' in a grove dedicated to Mars are miraculously suckled by a wolf, with the help of a woodpecker, rescued by a shepherd and raised by his wife Acca Larentia, who herself quickly acquires truly mythical status.[29] But before taking further the story of the youth of the twins, the restoration of their grandfather Numitor to his throne and the founding of Rome, to clarify some features of Romulus and Remus – such as the way they are constantly poised in their youth between 'nature' and 'culture' – it is essential to look more closely at the detail of their genealogy by reviewing their ancestry.

2. GRANDPARENTS AND ANCESTORS

This legend of Rhea Silvia conceiving the twins in a wood allows us to clarify some essential attributes of the kings of Alba Longa from whom the twins were descended. They constituted the dynasty of the Silvi, the 'men of the forests' (a highly artificial dynasty, as has often been stressed),[30] and these kings claimed as their ancestors mythical figures who were themselves delicately poised between the divine, the animal and the human. In fact, classical historiography tended to represent the earliest history of Latium, before the foundation of Rome, in typically Greek terms of homeland and colony (*metropolis* and *apoikia*). As Syracuse, for example, was a colony of the Dorians with Archias as its founder, and was in its turn a metropolis in relation to Acrae, Casmena and Camerinum, so Lavinium, a mixed colony of Trojans and natives, founded by Aeneas, was said to have produced Alba, a colony of Lavinium, founded by Ascanius; Rome, in its turn, originally a colony of the Albani, founded by Romulus, was said to have sprung from Alba. This interpretative model, the dominant model in classical historiography, although internally diversified by varying nuances, in what concerns Lavinium and Alba could be seen not only in an elaborate and stratified heritage of legend, but also in connections of a predominantly sacred nature, which still operated in the historical period and which at this level joined Rome indissolubly with the two oldest centres in Latium.[31]

Angelo Brelich, examining the first Latin kings and forebears of Romulus and Remus in a study which constitutes the sole truly comprehensive piece of research on the subject, emphasises their role as 'founding heroes'. In his view the role of the first kings of Latium was precisely this, to found cities and cults, establish laws and civic customs, and introduce agriculture. The genealogy taken by Brelich as pivotal to his research (Saturnus, Picus, Faunus and Latinus) corresponds substantially to that adopted by Virgil. Furthermore, taking Virgil's genealogy as his point of departure, Brelich could not help almost inadvertently introducing the myth of 'Saturnia regna', and working it into his own thematic scheme, while holding all the 'primitive' and 'wild' features of these kings to be of lesser consequence or, consistent with the nature of 'civilising heroes', necessarily located in 'pre-civilised conditions'.[32] Thus, concerning very early Latium before the birth of Lavinium and Alba and that of the twins themselves, historical and religious comparativism, through Angelo Brelich, replaces the interpretative model proposed in the Augustan epoch by Dionysius of Halicarnassus, based extremely coherently on the representation of a series of colonies, with a different interpretative model, based on an unbroken series of 'civilising heroes'.

Yet, with regard to the internal coherence of these two 'models', one substantial and inescapable reservation needs to be voiced: if a sequence of 'colonies' is theoretically valid, a sequence of 'civilising heroes' gives rise to almost insurmountable difficulties – arising within the series itself, since each individual should be understood as to all intents and purposes a 'civilising hero' – unless we can separate the different levels and various 'phases of development' and mythical segments in which these 'civilising heroes' played their particular roles. In Italia and earliest Latium, in the view of Angelo Brelich, Saturnus, Picus, Faunus and Latinus intervened constantly, not merely in similar ways but often in totally identical ways, as if the so-called 'stage of civilisation', of which these kings were supposed to be the bearers, was never quite reached.

However, side by side with the 'metropolis–colony' interpretative model proposed above all by Dionysius of Halicarnassus but also adopted by Livy, another representation must have existed, of which our documentation preserves no more than scant traces, although these traces were destined to emerge in highly significant ways. Indeed, in the documents which have come down to us, this latter representation appears in various combinations with the former or, rather, it has left within the former a series of 'intrusions' and clues which it is difficult to connect with the patterns and structures of Greek colonisation, and more generally with the world of the city, or at least with the world organised into cities as later represented by the Romans in the historical period.

The earliest evidence concerning the forebears of Romulus and Remus is found in some lines (often wrongly thought to be a later interpolation) of the *Theogony* of Hesiod, who lived at the beginning of the seventh century BC. In these lines mention is made of Agrius and Latinus: 'Circe, daughter of Helios the sun, son of Hyperion, one day bore to the patient Odysseus Agrius and Latinus, who, far away in a hidden part of the holy islands, ruled, excellent and strong, over all the illustrious Tyrrhenians.' Most discussion of these lines has centred on Agrius, the brother of Latinus, and whether Agrius, 'the Wild', 'the Untamed', is to be equated with 'Silvius', the founder of the Alban dynasty of the Silvi, and thus with the ancestor of Numitor, the grandfather of the twins, or directly with the god Faunus. Any attempt at a specific 'identification' for Agrius is sure to remain extremely problematic. Nevertheless the evidence of these lines from Hesiod remains fundamental: they correspond well, as Santo Mazzarino has noted, to 'the primitive nature of a Latin culture which may be defined as "woodland"'.[33]

The very name Agrius, 'the Wild', 'the Untamed', bears clear traces of this nature. As for Picus (the woodpecker), the father of Faunus and grandfather of Latinus, he is a bird-king who lives in the forests, so much a denizen of the forest world that his palace, later inherited by Latinus and described by Virgil as very grand, cannot fail to inspire fear thanks to the forests which surround it.[34] It is no surprise, then, that it is a woodpecker that is perched above the twins while they are suckled by the wolf on the Praenestine mirror from Bolsena, or that according to Plutarch it was again a woodpecker which helped the wolf feed and watch over them. Faunus, son of Picus, who lives in the forest (*silvicola*), may be defined as 'half-man, half-goat' (*semicaper*). In the historical period he is the god not only of agricultural land, but also of the untamed wilderness, that is, of those areas defined and characterised by being the antithesis of urban space, of that space which is, as we shall see, ritually defined. Latinus, the most 'human' of these kings – or at least the one who had shed all animal characteristics – either inhabits Picus' palace surrounded by forests which inspire fear or, still following Virgil, in striking but typically contradictory fashion, discovers a laurel tree when he founds the fortress of his city, and calls the inhabitants the Laurentes after it.[35]

As for Faunus, one of his highly typical talents may be observed. According to Varro, Faunus, with Fauna, was wont to foretell the future, speaking from the heart of a forest in Saturnian verses. Dionysius of Halicarnassus gives a much more alarming description of his prophetic powers on the eve of the decisive battle between the Romans and the exiled adherents of the Tarquins, supported by the Veientes and the people of Fidenae:

> The Romans attribute to this deity panic and all the
> apparitions which, when they appear to humans in one guise
> or another, inspire terror, or – they say – that the voices
> which disturb their ears are the work of this god. In the case
> in question, however, Faunus is said to have given heart to the
> Romans, and the consul Valerius, encouraged by his voice,

attacked the enemy camp and captured it (the 'voice' issuing from the Arsian forest was attributed by Livy to Silvanus, the counterpart, as is well known, of Faunus). Plutarch attributes similar powers not only to Faunus, but also to his father Picus, in a highly significant passage of his *Life of Numa*. The good king resorts to a stratagem to bring the two together on the Aventine Hill, which was not yet part of the city and was uninhabited. After Picus and Faunus had assumed numerous terrifying guises and found themselves unable to flee, they not only gave Numa many prophecies but also taught him the art of expiating thunderbolts.[36]

Virgil relates in detail how one addressed the 'oracles of Faunus' and consulted 'the groves beneath high Albumea, mightiest of forests': the priestess bears gifts, lies down on the skins of sacrificed animals, 'woos slumber, . . . sees many phantoms flitting with the gods in wondrous wise, hears many voices, holds converse with the gods, and speaks with Acheron in lowest Avernus'. We are in the presence of an incubation oracle, as Servius, the commentator on Virgil, properly underlined in another context. The *Fauni* were also known as *Fatui*, or fools, 'quod per stuporem divina pronuntiant' (because they pronounce divine things in a state of stupor). Above all, still according to Servius, Faunus received his own name 'from the voice' (*apo tes phones*) 'because he foretells the future through his voice, not through signs'.[37]

'Through his voice, not through signs': this indicates a fundamental distinction regarding the possibility the Romans had of knowing their future, emphasised by Theodor Mommsen when he briefly made the point that 'true oracles, as is well known, are alien to the primitive Roman faith and were never able to establish themselves firmly'. Mommsen underscored instead the intervention of Jupiter Optimus Maximus in human actions through *auguria*, whether these were *impetrativa* (in the sense of being a response to a specific request addressed to him by the magistrates) or *oblativa* (in the sense that they occurred in random fashion). Having taken the auspices within a ritually consecrated *templum*, the magistrate would proceed to the *spectio*, the observation of signs sent by the gods, and thence to the interpretation of these.[38]

If Faunus and, according to Plutarch, his father Picus foretold the future from the depths of the forests by means of voices which inspired terror, from this perspective too their practices can be seen to be quite opposite to those of the king-augurs of the monarchic period starting – as we shall see – with Romulus, and to those of the magistrates of the republican era, who required the gods to show themselves by sending signs and doing this within the confines of enclosed spaces designated by ritual.

Not even the arrival of Aeneas in Italy could break the links between this archaic form of kingship and the forest world, from which Faunus raised his prophetic voice: the Alban dynasty of the Silvi also had connections with this world, beginning with their name. According to Livy, the founder of the dynasty was given this name because Ascanius, the son of Aeneas, was 'born by some accident in the forest'; according to Dionysius, however, it was because Ascanius' half-brother was born to Lavinia, after the death of Aeneas, in a wood to which she had withdrawn for fear of Ascanius, her stepson. At this point we can understand why the twins Romulus and Remus, also sons of a Silvia and also conceived – as we have seen – in a wood, loved the forests during their adolescence and are irresistibly drawn to them: although reared in a world of shepherds, like the first Silvius, according to Livy they could not remain 'in the cowsheds or close to the flocks' but 'roamed and hunted in the mountain regions'.[39]

In a context such as this, and in the attempt to clarify the ways of the twins before the foundation of Rome, it is necessary to emphasise the great importance which the forests retained to a late date in the collective mind of the Romans: in Rome the forest world was perceived as the antithesis of the 'civilised' world: not only of the shaped and ritually delimited space of the city, but also of the domesticated or at least controllable space of cultivated land.[40] If the earliest history of Latium before the foundation of Rome could be depicted not only by Dionysius of Halicarnassus but also by Livy in terms of a typically Greek relationship (metropolis–colony: Rome as a colony of Alba, Alba in turn as a colony of Lavinium), we may note how this interpretative model, destined to become the dominant one, never succeeded in completely erasing traces which harked back in their entirety to a world of woodland and forest, a world of 'nature'.

Picus, Faunus and Latinus are in effect kings of the Aborigines, the original inhabitants of Latium. To Sallust, who describes their way of life, this was a 'race of rustic folk, without laws, without government, free and independent', whose characteristic features could be contrasted with those of Aeneas' more 'advanced' Trojans, when the two peoples met on his arrival and subsequently fused in one. The Aborigines as an ethnic group were defined on the basis of their indigenous status or their constant roaming (*errare*), whether because they had no permanent home or because they had 'a home in the mountains'. If this mountain-dwelling held connotations of complete wildness, within the framework of a 'harsh primitivism', the etymological investigations set forth above well characterise the way the mode of life of the subjects of Picus, Faunus and Latinus was depicted. They were said to have no fixed abode or were shown as simply inhabitants of the mountains who therefore knew nothing of the world of the city. This tradition was so firmly rooted that it reached down as far as a document of the late antique period, just after the middle of the fourth century AD (the *Chronographer of 354*): the chronographer stressed that the territory ruled by Picus not only possessed no urban centres (*oppida*), it also had no rural settlements (*vici*), and hence no form of organisational structure, urban or rural, at any level. Naturally, according to the same chronicler, the first town (*oppidum*) to appear on the territory of the Aborigines was Lavinium, which was founded by a foreigner, Aeneas the Trojan.[41]

3. AN ADOLESCENCE IN THE BOSOM OF 'NATURE': THE WORLD OF THE *LUPERCI*

Legend has it that the two twins, although descended from a god and the kings of Alba, grew up in poverty, raised with love by Faustulus and Acca Larentia, and grew to be strong and handsome. While, as Dionysius of Halicarnassus and Plutarch relate, a somewhat isolated tradition holds that 'the boys were taken to Gabii', a town in Latium, 'so that they could be educated there in the Greek manner', or in a more general sense 'to learn to read and write and learn all things proper to people of good family',[42] according to the more widespread traditions they became shepherds like their adoptive father Faustulus: they tended their flocks 'mostly in the mountains, in shelters which they built of timber and reeds'. The famous 'hut of Romulus' on the slopes of the Palatine Hill or rather on the Cermalus, one of the hills on which Rome would later rise, is one such shelter. This was a hut from the archaic period, held in a later Roman tradition to be the 'hut of Romulus', which the priests always took the trouble to repair, and religiously maintained until at least the end of the fourth century AD. Extremely generous, as Plutarch repeats, the twins loved 'bodily exercise, hunting, running, driving off robbers, capturing thieves, and rescuing the oppressed from violence'.[43]

One such encounter between the twins and some cattle thieves is related by Ovid in his *Fasti*, in which he describes the festivals of the Roman year. Here he writes of the origins of the Lupercalia, which were celebrated every year in Rome on 15 February (commemorating an episode in the youth of Romulus and Remus, to which we shall return). The festival was celebrated until about AD 500, and so in the historical period this may have been a somewhat alarming spectacle, when groups of young men clad only in loin-cloths ran at full tilt round the lower slopes of the Palatine Hill. Among the various versions of the origins of this most ancient festival (one of them connected to an embarrassing episode involving Hercules, Omphale and Faunus), Ovid reports the following, directly linked to the youth of the twins (*Fasti* II.359–80):

> To foreign reasons, add, my Muse, some Latin ones, and let my steed career in his own dusty course. A she-goat had been sacrificed as usual to hoof-footed Faunus, and a crowd had come by invitation to partake of the scanty repast. While the priests were dressing the inwards, stuck on willow spits, the sun then riding in mid heaven, Romulus and his brother and the shepherd youth were exercising their naked bodies in the sunshine on the plain; they tried in sport the strength of their arms by the gloves and javelins and by hurling ponderous stones. Cried a shepherd from a height, 'O Romulus and Remus, robbers are driving off the bullocks across the pathless lands.' To arm would have been tedious; out went the

brothers in opposite directions; but 'twas Remus who fell in with the freebooters and brought the booty back. On his return he drew the hissing inwards from the spits and said, 'None but the victor shall eat these.' He did as he had said, he and the Fabii together. Thither came Romulus foiled, and saw the empty tables and bare bones. He laughed, and grieved that Remus and the Fabii could have conquered when his own Quintilii could not. The fame of the deed endures: they [the *luperci*] run stripped, and the success of that day enjoys a lasting fame.

This tradition, then, identified the prototypes of the *luperci* – a brotherhood from the archaic period, still active in Rome well into the historical period – with Romulus, Remus and their companions. One day, having sacrificed a kid in honour of Faunus (a familial god to the twins, as we have seen), they were performing physical exercises 'in the nude' while the meat was roasting on the spits. When some thieves appeared and tried to make off with the livestock, the friends formed two groups and set off in hot pursuit. Remus with his companions the Fabii (or Fabiani) recovered the animals, and when they returned they tore the meat, still half-raw, from the spits and devoured it without waiting for the other group. Romulus, when he returned with his Quintilii, could only burst out laughing, as if greatly amused by the sight. For this reason the feast of the Lupercalia was established, commemorating the occasion which the *luperci* of the historical period enacted every year, preserving the memory of it in their rituals.

The rituals in which the *luperci* featured had their origins at the Lupercal, the cave where the she-wolf had suckled the twins. Dionysius of Halicarnassus is the only one to offer us a description of the Lupercal, either as it was presumed to have been originally, or as it was preserved in his own time. It was a cave surrounded by woodland, with springs rising from the rocks. Later the woodland was lost when houses were built. The cave and a spring remained, close to the Palatine Hill, on the road which led to the Circus Maximus. This situation, on the slopes of the Palatine Hill, places the Lupercal on the fringes of Romulus' future 'city'. This was indeed no temple, but a grotto, a cavern, which was said to have been originally dedicated by Evander the

Arcadian many centuries earlier to Pan Lykaios and his cult. Its marginal location with respect to Romulus' future 'city' was given a certain emphasis in the most comprehensive framework in which it was placed: a framework in which 'nature' was dominant, and therefore one which must have been agreed upon in the Augustan age, because Augustus, when he arranged for the refurbishment of the sanctuary, then completely surrounded by buildings, left its essential characteristics intact – the same characteristics which were again thrown into sharp relief in the Augustan age by Dionysius of Halicarnassus.[44]

The legends of the establishment of the sanctuary and the god who was venerated in it, Pan Lykaios and his Latin counterpart Faunus, the ancestor of the twins, lead back to pre-urban times and to a space which is the antithesis of the city in the historical period. In fact, in the historical period, all discussion of the origins of the festival notwithstanding (it was clearly of great antiquity), the Lupercalia could have been conceived, and were indeed shown as belonging, under the sign of Faunus, a deity who presided, in Georges Dumézil's elegant definition, over 'the nearby woodland, the countryside itself, considered not in the outlines of the farms which exploit it but as a whole, as a world to itself with its own surprises, its terrors, its rutting odors, its hidden forces of fertility'.[45] The rituals performed by the *luperci* at the Lupercal are described by Plutarch:

> The priests slaughter the goats, and then, after two youths of noble birth have been brought to them, some of them touch their foreheads with a bloody knife, and others wipe the stain off at once with wool dipped in milk. The youths must laugh after their foreheads are wiped.

The way in which the two boys are presented and the actions performed are clearly to be seen as an initiation rite, in which the pair stand for the two groups of *luperci*, the Fabiani and the Quintilii, just as their laugh was supposed to 'commemorate' the laughter of Romulus on seeing that Remus and his companions had already devoured all the meat. After these preliminary rites, under the sign of Faunus and in imitation of their god, the *luperci* would set out on their headlong naked run round the Palatine Hill. But here it was as if they were transformed into *creppi*, or 'he-goats', from the 'crepitio' (crackle) of the goatskin they clutched in their hands, taken from the freshly sacrificed goats. Their transformation was assisted most effectively by the strips of skin from the sacrificed beast, which they wore round their waists, and the thongs they held in their hands.[46]

The iconographic documentation in our possession shows the *luperci* wearing loin-cloths. In what sense, then, could they be described in Latin as *nudi* and in Greek as *gymnoi*? The contradiction is actually more apparent than real. The *luperci* were *nudi* not in the sense of being completely naked or not covered by a loin-cloth. In Latin they could be described in this way in a figurative sense, meaning that they did not have togas, and in Rome the toga was the quintessential urban garment. It was the dress that citizens had to wear in the city as a mark of their status, and which, precisely because it was city dress, was strictly prohibited not only to outsiders but also to Roman exiles. In effect the *luperci* were shown *nudi* in the same way as the good Cincinnatus (in a well-known story) tills his four *iugera* of land beyond the Tiber and welcomes *nudus* the envoys from the senate, who invite him to don the toga 'to listen to the Senate's instructions wearing the toga'.[47] It would be absurd to imagine the virtuous Cincinnatus (who, we understand, was also very bashful) working his land completely naked, since we are dealing here with a typical feature of the representation of 'nudity', more particularly, the 'civic' nudity of a citizen. This representation, with regard to the *luperci*, might be further illustrated by the scene in which Romulus and Remus perform their physical exercises in the open and then set off naked in pursuit of the cattle thieves, or by combining 'nudity' with other modes of behaviour banned to Roman citizens, or at best regarded as unbecoming.

With regard to the race itself – which is associated with the *luperci* along with the 'nudity' – it is above all Georges Dumézil who must be credited with showing at a more general level the contrast which existed in Rome 'between the mystique of *celeritas* and the morality of *gravitas*'.[48] While the essential contrast encapsulated here by Dumézil was exemplified in the figures of Romulus and Numa, from our point of view it is important to emphasise how even at the height of the historical period the race

– the same race which in Ovid lay at the basis of the 'nudity' of the *luperci* – was ill suited to the standing of a free man, and hence to that of a citizen of Rome. We have here a fragment of the history of a mentality, a fragment which is in many ways characteristic and verifiable over a very long period. In Plautus' *Poenulus* one of the *advocati* replies to Agorastocles, who calls to them to hurry up: 'it is more fitting that free men should walk with short steps in the city; I think that to hurry and run is typical of the slave'. From the same perspective, and emphasising the continuity of this core element, one might draw attention to a view expressed by the good emperor Severus Alexandrus (AD 222–35), who, according to *Historia Augusta*, as late as the first half of the third century always had only slaves as outriders. He explained this by saying that 'a free man should not run except in sacred contests'.[49]

In keeping with their style of life and modes of behaviour, the *luperci*, as we have seen, did not enter the 'city' of Romulus, the 'antiquum oppidum' of the Palatine: they only skirted it, remaining on the periphery. This ritual exclusion by a perimeter which is also ritual, like the pomerium laid down later, as we shall see, by Romulus, conforms well to the age group to which the *luperci* belonged.[50] As Valerius Maximus said, 'twice a year the young people of the equestrian order thronged Rome with crowds': first, at the feast of the Lupercalia, initiated by Romulus and Remus, when the crowd celebrated naked in an atmosphere of disorderly jollity, which imitated – so Valerius Maximus has it – the *hilaritas* and disorderly delight of the twins on receiving the news that their grandfather Numitor had given them permission to found a new city; then on the Ides of July, when, during the 'parade of knights' instituted in 304 BC by Quintus Fabius Maximus Rullianus, the young men of the equestrian order paraded on horseback sedately wearing the *trabea*, a short white toga. In fact the evidence of Valerius Maximus and a group of reliefs collected by Paul Veyne taken together suggest a whole world of young people.[51] Andreas Alföldi and Georges Dumézil have in different ways related this world of young people to a central point within the compass of their historical thinking: the Indo-European *Männerbund*. Other comparisons might also be suggested: restricting ourselves to the classical world with regard to the ritual exclusions which typify initiation rites and more generally rites of passage, we could suggest a comparison, for example, with the Athenian ephebes, termed *peripoloi*, 'those who circle the city', for whom, as Pierre Vidal-Naquet has so aptly shown, peripheral status was not solely topographical.[52] Here, however, apart from isolated comparisons with ritual exclusions in rites of initiation and passage which may be drawn from the most varied ethnographic contexts, the emphasis will be on features peculiar to Rome.

With regard to the *luperci*, the testimony of Cicero must be mentioned at this point. According to Cicero the *luperci* were 'a wild fraternity, entirely pastoral and agrarian', 'a sort of savage fraternity, quite rude and rustic' whose union (significantly termed *coitio*) was established in the forest 'before the time of *humanitas* and laws,' so long before them that the *luperci*, although belonging to the same fraternity, would prosecute one another even while declaring that they belonged to the same community.[53] The community of the *luperci*, then, was a somewhat strange one not only to Cicero, in not displaying any internal solidarity or any fraternal bonds, although solidarity and bonds were the norm in Rome and usual in any collegium and any fraternity. Indeed an examination of the individual components which typify the *luperci* shows that their style of life and behaviour must be described as the very opposite of those of the citizens. The *luperci*, young, *nudi*, and participants in a headlong race round the 'antiquum oppidum' of the Palatine Hill, thus place themselves on the side of 'nature', or more precisely, under the sign of Faunus, when re-creating every year a world which, according to Cicero, knew neither *humanitas* nor laws.

This extended consideration of the ancient Lupercalia and the behaviour of the *luperci*, for whom the twins and their two groups of companions were the prototypical models, may help to explain some essential aspects of the passage in Ovid, with which we began. In order to define their modes of behaviour we may note that, after the recovery of the animals, Remus and his Fabii (Fabiani) not only eat the half-raw meat but also deprive Romulus and his companions of that part of the sacrificial flesh to which the ritual would entitle them. Eating half-cooked meat and depriving one's table-companions of their share of the feast are two moderately grave 'sins' which need to be examined separately.

Taking as his starting point the term *exta*, used by Ovid of the flesh of the sacrificial kid that was roasted, Robert Schilling defines Remus' guilt as an act of extreme impiety: having taken nourishment, with his companions, from the parts of the animal due to the gods (the entrails), he incurs the gods' disfavour and those same gods then, at the moment of the foundation, mark him for death. This interpretation of the term *exta* may, however, be countered by a much broader use of the term, to denote not only the entrails but undoubtedly also the flesh of the sacrificial beast. This usage is attested not only in Plautus, highly significantly, but also in Virgil. Moreover, if we take *exta* to include the flesh, we can understand why in Ovid's account Romulus is so disappointed at finding the 'bare bones' on his return, bones which could not have formed part of the entrails, usually classified by the ancients as meaning the liver, lungs, spleen, kidneys and heart.[54] We may add, for later discussion of this interpretation, that in this particular case divine vengeance is visited only upon Remus and not on his companions the Fabiani (Fabii), the ancestors of those Fabii who in the republican age would become one of the most prominent *gentes* and among the most important in the Roman patriciate. The scene in which Remus and his companions eat the goat flesh on their own has been compared with other stories which feature the theft of *exta* from a sacrificial animal, but – with a single exception – without their being recovered or eaten by anybody. These are the well-known stories of a certain Octavius, an ancestor of Augustus of Velitrae, and a nameless Roman soldier at Veii, who suddenly emerges from an underground tunnel, takes from the altar the *exta* of a sacrificial beast, and carries them off to Camillus so that he can complete the sacrifice, so that the prophecy of the Etruscan haruspex could come to pass, the prophecy having stated that victory would go to whoever completed the sacrificial rite. In both cases the theft of the entrails and the completion of the rite ensured superiority and victory to the person responsible for this. The comparison with the fate of Remus is clearly not sustainable here, since Remus is not only inferior to his brother in reading the auspices, but above all is destined to be killed at the very moment when Romulus founds his city.[55]

Nevertheless, what is of much greater interest from our point of view is the fact that at the level of institutions and social practices the prototypical *luperci* seem not only to have no knowledge of the approved way to prepare meat (the way accepted among 'civilised' people),[56] but are also ignorant of the proper distribution of the meat during sacrificial feasts, which can be seen operating in Rome in the archaic period within the limits of the *curiae* established, according to tradition, by Romulus himself. On the site of the future Rome we know of only one feast at which equal sharing was ritually proscribed: that of the Potitii and the Pinarii, the two *gentes* charged with observance of the cult of Hercules at the *ara maxima*. Because the Pinarii arrived late for a feast which they should have prepared jointly with the Potitii, the Pinarii and their descendants were deprived in perpetuity of the right to the *exta*, although in a context such as this, entirely in the 'Greek rite', it is not clear whether *exta* refers only to the entrails or simply to the meat.[57]

4. AT THE CONQUEST OF ALBA

The twins' pastoral life (a carefree one consisting of races, hunting, and physical exercises while being *naked* in the sunshine and open air), however, would come to a fairly abrupt end on their eighteenth birthday. According to Livy a bandit attack took place while they were celebrating – highly significantly – the feast of the Lupercalia. Distracted by this, they were overwhelmed by the bandits, who were 'angry at having lost their booty'. In the ambush Remus was taken prisoner, while Romulus offered more determined resistance. According to Dionysius of Halicarnassus and Plutarch, however, the occasion was a dispute with Numitor's shepherds over pastureland. Such disputes were frequent, but this one attained the proportions of a real battle, in which Numitor's shepherds got the worst of it. Seeking vengeance, they proceeded to ambush the shepherds led by Romulus and Remus. Romulus was not present in the village, another version has it, because he had gone to Caenina, close to Rome, to offer 'sacrifices for the community according to the custom of the country' with 'the chief men of the village'. Remus went forth with his men when he learned of the attack, to take part in the defence. Numitor's shepherds feigned a withdrawal and deceived their opponents, who were incautious enough to advance too far and fall into a trap. They were captured and taken to Alba to be judged by Numitor.[58]

When Romulus learned on his return that his brother was in captivity, he decided to go at once to Alba with his companions. Faustulus, 'seeing that his haste was too frenzied', urged him to take more care.[59] Here is the account of a related event as recounted by Dionysius of Halicarnassus (I 83.1–3), who claimed to follow the chronicler Fabius Pictor. Dionysius tells of the life and adventures of Faustulus after he was taken prisoner when he went to Alba, while the twins, having endured various adventures, were both in the same town:[60]

But Faustulus, suspecting from the king's unaccountable mildness that his intentions were not in harmony with his professions, answered him in this manner: 'The youths are upon the mountains tending their herds, which is their way of life, and I was sent by them to their mother to give her an account of their fortunes; but, hearing that she was in your custody, I was intending to ask your daughter to have me brought to her. And I was bringing the ark with me that I might support my words with a manifest proof. Now, therefore, since you have decided to have the youths brought here, not only am I glad, but I wish you to send such persons with me as you wish. I will point out to them the youths and they shall acquaint them with your commands.' This he said in the desire to discover some means of delaying the death of the youths and at the same time in the hope of making his own escape from the hands of those who were conducting him, as soon as he should arrive upon the mountains. And Amulius speedily sent the most trustworthy of his guards with secret orders to seize and bring before him the persons whom the swineherd should point out to them. Having done this, he at once determined to summon his brother and keep him under mild guard till he had ordered the present business to his satisfaction, and he sent for him as if for some other purpose; but the messenger who was sent, yielding both to his good-will toward the man in danger and to compassion for his fate, informed Numitor of the design of Amulius. And Numitor, having revealed to the youths the danger that

24

threatened them and exhorted them to show themselves brave men, came to the palace with a considerable band of his retainers and friends and loyal servants. These were joined by the countrymen who had entered the city earlier and now came from the market-place with swords concealed under their clothes, a sturdy company. And having by a concerted attack forced the entrance, which was defended by only a few heavy-armed troops, they easily slew Amulius and afterwards made themselves masters of the citadel.

After the death of Amulius the twins restored to Numitor the throne usurped from him and naturally freed their mother from the dark dungeon in which she had languished for eighteen years. Then they took with them numerous companions from among the young herdsmen, as well as some members of the old families of Alba who claimed descent from the Trojans who were with Aeneas in Latium, and – with the permission of Numitor – resolved to found a city in the places in which they had been raised.[61]

Before moving on to the story of the foundation of Rome, some details which are of great importance from our point of view need to be clarified. It seems that there was never any urban centre bearing the name of Alba Longa, although there were scattered villages on the Alban hill, each with its own necropolis dating back to cultural *facies* of the Latium I and IIA periods (*c.*1000 to 900 and 930 to 830 BC respectively in the traditional chronology). It is very probable that the importance traditionally ascribed to a 'city' by the name of Alba must derive from the fact that on this hill Jupiter Latiaris (sometimes identified with King Latinus) was worshipped, and in his honour all the people of Latium, includ- ing – in the historical period – the magistrates of Rome, celebrated a most ancient annual festival (the *feriae Latinae*).[62]

Of course, as we have seen, the two twins named Romulus and Remus are 'figures of memory'. Romulus, the founder, was regarded as the eponym of Rome. His name was derived from that of his brother Remus (*Rhomos*, according to many Greek historians), with a diminutive suffix. Leaving aside some recent debate about the possibility of the names having separate origins,[63] emphasis needs to be given to the way the twins were seen as being linked even by name in the representations of the ancients. Thanks to a valuable entry in the encyclopedia of Verrius Flaccus, which has come down to us only through Paulus Diaconus, we learn that Romulus was also known as Altellus: again a diminutive suffix served to make him 'the diminutive other one' – 'other' (*alter*) by reference to his twin.[64]

In spite of being twins, Romulus and Remus were not identical in every respect. Besides the utterly reprehensible behaviour of Remus during the Lupercalia when he disregarded the principle of ritual sharing, a significant point made by Plutarch also helps to distinguish them:

> When they grew up, they were both of them courageous and manly, with spirits which courted apparent danger, and a daring which nothing could terrify. But Romulus seemed to exercise his judgement more, and to have political sagacity, while in his intercourse with their neighbours in matters pertaining to herding and hunting, he gave them the impression that he was born to command rather than to obey.

A significant indication of this is the fact that, according to Plutarch, Romulus was the one, at the moment of the attack on Amulius, who first made intelligent use of *manipulares*, or maniples, dividing his 'large army' into groups of a hundred men, while Remus caused those who were within the city to rise up. It should be added that Romulus seems to have given proof of greater religious devotion than his brother: when word came of the attack by Numitor's shepherds, which would eventually lead to his capture, Remus was content to remain in the village, not hastening to go with Romulus and the other 'chief men' to Caenina to offer 'sacrifices for the community according to the custom of the country', as Dionysius relates and as we have already recorded.[65] These are small hints but close attention must be paid to them when we have in mind later developments in their respective lives.

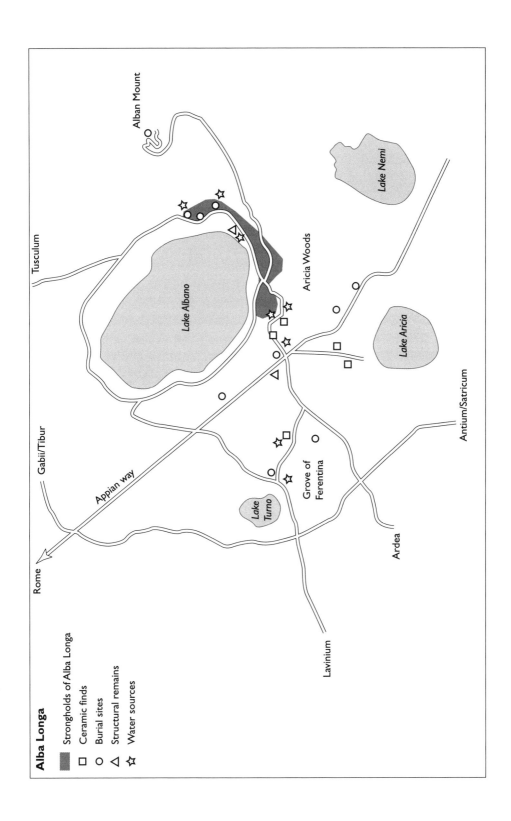

Alba Longa

◼ Strongholds of Alba Longa
☐ Ceramic finds
○ Burial sites
△ Structural remains
☆ Water sources

Tusculum

Gabii/Tibur

Rome

Appian way

Alban Mount

Lake Albano

Lake Nemi

Aricia Woods

Lake Aricia

Lake Turno

Grove of Ferentina

Lavinium

Ardea

Antium/Satricum

CHAPTER 2

The foundation

I. ON THE SITE OF ROME: TAKING THE AUSPICES, AND THE DEATH OF REMUS

According to Dionysius of Halicarnassus, after the restitution of Numitor to the throne of Alba it was Numitor himself who urged the twins to found a new city. He did this primarily in order to be free of that part of the population which he knew to be hostile to him. But perhaps the idea of establishing a new city, as Livy puts it, 'in the place where they had been exposed and brought up' should be attributed primarily to Romulus and Remus themselves, because they had been joined not only by many herdsmen but, as Plutarch adds, by 'slaves and many fugitives', whom the inhabitants of Alba were loath to welcome as true fellow citizens. Plutarch therefore hastens to make clear, with, from his standpoint, flawless logic:

When their city was first founded, they made a sanctuary of refuge for all fugitives, which they called the sanctuary of the God of Asylum. There they received all who came, delivering none up, neither slave to masters, nor debtor to creditors, nor murderer to magistrates, but declaring it to be in obedience to an oracle from Delphi that they made the asylum secure for all men. Therefore the city was soon full of people, for they say that the first houses numbered no more than a thousand.

Plutarch speaks here of a 'first foundation of the city' (*tes poleos ten proten hidrysin*), followed by a true 'synoecism' (*ton synoikismon*), or unification. This 'first foundation' is resolutely ignored by Livy and Dionysius of Halicarnassus (who are aware only of the foundation by Romulus and of the asylum which he

29

established), but for Plutarch Romulus was to be compared with Theseus, who – as we have seen – had brought about the unification of Attica, and Plutarch explains well the idea of a more gradual and phased foundation: a first foundation effected by the twins together, and a second by Romulus alone.[1]

Up to this point, with the exception of the feast *manqué* which is one of the *aitia* for the establishment of the festival of the Lupercalia, relations between Romulus and Remus have seemed nothing short of idyllic and based on the firmest fraternal solidarity. (We recall that Romulus hastened to Alba with his men to snatch his brother from the hands of Amulius.) But when they returned to 'the place where they had been exposed and brought up', some signs of tension began to appear in their relations, with a silent jealousy developing over the question of who was to be the founder and give his name to the new city. Livy attributes this jealousy to 'the curse of their grandsires, the greed of kingly power', the same greed which had led Amulius to depose his brother Numitor. Dionysius of Halicarnassus, on the other hand, attributes it to the division for practical purposes of 'the people into two parts', each led by one of the brothers, reaching the point of open rivalry concerning the site on which the city should be founded: the Palatine being the choice of Romulus, while Remus favoured another hill, which would have borne the name of Remoria.[2]

Wherever the settlement named Remoria was to be situated, the twins resolved, either on the advice of Numitor or on their own initiative, to settle the matter by consulting the gods, who gave their response by displaying auspicious birds. Romulus, according to the best-known traditions, selected the Palatine as his observation point, and Remus the Aventine, or precisely the spot named Remoria. On the Aventine, or at Remoria, Remus first sighted six vultures. Romulus on the Palatine then saw twelve. It was suspected that Romulus had deceived his brother by sending men to him to announce a flight of birds which had in reality not occurred, and that he saw the twelve vultures only after Remus had come to the Palatine to verify the appearance. From this a further dispute arose: should the founder be the one who had first seen the birds, or the one who had seen twice the original number? The quarrel became violent and in the struggle Remus was killed. According to another tradition, which Livy describes as 'the commoner story' (*vulgatior fama*), Remus was killed by the hand of Romulus himself for having mocked his brother by stepping over the wall that Romulus had marked out, or he was killed by Celer, one of Romulus' companions or one supervising the work. In the tussle Faustulus and his brother Pleistinus were also killed.[3]

We shall not linger on the stories – which apparently persisted in later times – of Remus sharing power with his brother for a period, at least, or even outliving him.[4] Here we shall pay more attention to certain highly typical features of this legend, those features related to the auspices and the death of Remus. With regard to the auspices, we should note those of the twins' attributes which we might describe as 'natural'. Without anyone ever having instructed them in the reading of the auspices and the relevant soothsaying skills, both prepare a true *templum* (a ritually defined space) on a preordained high point to receive 'auspicia impetrativa' (the auspices requested from Jupiter Optimus Maximus: Livy said that Romulus climbed the Palatine and Remus the Aventine 'ad inaugurandum templa'). And from these ritually defined spaces they set about observing the signs, just as later, in the historical period, observers would study the omens from the city's two *auguracula* (the one on the Arx and that on the Quirinal). The birds which Romulus sees are in exactly twice the number seen by his brother: this means that Romulus has better auspices, just as in the historical period the senior magistrates (consuls, dictators and praetors) possess 'auspicia maxima' relative to the junior magistrates such as aediles and quaestors, who hold 'auspicia minora'.[5]

We may now return to the *auguratorium* of the Palatine and its possible connections with 'Roma Quadrata' ('Square Rome'), founded by Romulus. With regard to the story of the foundation, it is essential to pause on the death of Remus – a death which even recently seemed to be an enigma and an utterly inexplicable one.[6] To Roman historians and poets of the late republic this was an event of such importance that it determined later developments in the history of the city, in particular the civil wars which so affected the last century of the republic: by killing his brother, Romulus had besmirched himself with such great guilt that it had to be expiated by his fellow-citizens, who, being engaged in combat on opposite fronts, were themselves stained with a brother's blood.[7]

The scene of the killing of Remus is sometimes interpreted by modern historians, however, as a true foundation rite: 'the first sacrificial victim to sanctify with his own blood the defence of the new city', a rite analogous to that described by John Malalas concerning the founding of Alexandria in Egypt or Antioch in Syria, when two virgins were sacrificed. In a more general way, some have seen the murder as a 'kind of offering of first-fruits', 'a precondition for the essential success of Romulus'.[8] We for our part prefer to follow a different path, bearing in mind that while one tradition places the death of Remus after he had stepped over the wall, another directly links his death with the fight which resulted from differences over the question of who was to be the founder.

From the fact that in one tradition Remus could die shortly before Romulus had traced the course of the walls we may deduce one further conclusion. If his death at the moment of stepping over the wall, whoever may have killed him (Romulus himself or the mysterious Celer), was to be seen as providing the basis for the inviolability of the walls of Rome,[9] then the 'purpose', the 'function' of his death must have been to forestall any possibility of his entering the city. If, as we have seen, in the period of their wild youth, spent amidst the forests, the twins enjoyed a life of equality, or if Romulus, known also as Altellus, could even be seen as 'the little Other' with regard to his brother, the two are now more sharply distinguished. Remus appears almost to combine in himself all the 'wild' features of both and is, it seems, compelled to depart the scene: he cannot enter the ordered and regulated world of the city, and is therefore driven out of it by force, whether in the conflict preceding the founding or after his brother has traced out the course of the walls. Being the prototypical *lupercus*, Remus cannot enter the Palatine city, just as every year the *luperci* of the historical period, whose race is kept to the perimeter of the *antiquum oppidum*, according to Varro, are excluded.[10]

Remus, who does not know the ordered and regulated life of the city, cannot understand the 'inaugural' significance of its walls. Not knowing the rituals of the sacrificial feast, he will not know the feasts which will be held in the *curiae* established by his brother. If the foundation of every city, as has been frequently noted, inevitably tends to assume aspects of a cosmogony, Remus, being removed from the creation of this 'new world' by his 'wild' nature, can never know the 'civilised' world, which thanks to Romulus will impel the Romans, as Quintus Ennius said, as far as the 'territories of light'.[11] In fact the attributes which Remus does not shed even after receiving 'lesser' auspices than his brother condemn him to be 'alien' to a new way of life, which will not include clashes with robbers or cattle thieves who make their own laws. If such clashes and such thefts persist, they will be judged first by kings and later by republican magistrates, as we shall see.

To conclude this treatment of the death of Remus we should consider the extremely distinctive features of the version of his death given by Ovid in his *Fasti* on 21 April, the day of the foundation of Rome and thus, at the same time, the day of the death of one of the twins. Noting the unequal taking of the auspices and the founding of the city by Romulus, with some details to which we shall return, Ovid cannot, of course, pass over the killing of Remus in silence. According to the poet, Celer, a kind of superintendent of works, receives an order from Romulus that nobody is to cross the newly traced walls. Remus either does not hear the order or, on purely patriotic grounds, questions the effectiveness of such low walls in protecting the citizens from enemy attack. Then, to make his point, he jumps over them. Seeing this, Celer at once strikes him down with a hoe. Romulus, as soon as he learns that his brother is dead, is about to burst into tears, but maintains his composure, well aware of the example of steadfastness that he must set. He kisses his dead brother, torn from him against his will ('Invito frater adempte'), and with Faustulus and Acca Larentia, their hair undone as a sign of mourning, he performs all the rites prescribed for the dead: he anoints the body with ointments and prepares the funeral pyre.

Naturally, if Faustulus took part, as Ovid tells us, in the funeral rites for Remus, he could not have been killed – as claimed by Dionysius and Plutarch – in the clashes following the reading of the auspices and the struggles between the supporters of the two rivals. Indeed in Ovid's account Faustulus and his wife Acca Larentia appear again in connection with a typical festival, the

Lemuria, which was celebrated in the historical period in the first half of May in honour of the spectres, the spirits of the unquiet dead who for three days returned to earth and terrorised the living. On their return from the funeral, exhausted and filled with sadness, Faustulus and Acca Larentia fell asleep (we should note that a funeral held some twenty days after Remus' death, which coincided with the Palilia, is highly unusual), but the bloody shade of Remus appeared to them, lamenting his sad fate and premature death, and asked them to request that Romulus should dedicate at least one festival to him. Romulus is said to have established the Lemuria, which, 'with a change of consonant', took its name from Remus.[12]

Having died a violent death, or perhaps because he died prematurely, Remus does not belong to the world of the *dii Parentes*, the peaceful dead, commemorated every year from 13 to 21 February in all families during the *novena* of the Parentalia. Rather he belongs to that of the *lemures*, the ghosts who returned to earth for three days in May and whom the *paterfamilias* placated by throwing on the floor behind him some black beans, on which the *lemures* fed.[13] As John Scheid has pointed out, if the feast which every family celebrated on the day of the Feralia, at the end of the Parentalia, was a feast of full communion (communion also with the departed of the family, the *dii Parentes*), the act of throwing the black beans to the *lemures* on the first night of the Lemuria must also have been interpreted as a feast, but a 'feast in reverse, perfectly inverted', in which the *paterfamilias* did not participate, confining himself to feeding the *lemures* with their own particular food – black beans. Remus, who in his youth had with his companions greedily devoured the half-raw flesh of the sacrificial goat, ignorant of the sharing principle, now, in death, like all the other *lemures*, must be content every year with the black beans dropped on the floor by the *paterfamilias* in what resembles a 'feast in reverse', as we have seen. The black beans are chosen – as the *paterfamilias* declares nine times in a loud voice – so that he can redeem himself and his kin, and also so that the *lemures* will withdraw from his house. In fact the figure of Remus will never be fully integrated in the urban sphere, except in eschatological forecasts of ultimate peace, such as the prophecy made by Jupiter to Venus concerning the descendants of Aeneas, in which, when wars have subsided (meaning principally the civil wars), the 'harsh centuries' will become myths: 'White-haired Faith and Vesta, and Quirinus together with his brother Remus, shall be lawgivers.'[14]

2. 'ROMA QUADRATA' AND THE POMERIUM

Having buried his brother with all due ceremony and honour, Romulus set about founding the new city. Dionysius of Halicarnassus (I.88) describes the founding in detail:

> He then in the first place took the omens, which were favourable. After that, having commanded fires to be lighted before the tents, he caused the people to come out and leap over the flames in order to expiate their guilt. When he thought everything had been done which he conceived to be acceptable to the gods, he called all the people to the appointed place and described a quadrangular figure about the hill (*tetragonon schema*), tracing with a plough drawn by a bull and a cow yoked together a continuous furrow designed to receive the foundation of the wall; and from that time this custom has continued among the Romans of ploughing a furrow round the site where they plan to build a city. After he had done this and sacrificed the bull and the cow and also performed the initial rites over many other victims, he set the people to work. This day the Romans celebrate every year even down to my time as one of their greatest festivals and call it the Palilia.

If Livy has less to say about the features of the new city, saying only that Romulus 'fortified the Palatine', Plutarch mentions the foundation of a 'Roma Quadrata', before the quarrel with Remus, then moves on to the 'true founding', extending the limits of the city from the Palatine as far as the area later known as the Comitium, where a circular ditch was dug. There has been much debate about the fact that in Plutarch the city of Romulus reached out to include the Comitium area.[15] Here we shall confine ourselves to noting that again we are dealing with representations, with topographic 'figures of memory': if, according to Plutarch, the ditch, in which 'were deposited first-fruits of all things the use of which was sanctioned by custom as good and by nature as necessary', was circular ('bothros ... kykloteres'), this does not necessarily mean that the city itself had a circular plan rather than a square one. Plutarch, after all, said only that, regarding the ditch as the centre, 'they marked out the city in a circle round it' ('periegrepsan ten polin'), just as Dionysius, speaking of 'Roma Quadrata', had maintained that Romulus 'described a quadrangular figure about the hill [evidently the Palatine]' ('topon perigrapsei tetragonon schema toi lophoi'). From this perspective it is highly significant that Ovid was also able to situate the ditch not in the Comitium but on the Palatine, although he does refer to identical rites.[16]

The possibility that the 'Roma Quadrata' of the historians and above all of the antiquarians should be considered to all intents and purposes a topographic 'figure of memory' becomes a certainty if one observes later developments of the term. According to Verrius Flaccus, 'Roma Quadrata' corresponded to a much smaller 'site' close to the temple of Apollo on the Palatine. It was a rectangular platform constructed of blocks of squared stone, beneath which had been laid 'everything that is used for good fortune in the foundation of a city'. As has been suggested, 'Roma Quadrata', understood as a monument, could correspond to the *auguratorium*, the point from which Romulus had taken the auspices for the first time at the moment of the foundation. It was certainly no coincidence that 'Roma Quadrata', which – if it can indeed be equated with the *auguratorium* – was a true commemorative monument, was later, in the Augustan age, fully incorporated into the house of the *princeps* on the Palatine, close to the 'house of Romulus'. Although in 27 BC the *princeps* Augustus rejected the name of Romulus, even for Augustus the reference to the founder figure was clearly central.[17]

There has been much debate concerning the period at which the original 'Roma Quadrata' arose. It has been suggested that it was probably as early as the age of the good king Servius Tullius, who had divided the city into four tribal territories (which came to be called 'regions' only much later).[18] What must be borne firmly in mind, however, is that 'Roma Quadrata' was understood to be surrounded by a pomerium, a sacred boundary which defined it as an *urbs* and distinguished it from the *ager*, while also separating the 'inner' zone of the city (*domi*) from the 'outer' zone (*militiae*): even after the subsequent extensions of the pomerium, this is a distinction of great importance, particularly in connection with the magistrates' direction of the auspices in the historical period.[19] Tacitus, in book XII of his *Annals*, provides some information on the extent of the original pomerium marked out by Romulus, in the context of an extension of it inaugurated by the emperor Claudius in AD 49:

> 23.2. The emperor likewise widened the pomerium of the capital, in conformity with the ancient usage, according to which, those who had enlarged the empire were permitted also to extend the boundaries of Rome. But Roman generals, even after the conquest of great nations, had never exercised this right, except Lucius Sulla and the Divine Augustus.

> 24.1. There are various popular accounts of the ambitious and vainglorious efforts of our kings in this matter. Still, I think, it is interesting to know accurately the original plan of the pomerium, as it was fixed by Romulus. From the ox market, where we see the brazen statue of a bull, because that animal is yoked to the plough, a furrow was drawn to mark out the town, so as to embrace the great altar of Hercules; then, at regular intervals, stones were placed along the foot of the Palatine hill to the altar of Consus, soon afterwards, to the old Courts, and then to the shrine of Larunda.

> 24.2. The Roman Forum and the Capitol were not, it was supposed, added to the city by Romulus, but by Titus Tatius.

If we follow the pointers provided by Tacitus and by the boundary stones, which had to be religiously preserved and which he could probably still see, the result is a 'square' pomerium line which, starting from the two ends of the Circus Maximus (the *ara maxima* of Hercules before the *carceres* and the altar of Consus at the opposite end of the Circus), then extended from the *curiae veteres* to the eastern fringe of the Palatine, and on the other side to the 'shrine of the Lares' or, as has been suggested, 'of Larunda'.[20] Andrea Giardina has made the point about the 'disconcerting nature' of the ancient documentation relating usually to the line of the pomerium, variously placed outside and inside the walls or on both sides of them. We for our part will do no more than stress the enormous value of the information furnished by Tacitus about Romulus' pomerium, information which is sometimes greatly undervalued, yet highly significant for a very simple reason: the presence of the boundary stones, still visible. If the pomerium line had really been extended by Servius Tullius, then by Sulla, and perhaps by Caesar and Augustus, Romulus' boundary stones must have remained in place not simply for 'historical reasons' but also, and perhaps above all, because they marked the original perimeter of the city: the original 'Roma Quadrata', the sacred walls first laid down by Romulus at the moment of the foundation.[21]

3. THE CIVIC BODY AND ITS ORGANS

To understand how, after the foundation, ancient historiography represented the birth of the most important organisms of the city of Rome, we have Livy's account to follow. When Romulus had made his sacrifices to the gods, 'according to the Alban rite' – he had plainly not forgotten his origins or those of the city which was the metropolis of Rome – and to Hercules, according to the Greek rite, as the cult of Hercules had been established in Latium by the Arcadian Evander, he summoned his companions *ad concilium*. Since his companions were unable 'to form themselves without the benefit of laws into a single body politic', he gave them laws, thus effecting a change from *multitudo* into *populus*. And what is the *civitas*, after all, if not 'an association or partnership in justice', according to Cicero's well-known formulation? Romulus defined his now undisputed royal status by adopting suitable regalia (the curule seat and toga praetexta), and an escort of twelve lictors. At the Capitol, between two woods, he opened his asylum, where men of all conditions could find refuge.[22]

Then, in order to control and direct the new forces and at the same time establish a 'council' for himself, he created one hundred senators from among the people. As they were termed *patres* 'for the dignity conferred upon them', their successors became the *patricii*. Thus a fundamental division was produced

38

within the body politic. During the new festival of the Consualia (in honour of the god Consus), the abduction of the Sabine women, as we shall see, not only brought women into a predominantly male society, but also, in Livy's account, brings the first mention of the existence of the plebeians: some plebeians ('ex plebe homines') were entrusted with the task of taking the most beautiful of the abducted women to the houses of the most illustrious senators ('primoribus patrum'). The war against Caenina and the killing by Romulus of their king Acron signalled the institution of *spolia opima* and the dedication of the temple of Jupiter Feretrius where the spoils would be deposited. The war against the Sabines, who occupied the Capitol and moved from there towards the marshy plain where the Forum would later be built, gave birth to the cult of Jupiter Stator and one of the aetiological myths of the *lacus Curtius* (as we shall see further on). The peace with the Sabines and the joint reign of Romulus and the Sabine Titus Tatius led to the birth of the 'doubled city' (*geminata urbs*), whose inhabitants took the name of Quirites and were distributed over thirty *curiae*. Although Livy derives the term *Quirites* from the Sabine city of *Cures*, it can be seen that this etymology does not, even in Livy's account, at least at the level of narrative sequence, appear to affect the close relationship between the Romans who were Quirites and the *curiae* established by Romulus.[23]

While Livy attributed the institution of the *curiae* to the moment of the 'refoundation' of the 'doubled city', as Plutarch would do at a later date, Dionysius of Halicarnassus in a much fuller account, in view of the parallels so frequently drawn between Roman institutions and those of Greek cities, as we shall see, attributed to Romulus alone, at the moment of foundation, the creation of the three 'genetic' tribes and thirty *curiae*, as the further subdivisions of the tribes. The three 'genetic' tribes were those to which all citizens of Rome belonged by birth. Their names were the Ramnes, from the name of Romulus, or so it was thought, the Tities from Titus Tatius, and the Luceres, which Plutarch linked with the wood (*lucus*) in which Romulus had received the fugitives in the asylum, though others held that this name was given by an Etruscan called Lucumo, an ally of Romulus during the war against the Sabines. Livy very wisely seems to ignore any such distribution, attributing the names (as he has them, Ramnenses, Titienses and Luceres) purely to the three equestrian centuries established when that war ended. As for the three 'genetic' tribes, Livy in this part of his work shows only that he knows that they 'survived' from the republican period, when the names Ramnenses, Titienses and Luceres, after the duplication effected by the king Servius Tullius, according to tradition, designated only the 'six voting units' (*sex suffragia*), the six most venerable equestrian centuries, intended exclusively for the patricians.[24]

The nature of this tripartite origin of the Roman civic body has been much debated. In the nineteenth century their presumed ethnic character was given much emphasis: the Ramnes on the Palatine became the Latins by association with Romulus, the Tities the Sabines of Titus Tatius, who lived on the Quirinal, and the Luceres the Etruscans, who at a certain point, though still in the age of Romulus, moved to the Caelian Hill. Georges Dumézil believed it possible to separate within the three tribes the three social functions (priests, warriors, producers) according to his reconstruction of the Indo-European ideology. At present, however, some prefer to emphasise their nature as artificial creations, of a kind commonly found in ancient city-states. If, in addition, according to Varro, we are dealing with subdivisions not of the Roman people but of their land and thus the inhabitants into three territorial districts, it cannot be ruled out – indeed, it is very probable – that this representation of the three 'genetic' tribes is to be connected, in Varro's account, with the later subdivision by Servius Tullius, of the territory of the *urbs* and the 'Roman land' into tribal territories. One thing that is certain, however, is the direct connection between primitive tribes and army corps, a connection demonstrated – as we have seen – by Livy when he linked the Ramnenses, Titienses and Luceres to the three centuries of horsemen instituted after the birth of the 'doubled city'.[25]

If, therefore, the division of the population into three tribes during the monarchic period still seems somewhat mysterious, as we have stressed, this division was followed by a further division of each tribe into ten *curiae*, giving a total of thirty, whether this subdivision was the work of Romulus alone or of Romulus and Titus Tatius, after the city had been 'doubled' by the arrival of the

Sabines. While the criteria of membership of a tribe remain obscure, we do know that membership of the *curiae* was decided by birth, since, according to a famous definition by Laelius Felix, the jurist of the age of the Antonines, anybody who voted in the *comitia curiata* (the assembly of the thirty *curiae*) gave his vote *ex generibus hominum*. Leaving aside any discussion of the exact meaning to be attributed to the term *genera*, as has been pointed out most opportunely by Jean-Claude Richard, '*genus* is used of any group with its own identity determined by a totality of well defined characteristics'.[26]

If the *comitia curiata* were established by Romulus and continued to function as 'fossils' in the late republican period, but with purposes which were as much specific as fundamental, it may be seen that the term *curia* could also stand for something else: for the places where the members of the *curiae* met to share feasts for cult purposes – feasts described in the Augustan period by Dionysius (II.23.1–2 and 4–5), who attributed their establishment to Romulus himself:

> After he had made those regulations concerning the ministers of the gods, he again . . . assigned the sacrifices in an appropriate manner to the various *curiae*, appointing for each of them gods and genii whom they were always to worship, and determined the expenditure for the sacrifices, which were to be paid for them out of the public treasury. The members of each *curia* performed their appointed sacrifices together with their own priests, and on holy days they feasted together at their common table. For a banqueting-hall had been built for each *curia*, and it there was consecrated, just as in the Greek *prytaneia*, a common table for all the members of the *curia*. . . . And not alone for his wisdom in these matters does Romulus deserve praise, but also for the frugality of the sacrifices that he appointed for the honouring of the gods, the greatest part of which, if not all, remained to my day, being still performed in the ancient manner. At any rate, I myself have seen in the sacred edifices repasts set before the gods upon ancient wooden tables, in baskets and small earthen plates, consisting of barley bread, cakes and spelt, with the first-offerings of some fruits, and other things of like nature,

simple, cheap, and devoid of all vulgar display. I have seen also the libation wines that had been mixed, not in silver and gold vessels, but in little earthen cups and jugs, and I have greatly admired these men for adhering to the customs of their ancestors and not degenerating from their ancient rites into a boastful magnificence.

In the *comitia curiata* the citizens, both patrician and plebeian, all voted in their own *curia* and each *curia* constituted a voting unit, so that a majority was reached not by the sum total of single votes but by those of the *curiae*, with sixteen as the minimum, which had voted together on a motion of the king. The basic characteristic of the *comitia curiata*, then, was that within them all votes had the 'same weight', those of rich and poor, patrician or plebeian. The characteristic was so fundamental that Dionysius of Halicarnassus gave it particular emphasis in contrasting it with the new system of *comitia centuriata* created by Servius Tullius. King Servius Tullius, 'whenever he thought proper to have magistrates elected, a law considered, or war to be declared, he assembled the people by centuries instead of by *curiae*'. If, thanks to his new system, Servius Tullius had made the more affluent classes 'masters of all the city, while distancing the poor from government', the 'democratic' system of the *comitia curiata*, in which all votes had equal weight, apparently seemed to guarantee less than a voting system dominated by wealth and personal prosperity.[27]

If this feature of the *comitia curiata*, in which votes were reckoned at 'one for one' (*viritim*) and therefore equally, makes it very easy to understand why Romulus was always 'dearer to the crowd than he was to the senators', the banquets held on feast days in the buildings which housed the individual *curiae* are also a very clear indication of a wish to establish 'parity' among the citizenry. At these banquets the citizens, seated side by side, again demonstrated their status as 'equals' (*pares*), overcoming not only disparities in wealth but also of membership of the patriciate or the plebs, since (as is clear), if they belonged to their *curiae* by birth, one and the same *curia* could include, according to birth, both patricians and plebeians. Attention has also been paid to the connection between the number of *curiae* – thirty – and the thirty peoples of Latium, which as members of the Latin league customarily marked the *feriae Latinae* by feasting together on the Alban Hill after the sacrifice to Jupiter Latiaris. Just as these 'peoples', having equally shared the meat of the sacrificial ox, reaffirmed their equality within the league, so the Quirites, it is clear, being members of the *curiae* and feasting together, re-affirmed their 'equality' as citizens.

The accounts of the birth of Rome by Livy and Dionysius of Halicarnassus in the age of Augustus are largely typical of what is understood by 'the foundation of the city' in the historio-graphic tradition that developed from at least the beginning of the final decades of the third century BC. There has been much debate on the genesis of this tradition, its value, and its possible projec-tions into the Romulean epoch of problems and trends which at times would seem to date from much later periods: only think, for example, of Dionysius' figure of Romulus the 'good legislator', to which we shall return in detail later. Note also that – as we have seen – Dionysius, unlike Livy, traced to Romulus alone the divi-sion of the Romans into three tribes and thirty *curiae*, well before the arrival of the Sabines of Titus Tatius. Nevertheless, beyond any differences in the accounts of individual episodes in the life of Romulus and the establishment of particular institutions, his foundation on the Palatine Hill signalled for the ancients the birth of a real city, with the organisms we have recorded, thanks to the cults he established. These, with the exception of the cult of Hercules in the Forum Boarius, for which the 'Greek rite' of the Arcadian Evander was religiously retained, were practised typi-cally according to the 'Alban rite', since Romulus was descended from Alba and Alba was a metropolis of Rome.[28]

In parallel with this general description, the inhabitants are transformed from herdsmen into farmers to whom Romulus granted the famous two *iugera* of land. On the basis of the absence of farmers in the story of the infancy and childhood of the twins, and more generally in the Alban saga, it has been sug-gested that we should see the birth of Rome as the mythical memory of a socio-economic revolution which would have sig-nalled the change in Latium from a type of economy founded on grazing to a type of agricultural economy, or rather, a mixed economy.[29] If this last hypothesis seems difficult to support, the observation on which it is based may, on the contrary, prove extremely interesting: it points to the conclusion that, at least in one sector of ancient tradition, the foundation of Rome indicated a qualitative leap that coincided, explicitly or implicitly, with the beginning of agricultural practices by its inhabitants. This concurs with the image already elaborated of ancient Latium, before the foundation of Rome, as a world of woods and forests, which, according to the annalist tradition, was inhabited by herdsmen, but in which farmers at any rate did not seem to be much in evidence.

The companions of Romulus, transformed from *multitudo* into *populus*, changed not only their 'way of life' but also, above all, their social practices. The young shepherds who hunted, formed bands and clashed with raiders became citizens and members of a political community; they abandoned the vast territory in which they had moved for the religiously determined space of the city. While, as prototypical *luperci*, Remus and his companions had no concept of equitable distribution of the sacrificial flesh and could even eat half-cooked meat, now as citizens the Romans held banquets together in the *curiae* into which they had been divided. The birth of Rome, then, could be made to coincide with the creation of a 'new world', not only on the level of community practices, but also on that of techniques of land tillage, as though from this perspective the passage of the inhabitants from a 'state of nature' to one of 'culture' could once and for all be deemed accomplished thanks to Romulus' foundation.

4. THE ABDUCTION OF THE WOMEN AND THE WAR AGAINST THE SABINES

Despite this change the city still had difficulty growing, primarily because there were too few women to produce prospective new citizens. All of Romulus' attempts to encourage marriages by sending ambassadors to the neighbouring peoples were unsuccessful: no one wanted to give a daughter to the inhabitants of a city which was newly founded and also composed of men of very obscure origin, some of whom had even taken refuge in the Asylum. To this main reason – the objective lack of women – Dionysius added the wish on the part of Romulus to establish more solid alliances with the nearby cities thanks to 'blood' ties.

However, faced with repeated rejections, Romulus devised as an expedient the course of abduction. The neighbouring peoples from Antemnae, Caenina, Crustumerium and the Sabines were invited to Rome with their families to attend the Consualia, a festival in honour of Neptune which had been established on purpose by Romulus, and which promised horse races on the Circus Maximus. While the spectacle was taking place the Romans at a given signal flung themselves on the daughters of their guests and carried them off by force while the enraged parents and brothers, prevented from protecting them, fled.[30]

We shall return later to Romulus' wars against the Antemnates, Caeninenses and Crustumerians. First, however, because of the consequences it had for the formation of the 'doubled city', we shall examine the – to all appearances – rather slow reaction of the Sabines. After the Romans have defeated the people of Antemnae, Caenina and Crustumerium, the Sabines, led by Titus Tatius, the king of Cures, finally attack Rome and besiege the Palatine Hill. Thanks to the controversial treachery of Tarpeia (see below), they even occupy the Capitol and from there engage the Romans in the valley of the Forum. The Roman army is led by Romulus and the Etruscan Lucumo, who hastened to support him. While an early battle is raging, the Sabine Mettius Curtius, having managed to force Romulus to retreat, is himself pressed to withdraw. He flees towards a part of the Forum which was then particularly swampy, and his horse falls into a large pool of water out of which he manages to clamber. That spot in the Forum, later marked by a monument, will come to be called 'Lacus Curtius'. Hostus Hostilius, an ancestor of the king Tullus Hostilius, dies in combat and, according to some sources, his tomb is where he fell. Romulus, seeking to halt the Sabines who are attempting to reach the Palatine Hill, promises a temple to Jupiter: the future temple of Jupiter Stator. After further battles it is the abducted Sabine women themselves, now the happy wives of Roman husbands, who separate the adversaries, either by throwing themselves between the combatants, their hair dishevelled and their clothes torn as a sign of mourning, or, with the express permission of the senate, by sending a delegation to their relatives.[31]

If the abduction of the women clearly constitutes an *aition* of the ancient practice of marriage by rape, which was then supplanted by the customary Roman matrimonial practices, it may be observed that the whole course of encounters between Romans and Sabines in the valley of the Forum itself builds a series of *aitia*, connected with famous monuments present in historical times in the Forum. As we shall see, according to one tradition the Lapis Niger indicated the tomb of Hostus Hostilius, while according to a different tradition it identified the tomb of Faustulus. In its turn the 'Lacus Curtius' was supposed to indicate the swamp into which Mettius Curtius and his horse had plunged. The *lacus*, which evidently was by then drained, was in the centre of the Forum and was marked by a pavement of tufa (porous stones) in the centre of which stood a circular well. Cavities which held tombstones or altars have been found inside the paving. Just as the Lapis Niger, as we have seen, could have indicated not only the tomb of Hostus Hostilius but also that of Faustulus, so were there also different traditions in ancient times as to the origin of the *lacus*. Besides the Sabine legend, the story was passed down that in 362 BC the Roman knight Marcus Curtius had thrown himself into an abyss which had miraculously opened in the Forum. He had done so to fulfil the advice of the haruspices, according to whom, in order for the abyss to be closed, the offering of the most valiant Roman citizen was demanded in expiatory sacrifice by the Manes. According to a third tradition the monument marked the spot struck in 445 BC by a bolt of lightning and enclosed by senate decree by the consul Curtius, colleague of M. Genucius. Evidently the dedication by Romulus of the temple of Jupiter Stator on the Via Sacra was connected to the presence of the temple consecrated later, in 294 BC, by the consul M. Atilius Regulus after Lucerius' victory over the Samnites.[32]

If the Romans held the Palatine Hill and the Sabines the Capitol, the place where the Via Sacra later appeared then becomes a sort of boundary zone. Note, however, that this Via Sacra, after the birth of the 'doubled city' thanks to Romulus and Titus Tatius, will become the principal axis of the Forum, taking its name from the path on which 'offerings are brought every month to the citadel, and by which the augurs regularly set out from the citadel for the observation of the birds'.[33] The centrality of the Via Sacra during the Roman–Sabine clashes thus seems to foreshadow the new centrality this Via Sacra acquires in the 'doubled city' of Romulus and Titus Tatius. Indeed, once a peace agreement had been reached the two peoples fused together, after they 'consecrated altars to those gods to whom they had addressed their vows' 'in the middle of the so-called Sacred Way'. While Romulus continued to live on the Palatine Hill and also occupied the Caelian Hill, Titus Tatius chose for his own residence the Capitol and the Quirinal. So, by draining the swamp which had seen their battles, they prepared the Forum.[34] There was therefore an extended city, not only as regards its political institutions (according to one tradition it was only then, as we have seen, that the establishment of the *curiae* occurred, as well as the expansion of the senate to include Sabine notables), but also in its territorial dimensions, so that then, at least according to Dionysius of Halicarnassus, it also possessed its own Forum.

5. FROM THE DOMESTIC FIRES OF THE *CURIAE* TO THE HEARTH OF VESTA

In 1952 Louis Gernet retraced the history of the 'common hearth', the *hestia*, as a 'characteristic symbol *par excellence* of the Greek city'. While in his work there is no lack of comparisons and parallels with the Roman cult of Vesta, there is no mention of his most illustrious predecessor, Fustel de Coulanges, who not only defended his Latin thesis on the cult of Vesta in 1858, but also, primarily in his *Cité antique* in 1864, singled out in the 'common hearth' a – perhaps the – most important characteristic sign of the birth of the city. Later Fustel de Coulanges was also the first to make a sound comparison between the *prytaneion* of the Greeks and the *regia* of the Romans. Ever since then, that comparison has been a strong argument for those who support a substantial degree of correspondence between two concepts of a city: the Greek *polis* and the Roman *urbs*; a correspondence, however, that was not always welcomed or even discussed on various levels by those who instead sought to point out the specific nature and workings of two ways of understanding and practising politics.[35]

In reality, if the comparison seems rather abstract, at least in the terms in which it has sometimes been proposed, the debate about the role of the 'common hearth' and therefore the cult of Vesta in Rome and its distinctive characteristics with reference to the *koine hestia* of Greek cities is much more ancient than is commonly believed. It was neither Fustel de Coulanges nor the nineteenth-century supporters of a Greek loan of the Roman cult of Vesta who first opened the discussion.[36] Rather, the first to pose the problem was an ancient historian who was, most significantly, a Greek: Dionysius of Halicarnassus. Dionysius discusses the 'common hearth' with regard to the religious reforms introduced by Numa (II 65–66.1):

LXV.1. At any rate, as regards the building of the temple of Vesta, some ascribe it to Romulus, looking upon it as an inconceivable thing that, when a city was being founded by a man skilled in divination, a public hearth should not have been erected first of all, particularly since the founder had been brought up at Alba, where the temple of this goddess had been established from ancient times, and since his mother had been her priestess. And recognising two classes of religious ceremonies – the one public and common to all the citizens, and the other private and confined to particular families – they declare that on both these grounds Romulus was under every obligation to worship this goddess. 2. For they say that nothing is more necessary for men than a public hearth, and that nothing more nearly concerned Romulus, in view of his descent, since his ancestors had brought the sacred rites of this goddess from Ilium and his mother had been her priestess. Those, then, who for these reasons ascribe the building of the temple to Romulus rather than Numa seem to be right, in so far as the general principle is concerned that, when a city was being founded, it was necessary for a hearth to be established first of all, particularly by a man who was not unskilled in matters of religion; but of the details relating to the building of the present temple and to the virgins who are in the service of the goddess they seem to have been ignorant. For, in the first place, it was not Romulus who consecrated to the goddess this place where the sacred fire is preserved (a strong proof of this is that it is outside of what they call Roma Quadrata, which he surrounded by a wall, whereas all men place the shrine of the public hearth in the best part of a city and nobody outside of the walls); and, in the second place, he did not appoint the service of the goddess to be performed by virgins, being mindful, I believe, of the experience that had befallen his mother, who while she was serving the goddess lost her virginity; for he doubtless felt that the remembrance of his domestic misfortunes would make it impossible for him to punish according to the traditional laws any of the priestesses he should find to have been violated. For this reason, therefore, he did not build a common temple of Vesta nor did he appoint virgins to be her priestesses; but having erected a hearth in each of the thirty *curiae* on which the members sacrificed, he appointed the chiefs of the *curiae* to be the priests of those hearths, therein imitating the customs of the Greeks that are still observed in the most ancient cities. At any rate, what are called *prytaneia* among them are temples of Hestia, and are served by the chief magistrates of the cities.

LXVI.1. Numa, upon taking over the rule, did not disturb the individual hearths of the *curiae*, but erected one common to them all in the space between the Capitoline and the Palatine . . ., and he enacted, in accordance with the ancestral custom of the Latins, that the guarding of the holy things should be committed to virgins.

In this particular case it is highly probable that Dionysius is questioning the conflicting opinion of Varro, whose works were well known to the author of *Roman Antiquities*; the very name 'Varro' would indicate the high level of the 'debate' entered into by Dionysius. In *Antiquitates rerum divinarum* Varro describes Vesta as 'the fire (*ignis*) which belongs to the hearths (*foci*), without which the *civitas* cannot exist'. Furthermore, with geometrical precision he makes the priesthood of Vesta, and hence the cult of the goddess, date back to the period of Romulus. The point is sound when one reflects that Varro portrays Tarpeia, a figure inextricably linked to the war between Romulus and the Sabines of Titus Tatius, to all intents and purposes as a Vestal Virgin.[37]

A brief examination of the saga of Tarpeia will show how her possible characterisation as a Vestal as far back as the Roman–Sabine war influenced the debate on the birth of the priesthood of Vesta in antiquity. Greedy for Sabine gold or madly in love with king Titus Tatius; a traitor to her city; more rarely, an unfortunate heroine or even one of the Sabine maidens abducted by Romulus; the young daughter of the commander of the citadel on the Capitol, or herself the citadel's guardian; or else a priestess of Vesta – despite these contradictory and sometimes even antithetical characteristics, there is unanimity about how Tarpeia dies. Once the Sabines, thanks to her, had entered the stronghold, they buried her alive under their shields.

This consistent element, having emerged from among the wide range of variants of the saga, is of considerable importance. We shall not enter into the debate over the origins of the legend – which is as long as it is filled with contradictions – that is linked with the widespread mythic theme of the maiden who betrays her city out of greed or love. As for the many and individual variants, sometimes it cannot be denied that they are real 'author's variants'. One has only to think of the radical transformation of Tarpeia from traitor to heroine by the annalist Calpurnius Piso, the censor of 120 BC. In this case Piso is openly at odds with Cincius Alimentus and Fabius Pictor, as Dionysius of Halicarnassus implicitly testifies when, in writing of Tarpeia, he relates and compares the two versions.[38]

What must be emphasised is the way Tarpeia dies: she is buried alive beneath the shields of the Sabine warriors. In fact, following Varro, Propertius and Silus Italicus portray Tarpeia as a Vestal, Silus Italicus accusing her of having dishonoured her own priesthood. It may be deduced from this that, although she was buried alive under the shields and not in an underground cell, Tarpeia still received the punishment meted out to Vestals who compromised their chastity in historical times: interment alive. There is remarkable agreement on this point in the literature. According to Livy 'they (clearly the Sabines) killed her', they 'heaped their shields upon her'; Dionysius writes that she died 'overwhelmed by the shields'; and Plutarch says, 'smitten by the gold and buried under the shields, [the girl] died from the number and weight of them', and also, more simply, that 'the Sabines' 'buried her alive'.[39]

While Plutarch later reports the opinion of those who believed that Romulus 'first introduced the consecration of fire, and appointed holy virgins to guard it, called Vestals', Dionysius for his part attributed the foundation of the cult of Vesta to Numa, and argued against those who held that it had been instituted by Romulus. The Greek historian who – as we have seen – described the earliest events of Rome and ancient Italy in the light of the relationship between metropolis and colony, almost paradoxically from his own viewpoint did not agree in this instance with those who, rigorously imposing such a relationship, claimed that it had been the founder Romulus who introduced the Alban cult of Vesta to Rome, a colony of Alba.[40] If Dionysius in principle had to agree with his opponents because 'nothing is more necessary for men than a public hearth', nevertheless, in his opinion, Rome was a very special case from this point of view.

His proof – a 'grand testimony', as he himself maintains – is unexceptionable as part of his reasoning: the temple of Vesta 'is outside of what they call Roma Quadrata, which he [Romulus] surrounded with a wall, whereas all men place the shrine of the public hearth in the best part of a city'. Therefore the institution of the common hearth cannot be attributed to the founder. But Romulus did something else:

> Having erected a hearth in each of the thirty *curiae* on which the members sacrificed, he appointed the chiefs of the *curiae* to be the priests of those hearths, therein imitating the customs of the Greeks that are still observed in the most ancient cities. At any rate, what are called *prytaneia* among them are temples of Hestia, and are served by the chief magistrates of the cities.

It may seem remarkable that for the Greek Dionysius – unlike modern historians after Fustel de Coulanges – the function of the *prytaneia* was assimilated into the functions of the *curiae* rather than into the functions of the temple of Vesta (note that he first stresses the masculine gender of those who serve the goddess).[41] More remarkable still is the observation which follows from this: Numa, the founder of the cult of Vesta and her female priesthood,

> did not disturb the individual hearths of the *curiae*, but erected one common to them all in the space between the

Capitoline and the Palatine (for these hills had already been united by a single wall into one city, and the Forum (*agora*), in which the temple is built lies between them).[42]

Gaetano De Sanctis detected the common hearth of the 'city of Romulus' in the cult of Caca, describing this very obscure figure as the 'Vesta of the Palatine'. Dionysius' version is undoubtedly preferable: less because of the almost total absence of information about a goddess Caca connected with the hearth[43] than for reasons of a more general order. Indeed, Dionysius' method may be considered typical of the way in which ancient historiography often worked in attempting to reconstruct what we are accustomed to calling 'the foundation of the city'. Removing from Romulus the institution of the common hearth, not only Dionysius but others – the great majority (including Livy) agree with him – made themselves bearers of a common heritage of knowledge, very probably a piece of collective memory, regarding the Romulean foundation, in which is preserved a trace of the later nature of the temple of Vesta, and therefore the common hearth. This clue naturally led to the attribution of the 'aedes Vestae' to the second king, Numa Pompilius, since it was he who established the most important priesthoods and religious rites, which later characterised the city in historical times.[44]

Archaeological evidence has shown itself to be crucial here. The most ancient materials discovered in the temple of Vesta date only from 560 BC, while a well in the immediate vicinity – if the objects found in it are really connected to the temple – allows the cult of the goddess to be traced to the second half of the seventh century. The first remains that can be referred to the *regia* are traceable to the end of the seventh century, but its outline, with a plan similar to that of ancient houses, is only traceable to the end of the sixth century. In one of the three rooms, the largest, there seems from the outset to have been a hearth, which, in the context of a structure destined to remain as if fossilised for ever, stands in the sacrarium of Mars and connects, very significantly, with the ceremonies of the 'equus October'.[45]

In Rome the birth of a common hearth, a temple of Vesta, immediately behind the *regia*, evidently signals a transformation and change in many significant aspects. Even if the hearths of the thirty *curiae* remain, even if the members of the *curiae* continue later to feast together around their own hearth, the emergence of a community city hearth *par excellence* (*koine hestia*) – one notes its close proximity to the house of the *rex* – must coincide on a socio-political level with an objective (at least) weakening of the curial organisation. We shall return later to some of the points associated with this series of problems. For now we observe how the birth of the temple of Vesta was preceded by – or in any case appeared in parallel with – the construction of another eminently political space: the Comitium, thanks to the extension of the Forum over a second structure that is datable to the last decades of the seventh century. While many details of the purpose of the site escape us, around the end of the sixth and beginning of the fifth centuries the Comitium was rebuilt. In it was the sanctuary of the Lapis Niger (see below), the source of the famous stone with an ancient inscription recording the development of some functions of the *rex*.[46]

6. ARCHAEOLOGY AND THE 'RIGHTS' OF CRITICISM

If what we have sought to outline primarily through the accounts of Livy and Dionysius of Halicarnassus is the 'birth of Rome' in the collective representation of Romans and Greeks in the Roman epoch, such a representation has been disputed by modern criticism on a two-fold level. One, rather more ancient and quasi-secular, sought to revise the literary tradition relating to ancient and late republican Rome as a whole, beginning with the figure of the founder. As already noted, this trend was linked at first with the names Giambattista Vico and Barthold Georg Niebuhr, and it continued in the nineteenth and twentieth centuries with various degrees and shades of 'hypercriticism' and 'moderated criticism'.[47] The other, relatively recent, level tackles the problem of the origins and formation of the city from archaeological research, in particular since the 1950s, when Einar Gjerstad initiated the systematic publication of archaeological material relevant to ancient Rome as a whole.[48]

At the time it seemed to fulfil the great hope of being able to reconstruct the origins of Rome at last in a more concrete way, on the basis of finds and documents, which, as 'material' from those obscure centuries, gave the appearance of greater certainty than a literary tradition in which everything had been called into question and everything seemed subject to 'criticism'. As to the date of the birth of Rome – the city's political, as much as formative, moment *par excellence* – Einar Gjerstad had no scruples about moving it drastically from Varro's date of 754/53 to circa 575, the date, in his opinion, of the first paving of the Forum. In a parallel, very drastic fashion, though for reasons of a different order, the fall of the monarchy was shifted from the canonical 510 to the years around 450 BC.

The difference in reactions to Gjerstad as perceived by Massimo Pallottino may be seen as typical: in Pallottino's opinion, while 'there was a general outcry' from topographers and archaeologists, 'the historians, accustomed to much worse, were not excessively perturbed'.[49] Nevertheless, it was not simply a matter of 'habit' on the part of the historians, and of their being 'accustomed' to hypotheses that were sometimes even more 'adventurous'. In the first place, Gjerstad's reconstruction, which aimed to make the birth of Rome coincide with the creation of an urban space identifiable through the first paving of the Forum, had the undoubted merit of stimulating worthwhile investigations into explanatory models of the birth of Rome as a city and, as such, a politically favoured place. In the second place, and in a wider historiographical perspective, the reductive attempts of Gjerstad could be easily inserted into the long process of 'critical' revision of the more ancient history of Rome already mentioned.

There is, though, one profound difference. In setting a new foundation date for the city, Gjerstad replaced criticism of literary documents and the notorious *Quellenforschung* with the archaeological dates of the paving of the Forum, dates that, being 'archaeological', were – and were meant to be – not 'open to criticism' and thus constituted a privileged reference grid. Once again the literary tradition with its seven kings was to be grandly sacrificed; however, Gjerstad continued to accept the kings, but he compressed their period to the years from approximately 575 to around 450, which is less than half the period traditionally assigned to them.[50]

Criticisms of this interpretation have been numerous and sweeping, aimed at attacking not only the criteria on which

Gjerstad based his chronology (in particular the first paving of the Forum) but also his reconstruction of the more comprehensive conditions of the birth of Rome, which, he claimed, occurred according to a 'synoecistic' process, thanks to the unification around the Forum of individual and different villages. On the contrary, Gjerstad's great opponent, Hermann Müller-Karpe, maintains that Rome is not only already a true city in the eighth century, but its 'becoming a city' (*Stadtwerdung*) is achieved by slow and gradual development, with a progressive, hegemonic expansion of the Palatine settlement, or, more precisely, the Palatine–Velia settlement.[51]

7. SETTLEMENTS AND FESTIVE RITUALS: FROM ROMULUS TO TULLUS HOSTILIUS

Because of the importance and prominence it has recently assumed, the debate over 'mononuclear development' and 'syn-oecism' provides the opportunity to re-examine two festive rituals in this context. These rituals, by 'photographing' and reproducing – as rite – situations that, thanks to their extremely faithful and unbroken repetitiveness, are almost paradoxically more 'concrete', will perhaps make it possible to explain the great inadequacy of interpretative schemata that are too rigid and too bound to the search for and formalisation of a 'model' of 'the city' that is unequivocal and comprehensive: a 'model' which, however it is reconstructed, displays wide margins of abstractness, especially compared with a body of documentary material which is often much richer and more articulate – and sometimes even much more ambiguous.

We shall therefore take the actions of the festival of the Lupercalia, which has already been dwelt on at length. As we have seen, every year on 15 February the race of the *luperci* skirted the 'antiquum oppidum' of the Palatine, winding along the side of the Forum on the Via Sacra. The very close relationship between the Lupercalia and the perimeter of the 'city of Romulus' can obviously be considered certain.[52] As regards the role of the Palatine we observe that this festival, originally connected to that 'hill' alone, became the common heritage of the entire city in historical times. We may add that the role of the Via Sacra in the race of the *luperci* evokes in a secondary sense the city of Romulus from which the *luperci* were excluded. From this perspective the ritual marginality of the Via Sacra during the Lupercalia equates well with its legendary marginality: as we have seen, during the clashes between Romulus and the Sabines of Titus Tatius, the Via Sacra represents a true borderline, given that the Porta Mugonia opens onto it and the most significant episodes and encounters are situated along its route. It follows from our discussion that its character as *via*, in the original sense of a sub-urban – or perhaps, rather, extra-mural – pathway, must be related to the Palatine.[53]

The Septimontium, the festive ritual of 11 December, presents a much more complex situation, at least in the terms in which this ritual was described in a fragment by Antistius Labeo, the great jurist of the Augustan era. In Varro there are seven 'hills' of Rome. Antistius Labeo, on the other hand, records eight: Palatium, Velia, Fagutal, Subura, Cermalus, Oppius, Caelius, and Cispius. Labeo, however, made it clear that, if the Septimontium was a 'festival for these hills' (and not of the whole city), on the day it was celebrated only the Palatine received 'a sacrifice, which is called *Palatuar*', and 'the Velia, to which equally a sacrifice is made.' The Palatine and the Velia, the only two 'hills' to receive sacrifices, remained of greater sacred importance in historical times than the other 'hills', for which Antistius Labeo only records *feriae*. Indeed – and this is evidently a significant point in characterising the kind of meeting reached at this stage – they must have been *feriae* which, even though celebrated on the same day, nevertheless occurred separately on individual and different 'hills', since Varro definitively states that at least originally, and still in the late republican period, it was a 'holiday not of the people generally, but only of those who live on the hills, as only those who are of some *pagus* "country district" have a holiday at the Paganalia "Festival of the Country Districts"'.[54]

Thanks to their being 'fossils', the two festive rituals (the Lupercalia and the Septimontium) also serve to render improbable the hypothesis that the city of Romulus was born according to the linear schema of one of the two proposed models. The 'synoecist' model can easily be refuted by the leading role that was always unanimously accorded to the Palatine in the ancient tradition. In relation to the Lupercalia, which was originally a festival of the Palatine and then, highly significantly, of the whole city (according to Varro, a festival of the people generally), and, more particularly, in relation to the race of the *luperci*, it must be strongly emphasised – and this is an important point that is too often forgotten – that the community of the Palatine ('Roma Quadrata') was ritually delimited by a pomerium, a sacred boundary (which ran, as we have seen, from the Forum Boarius to the altar of Consus, to the *curiae veteres* and the shrine of the Lares, or Larunda). This was replaced only later by the new pomerium traditionally attributed to Servius Tullius. Note too – again a point that is perhaps too often forgotten – that according to the ancient tradition the community on the Palatine also made use of an absolutely characteristic political space: the *curiae veteres*, whose members evidently not only banqueted together but also debated common problems before going to the *comitia*.[55]

With regard to the model of a 'mononuclear' development centred on the Palatine alone, after our consideration of the Septimontium this model cannot account fully for the subsequent role of the Velia in the festival. This role on the sacred level may be shown to parallel that of the Palatine, to the extent that the Velia, like the Palatine, received a sacrifice, and even in the most reductive hypothesis seems at least to have played a role that was superior to that of the other seven 'hills' in Antistius Labeo's list. As to the Velia, it is not, however, just a matter of the fossilisation in a later epoch of an eminent sacral role played by this hill. Without an accurate assessment of its importance (we may also add the importance of the Velienses recorded in the list of Pliny the Elder as one of the *populi* which participated in the *feriae Latinae*),[56] many aspects of the topography of ancient Rome are destined to remain obscure.

A topography of the royal buildings must highlight the rise – on the slopes of the Palatine but immediately adjoining the Velia – of public buildings of evidently extreme importance, such as the *regia* and the temple of Vesta. Moreover, in the ancient tradition the continuous and progressive siting of the houses of the kings within a clearly defined zone – again from the Palatine downwards, in the direction of the Velia – may be observed. While Romulus lives on the Palatine (to be precise on the Cermalus) and Numa in the *regia*, Tullus Hostilius takes up residence on the

Velia, where later the temple of the Di Penates was erected. Ancus Marcius and Tarquinius Priscus return to the Palatine but near the Velia, and both are somewhere close to the Porta Mugonia.[57]

The dominant character of the Palatine–Velia zone with respect to the other 'hills' listed by Antistius Labeo can also be deduced by other means. Consider the false etymology of Subura ('from the fact that it was at the foot of the ancient city'). This 'ancient city' mentioned by Junius Graccanus must be identified with the zone of the Palatine and the Velia. Or consider the real etymology ('outside the settlement') of the Esquiline (Oppius, Cispius, Fagutal), together with two ancient false etymologies that are absolutely analogous in their final value (as we shall see), in which the settlement, in relation to the Esquiline which remained outside it, must again be identified with the Palatine and Velia zone. This last point of view is another reminder of the Varronian tradition of the 'murus terreus Carinarum', an earthwork which, while it was necessary to separate and defend the Velia from the Esquiline side, acquired a much more profound value thanks to the presence nearby of the 'tigillum sororium' (the 'Sister's Beam'). Beneath this beam had passed the survivor of the three Horatii – who killed the three Curiatii of Alba – shortly after he murdered his sister, and its connection with rites of passage in general was guaranteed by the altars which stood on either side of it: the altar of Juno Sororia and that of Janus Curiatius.[58]

As we shall see, it is significant that the episode of Horatius and the 'Sister's Beam' near the 'earth wall of the Carinae lands' has been traditionally placed under the reign of Tullus Hostilius, the king who lived on the Velia. It is also characteristic that the passage of Horatius beneath the beam took place after his 'appeal to the people' ('provocatio ad populum': an institution founded then) following his absolution. If Janus is the god who watches over doorways and passages, the god who, in this case, as a Curiatius, oversees the passage of young men into the *curiae* (as, in a parallel fashion, Juno Sororia watches over female – mainly sexual – initiations), then the passage of Horatius beneath the 'beam' does not indicate simple expiatory values alone, or at least it also has expiatory connotations, in so far as these are active in every initiation ritual.[59]

Horatius' father also made other expiatory sacrifices for the purification of his son which were later traditional among members of his *gens*. However, when he makes his son, head covered, pass beneath the 'beam', he as father performs a much more important and significant act: after the absolution granted by the people, he reintroduces his son materially and symbolically into the political community – the community of citizens organised into *curiae* – from which Horatius, after he had been condemned by judges who were expressly appointed (the 'duumviri perduellionis', instituted for the first time by king Tullus Hostilius), had had to be implicitly excluded.[60]

It did not take long to recognise in the 'Sister's Beam' an ancient gate next to the earthwork fortified in the direction of the Esquiline. This gate had evident initiatory functions for the young men thanks to the two cults documented at its sides and the saga of Horatius, which founded both the institution of the 'beam' and that of the two altars. Besides, only by taking account of these very ancient ritual values can the continued restoration of the 'beam' down to a late epoch be explained, as well as the sacrifices that were celebrated every year on 1 October.[61] In the collective memory of the Romans, in their historical and antiquarian traditions, Tullus Hostilius was not merely a 'copy' of Romulus in the terms in which such a characteristic has been explained by Ettore Pais, nor was he merely the exponent of a lifestyle centred on the fury and pursuit of war (and, consequently, on the founding of the temple of Pavor and Pallor), as proposed by Georges Dumézil.[62]

Beside this complex of elements which turn on war and conquest, a whole series of clues around the figure of the third king points to the expansion of the ancient Roman settlement in a definite direction. If, as we have seen, Tullus Hostilius is the only king of whom it is told that he lived on the Velia, the hill must have been considered to all intents and purposes an integral part of the city in this period. The false etymology of Esquiline preferred by Varro, according to which the name derived 'from the fact that the area was planted with oaks (*aesculi*) by king Tullus', closely fits this information. The Esquiline, which according to another false etymology was called thus 'from the king's guard posts (*excubiae*)', became consistently an area at the edge of the inhabited centre, which Tullus Hostilius, leaving for the campaign against Veio, placed under the protection of Opiter Oppius of Tusculum and Laevius Cispius of Anagni. If the Oppius and the Cispius took their names respectively from these two leaders, following the remarks about the 'murus terreus Carinarum' and the 'tigillum sororium' which is somehow connected to it, it is not surprising that Opiter Oppius claimed to have defended the city from the Carinae.[63]

The reported information comes from a first-rate ancient tradition attributable with certainty to Varro. From this we can conclude, then, that the collective memory of the Romans, expressed in this tradition with false etymologies and legendary eponyms, placed under the third king a development of the earlier site of habitation identifiable on the whole in the Palatine–Velia area, with the Esquiline – and, we can add, the Subura – as an immediately 'extra-urban' territory. On the other hand, the Varro chronology places the reign of Tullus Hostilius between c.672 and 641 BC and thus within a period conventionally known as Latial Period IV A (730/20 to 640/30 BC). In this period, while there is continued occupation on the Palatine, 'the village connected with the infant tombs of the Via Sacra developed'; more particularly, with regard to the decades which interest us, to 'this same period (679 BC by Carbon 14 dating) are attributable ten or eleven huts below the Palace, perhaps not all intended as dwellings; in the mid-eighth century the first "rough pavements" of the Via Sacra and the Forum are reported . . ., following the demolition of huts in this last area'; 'on the Velia, . . . huts arose in the area prepared for the construction of the present Via dei Fori Imperiali'; the Esquiline, for its part, continued to be described in this period, and then again later, as a district of necropolises.[64]

Although it is not intended to propose 'combinatory' solutions, which are often as facile as they are vague, one nevertheless cannot avoid highlighting the substantial concurrence of two orders of dates (those of the antiquarian tradition and those that are relevant, for this period, to the settlements). They converge, in fact, in the description of the Rome of Tullus Hostilius, which hinges on the Palatine and the Velia, as a by then rather large, compact and organised nucleus, according to a typology common to the other settlements of ancient Latium. If this characteristic formative process explains the sacred prominence of the Palatine and the Velia in the Septimontium of historical times, it also concurs with the initiatory characteristics of the 'Sister's Beam'. It is clear, then, that it is impossible to establish whether these functions were connected originally to the single community on the Velia (the Velienses of Pliny the Elder's list), while the ceremonies conducted at the Lupercal, which were also of an initiatory nature in the ancient epoch, had to be connected, at least in origin, to the single community on the Palatine.

After considering the role attributed to the Esquiline by the antiquarian tradition in this period, and given that the Esquiline had a necropolis district, we must record a displacement. Thanks to the saga of Horatius, who killed his sister and who, condemned by the *duumviri*, was absolved by the people, the 'Rome of Tullus Hostilius' (the king who lived on the Velia) takes possession of a new initiatory site, the 'tigillum sororium', whose location emerges as fully functional in relation to the development of the place of habitation in this particular phase of the Latial Period IV A. The appearance of the beam and the relevant annual ceremonies did not replace the functions of the Lupercal or those of the annual rites which took place in the grotto. While this fact may be considered a typical element in the history of the mental structures in Rome, the displacement still proves to be rich in significance: not only – as we have already emphasised – with regard to the site of habitation but also, and perhaps above all, for the clues it gives regarding a new socio-political structure.

As for the place – and the shift is notable – we come from a sacred grotto in the state 'of nature' on the slopes of the Palatine to a sacred 'gate' of great symbolic value on the edge of the Velia, close to a fortified earthwork. On the level of cult, from archaic ceremonies linked to a world of herdsmen, which are still under the sign of Faunus in the historical period and which see the *luperci* separate into two brotherhoods that were at least originally gentilitial, we arrive at the cults of Janus Curiatius and Juno Sororia, which from the beginning appear as public cults differentiated according to the sexes. On the level of the myth and legend of foundation: from the *luperci* who run nude around the edge of the 'city of Romulus', eat half-raw meat and know nothing of ritual sharing, we reach a rite of passage from outside to inside the settlement. For males – beginning with the saga of Horatius – on the one hand it functions with the active participation of the father, and on the other it is conducted symbolically under the sign of the god (Janus Curiatius) who watches over the entrance of young men into the *curiae*, where common sacrifices are performed and the Quirites banquet together. The rite of passage for the maidens takes place under the sign of Juno Sororia, the goddess who protects their sexual development.[65]

Clearly in this context the idea of 'formation' of the city is preferable to that of 'foundation', irrespective of any debate about who could be the possible 'founder'.[66] According to ancient tradition this 'founder' was a figure called Romulus, whose name was always linked by the ancients to that of Rome.

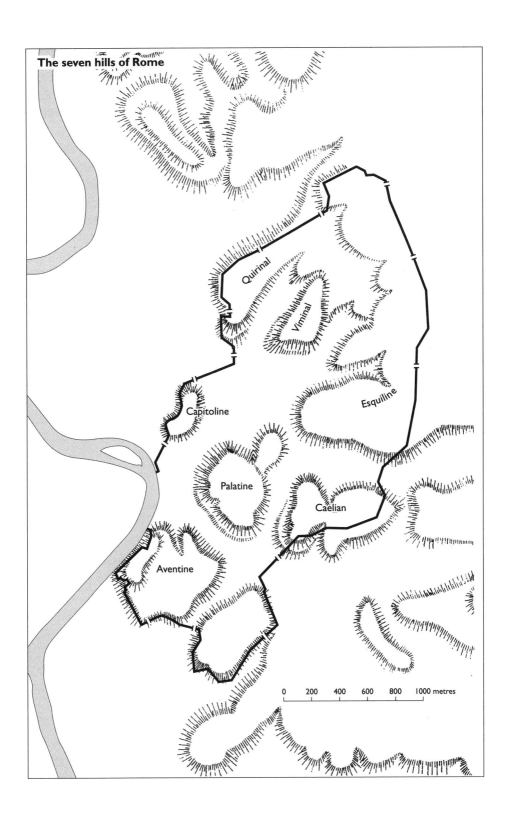

The seven hills of Rome

Quirinal

Viminal

Capitoline

Esquiline

Palatine

Caelian

Aventine

0   200   400   600   800   1000 metres

CHAPTER 3

Romulus' government and his wars

I. ROMULUS 'THE LAWGIVER'

As we have already seen, Livy was rather reserved and he did not dwell on Romulus' mode of government. After the foundation, Livy attributed to Romulus essentially the institution of the lictors, the regal insignia and the senate, as well as implicitly – as we have observed – the bipartition of the body civic between patricians and plebeians. However, Livy placed the institution of the thirty *curiae* later, in Romulus' joint reign with Titus Tatius. As for Ramnes, Titienses and Luceres, Livy mentions them here not as the names of the three 'genetic' tribes, but more simply as the titles of the three 'centuries' of knights formed under the same circumstances after the peace with the Sabines and the 'doubling' of the city. After a brief reference to the death of Titus Tatius, to which we shall return, Livy simply described the wars against the people of Fidenae and Veii.[1] Dionysius of Halicarnassus, very differently, dwelt extensively on the activity of Romulus 'the lawgiver', which he attributed to the very beginning of his reign; that is, immediately after the foundation.

In specifically comparing Romulus' actions to those of famous Greek lawgivers (Solon, Pittacus and Charondas), Dionysius starts by claiming that straight after the foundation Romulus had called an assembly of the Romans and given them the choice of a 'system of government' (monarchy, oligarchy or democracy: a topic that was very dear to Dionysius' predecessor Polybius).[2] Immediately he dangled before them the fear of 'civil commotions' ('emphyloi tarachai'), which were much more dangerous for the community than foreign wars (this theme was also very dear to Polybius). Cassius Dio, the historian and senator, in a lengthy excursus likewise attributed a discussion on the choice of

65

government – monarchy, oligarchy or democracy – and on the
merits and drawbacks of these forms of government, to Augustus
and his friends Maecenas and Agrippa after the end of the civil
wars.[3]

After Romulus had stressed the necessity for 'unanimity
among the citizens' ('en ton polyteumaton homophrosynen') in
the event of 'civil commotions', the Romans, faced with the alter-
natives of monarchy, oligarchy and democracy, chose the 'consti-
tution' of the city of Alba (the home of their ancestors), and
bestowed the kingdom on Romulus himself. Having consulted
the auspices concerning 'the rule' ('peri tes arches') of the city,
Romulus, according to Dionysius – as we have seen – then
divided the people into three tribes and thirty *curiae*, and provided for the subdivision of the inhabitants into patricians and
plebeians (the latter distributed among the clients of the patricians), diversifying their duties and establishing appropriate
norms of reciprocal conduct. The plebeian could choose for his
patron the patrician he preferred, who then acted towards him
like a father towards his children:

> Accordingly, the connexions between the clients and patrons
> continued for many generations, differing in no wise from the
> ties of blood-relationship and being handed down to their
> children's children. And it was a matter of great praise to men
> of illustrious families to have as many clients as possible and
> not only to preserve the succession of hereditary patronages
> but also by their own merit to acquire others.

Romulus' actions would thus have led to a general 'harmony'
('homonoia') of the orders. Here Dionysius appears almost to
forget the extremely hard struggles of the plebeians to be admit-
ted to the consulship, about which he himself had written at
length, painting a gloomy picture, in successive books. According
to him, the 'harmony' between patricians and plebeians would be
shattered in Rome only 'six hundred and thirty years' later (so he
calculated), in 123 BC, during the first tribunate of Gnaeus
Gracchus.

Romulus then decided to organise a council of 'assistance' (the
senate). He appointed the leading senator, who would be respon-

sible for command in the city whenever the king was absent from Rome: the *praefectus urbi*. (Significantly, the first *praefectus urbi* had the name Denter Romulius, and was thus almost a member of Romulus' *gens*.) Later, in a substantially democratic fashion (note that in Livy and Plutarch it was Romulus who, on his own initiative, chose the first hundred senators), each tribe chose another three senators, and each *curia* nine, to bring the number to one hundred. Romulus established his own bodyguard: three hundred *celeres* appointed by the *curiae* in the same way as they had appointed the senators. Then he provided for the division of tasks between king, senate and people. The king was responsible for religious and legislative tasks, asking the senators to judge on crimes of minor importance. The king was always responsible for command during war. For their part, the senators examined the king's proposals in council and held religious and mysteriously 'magisterial' offices. The people, gathered in curiate assemblies, in turn chose the 'magistrates', ratified laws and, at the king's suggestion and in accord with the senate, examined problems related to wars.

So Romulus instituted the priesthoods, cults and feasts of the *curiae*, besides drawing up the most important laws that later guided the daily life of the Roman people; in particular, those relating to matrimony, children, the *patria potestas* and the work of the camps, transforming all the Romans into farmer-soldiers by granting two *iugera* of land to every family.[4] He also introduced the Asylum, but there is a fundamental difference between the Asylum to which Livy and Plutarch refer and the one described in Dionysius. According to Plutarch, the Asylum had been introduced by the twins directly after the 'first foundation' in a wood on the Capitol for the precise purpose of providing asylum to rebels, runaway slaves, insolvent debtors and murderers. Livy, attributing the institution of the Asylum to Romulus alone after the foundation of the city, also spoke of it as an asylum which attracted 'a miscellaneous rabble, without distinction of bond or free'. Dionysius, however, presents this institution in different, much more 'political' terms:

> Secondly, finding that many of the cities in Italy were very badly governed, both by tyrannies and by oligarchies, he

undertook to welcome and attract to himself the fugitives
from these cities, who were very numerous, paying no regard
either to their calamities or to their fortunes, *provided only
they were free men*. . . . For he consecrated the place between
the Capitol and the citadel . . . and made it an asylum for
suppliants. And building a temple there . . . he engaged, under
the colour of religion, to protect those who fled to it from
suffering any harm at the hands of their enemies; and if they
chose to remain with him, he promised them citizenship and a
share of the land he should take from the enemy.[5]

Obviously it has not been very difficult to highlight the
extremely artificial nature of Dionysius' lengthy excursus (II.
7–29) on Romulus 'the lawgiver'. So ideologised and artificial was
it that it was assumed that it had been based on a pamphlet from
the late republican or even the Augustan period, which Dionysius
had obtained directly, with almost nothing added or, perhaps,
with some changes. As for dating this pamphlet, the existence of
which Pohlenz was the first to hypothesise, Pohlenz himself
places it in Caesar's time, von Premerstein in the age of Augustus,
and Gabba puts it under Sulla.[6] The first and third of these periods
seem to correspond little with those ideals of harmony between
king, senate and people for which the pamphlet is supposed to be
the vehicle, while the second period (the Augustan age or, to be
exact, the years 28 to 27 BC) as shown in that pamphlet does not
seem to reflect any of the religious fervour of Augustus by projecting it onto the founder figure. Dionysius does not appear to
dwell on the religious institutions established by Romulus, attributing the creation of the most important Roman priesthoods, and
– as we have seen – even the construction of the temple of Vesta,
to his successor Numa instead.[7]

If we examine all the information about Romulus 'the lawgiver'
recorded by Dionysius, we can perhaps challenge the proposition
that it was contained in a real pamphlet and, consequently, query
the likelihood of determining exactly when this pamphlet was
produced. The insistence on the necessity of harmony and on the
danger of civil commotions, with which Dionysius opened his
excursus, can in fact be related to a very long period of late republican history, beginning with the 'black' year of the first tribunate

of Gnaeus Gracchus (or rather, his brother Tiberius), which according to Dionysius had destroyed 'the harmony of the government' ('ten tou polieumatos harmonian'). The reference to harmony between king, senate and people, with their diverse duties and tasks, which fits as badly in the age of Sulla as in the age of Caesar, must be understood, in that context, to all intents and purposes not only as an ideal, but also as a result of the wise and far-sighted works attributed by Dionysius to the character Romulus.[8]

The regulations regarding matrimony and *patria potestas*, and those which made the Romans into farmer-soldiers, were evidently so well known and widespread that they did not need to be stated in a special pamphlet. We shall do no more than observe that, according to Dionysius – unlike Livy and Plutarch – it was Romulus who, straight after the foundation of Rome, instituted both the tribes and the curiate system. Here Dionysius almost certainly followed Varro, who had claimed that the names of the *curiae* did not derive from the abducted Sabine women, but that Romulus had assigned 'the names to the *curiae* earlier than this, when he first divided the people, some of these names being taken from men who were their leaders and others from districts'.[9] The institution of the *curiae* by Romulus, already present in Varro's account, is a detail which must be emphasised. It is in harmony with the establishment, again according to Varro – as shown – of the cult of the common hearth of Vesta by the founder himself. If Livy and Plutarch dated the curiate system only after the birth of the 'doubled city', it must be concluded that in their reconstructions the *comitia curiata* simply did not exist before that date. We merely observe that the Greek Dionysius, on the contrary, attributed directly to Romulus all the essential institutions of the city in the age of kings, apart from the creation of the *comitia centuriata*, which would have constituted the surpassing of the curiate system by Servius Tullius. Extremely significant, moreover, still from this point of view and viewing it in perspective, is the point that it was Romulus who conferred on the patricians the right of 'holding magistratures' ('archein') which, evidently, apart from the *praefectus urbi* in the case of the king's absence, and apart from certain powers that could be termed 'delegated', obviously could not exist in the monarchic period.[10]

2. THE CALENDAR

In Dionysius of Halicarnassus' long digression on Romulus the lawgiver one would search in vain for an explicit reference to the institution of a true civic calendar by Romulus. This is a rather serious lacuna. Dionysius, in fact, limited himself to recording that Romulus instituted some festivals, the days on which work was to be suspended, the days of solemn assemblies and rest, following the 'best customs in use among the Greeks'.[11] This scanty information shows that even Dionysius had to attribute to Romulus at least an 'embryo' of a calendar, since a city could not exist without a calendar of its own. Other ancient authors would be far more explicit with regard to such an attribution, beginning with Varro, through Aulus Gellius and Censorinus down to Macrobius and the Byzantine Johannes Lydus in the late classical period.[12] In view of its importance among the many accounts, we shall quote in full that of Ovid, who evidently could not fail to describe the 'Romulean' year in his *Fasti*. We may note that Ovid himself held that the institution of such a calendar had been the first act of the new king immediately after the foundation of the city (*Fast*. III. 71–166):

And now what of late had been woods and pastoral solitudes was a city, when thus the father of the eternal city spake: 'Umpire of war, from whose blood I am believed to have sprung (and to confirm that belief I will give many proofs), we name the beginning of the Roman year after thee; the first month shall be called by my father's name.' The promise was kept; he did call the month by his father's name: this pious deed is said to have been well pleasing to the god. And yet the earlier ages had worshipped Mars above all the gods; therein a warlike folk followed their bent. Pallas is worshipped by the sons of Cecrops, Diana by Minoan Crete, Vulcan by the Hypsipylean land, Juno by Sparta and Pelopid Mycenae, while the Maenalian country worships Faunus, whose head is crowned with pine. Mars was the god to be revered by Latium, for that he is the patron of the sword; 'twas the sword that won for a fierce race empire and glory.

If you are at leisure, look into the foreign calendars, and you shall find in them also a month named after Mars. It was the third month in the Alban calendar, the fifth in the Faliscan, the sixth among thy peoples, land of the Hernicans. The Arician calendar is in agreement with the Alban and with that of the city whose lofty walls were built by the hand of Telegonus. It is the fifth month in the calendar of the Laurentes, the tenth in the calendar of the hardy Aequians, the fourth in the calendar of the folk of Cures, and the soldierly Pelignians agree with their Sabine forefathers; both peoples reckon Mars the god of the fourth month. In order that he might take precedence of all these, Romulus assigned the beginning of the year to the author of his being.

Nor had the ancients as many Calends as we have now: their year was short by two months. Conquered Greece had not yet transmitted her arts to the victors; her people were eloquent but hardly brave. The doughty warrior understood the art of Rome, and he who could throw javelins was eloquent. Who then had noticed the Hyades or the Pleiades, daughters of Atlas, or that there were two poles in the firmament? and that there are two Bears, of which the Sidonians steer by Cynosura, while the Grecian mariner keeps his eye on Helice? and that the signs which the brother travels through in a long year the horses of the sister traverse in a single month? The stars ran their courses free and unmarked throughout the year; yet everybody agreed that they were gods. Heaven's gliding ensigns were beyond their reach, not so their own, to lose which was a great crime. Their ensigns were of hay, but as deep reverence was paid to hay as now you see paid to the eagles. A long pole carried the hanging bundles (*maniplos*); from them the private (*maniplaris*) soldier takes his name. Hence through ignorance and lack of science they reckoned lustres, each of which was too short by ten months. A year was counted when the moon had returned to the full for the tenth time: that number was then in great honour, whether because that is the number of the fingers by which we are wont to count, or because a woman brings forth in twice five months, or because the numerals increase up to ten, and from that we start a fresh

71

round. Hence Romulus divided the hundred senators into ten groups, and instituted ten companies of spear-men (*hastati*); and just so many companies there were of first-line men (*principes*), and also of javelin-men (*pilani*); and so too with the men who served on horses furnished by the state. Nay, Romulus assigned just the same number of divisions to the tribes, the Titienses, the Ramnes, as they are called, and the Luceres. Therefore in his arrangement of the year he kept the familiar number. That is the period for which a sad wife mourns for her husband.

If you would convince yourself that the Calends of March were really the beginning of the year, you may refer to the following proofs: the laurel branch of the flamens, after remaining in its place the whole year, is removed (on that day), and fresh leaves are put in the place of honour; then the king's door is green with the tree of Phoebus, which is set at it; and at thy portal, Old Chapel of the Wards, the same thing is done; the withered laurel is withdrawn from the Ilian hearth, that Vesta also may make a brave show, dressed in fresh leaves. Besides, 'tis said that a new fire is lighted in her secret shrine, and the rekindled flame gains strength. And to my thinking no small proof that the years of old began with March is furnished by the observation that Anna Perenna begins to be worshipped in this month. With March, too, the magistrates are recorded to have entered on office, down to the time when, faithless Carthaginian, thou didst wage thy war. Lastly, the month of Quintilis is the fifth (*quintus*) month, reckoned from March, and with it begin the months which take their names from numbers. (Numa) Pompilius, who was escorted to Rome from the lands where olives grow, was the first to perceive that two months were lacking to the year, whether he learned that from the Samian sage who thought that we could be born again, or whether it was his Egeria who taught him. Nevertheless the calendar was still erratic down to the time when Caesar took it, like so much else, in charge. That god, the founder of a mighty line, did not deem the matter beneath his attention. Fain was he to foreknow that heaven which was his promised home; he would not enter as a stranger god mansions unknown.

He is said to have drawn up an exact table of the periods within which the sun returns to his proper signs. To three hundred and five days he added ten times six days and a fifth part of a whole day. That is the measure of the year. The single day compounded of the (five) parts is to be added to the lustre.

Ovid then, after the invocation to Mars, from whom the month of March took its name, and having recorded the conception and adventures of the twins, shows us Romulus who dedicates the first month of his year to his father, calling it *Martius* – a widely used month name, according to Ovid, even among the peoples of Latium and Italia, although at different times of the year. But the ancients, 'through ignorance and lack of science', without observing the stars, divided the year into ten months; in Rome, thanks to Romulus, it began with March. To prove that the Calends of March was the first day of the Roman year in Romulus' time, Ovid adduces much evidence: on that day the laurels that decorated the houses of the flamens and the *rex sacrorum*, the *curiae* and the temple of Vesta were renewed, and in that temple the fire was also rekindled; and on that day, until the third Punic war, the magistrates took office. Numa, Romulus' successor, added the months of January and February to the year, thus moving to a calendar of 305 days. 'Nevertheless the calendar was still erratic' until the reform of the *pontifex maximus*, Caesar, who wanted 'to foreknow that heaven which was his promised home'.[13]

It is not possible to review the history of the ancient Roman calendar here;[14] however, it must be pointed out that Gaetano De Sanctis considered the 'Romulean' calendar a rather absurd legend.[15] We shall point out only that the attribution of a civic calendar to Romulus was – in the context of his depiction as the founder – an unavoidable necessity, and that the number ten, in Ovid, corresponds not only to the ten months of a woman's gestation or the *tempus lugendi* of widows,[16] but also to what he considered essential components of the body civic in the ancient period: the subdivision of Romulus' 'hundred senators into ten groups', the ten companies of spear-men, and the division into ten *curiae* of the tribes of the Titienses, Ramnes and Luceres.

3. THE JOINT REIGN OF ROMULUS AND TITUS TATIUS

The 'doubled city' saw the new king, Titus Tatius, install himself on the Capitoline (which he had already occupied during the war) and the Quirinal, while Romulus occupied the Palatine and Caelian. Both kings then provided for the construction of the Forum, the Comitium, and the temple of Vulcan, consulting both each other and the senate. The senate was enlarged to admit the influential Sabines and grew from one hundred members to one hundred and fifty or two hundred (the number was disputed). Romulus also built the temple of Jupiter Stator, while Titus Tatius raised altars to a number of gods (and, as we have seen, very significantly, to Vesta). Plutarch recorded that the two kings sat with their own patricians separately and then united them all. The festivals and sacrifices were celebrated in common; moreover, the Matronalia had been introduced, in honour of the 'women [obviously the Sabine women] to commemorate their putting a stop to the war', as well as the Carmentalia (he discusses the goddess Carmenta, in whose honour the festival was celebrated). Finally he, too, mentions Romulus 'the lawgiver', in particular regarding matrimonial practices and the crime of parricide: 'It is also a peculiar thing that Romulus ordained no penalty for parricides, but called all murder parricide, looking upon one as abominable, and upon the other as impossible.'[17]

However, after some years this absolutely unanimous reign suffered a dramatic rift because a rather 'tyrannical' trait of Titus Tatius was revealed. Livy says that 'some years later' envoys of the Laurentians who had come to Rome for reasons unknown were assaulted by relatives of Titus Tatius, and that the envoys, who appealed to the law of nations, obtained no justice from the Sabine king. So, when Titus Tatius went to Lavinium to conduct a solemn sacrifice, he was killed by an angry mob in revenge. Romulus did not seem greatly upset by the incident, either because he was by then tired of their joint reign, or because he was convinced that his colleague had not been wrongly killed.[18] Dionysius of Halicarnassus' version of the episode (II. 51–2), which is much more complex, much more tragic even, should be given in full:

LI. But in the sixth year, the government of the city devolved once more upon Romulus alone, Tatius having lost his life as the result of a plot which the principal men of Lavinium formed against him. The occasion for the plot was this. Some friends of Tatius had led out a band of robbers into the territory of the Lavinians, where they seized a great many of their effects and drove away their herds of cattle, killing or wounding those who came to the rescue. Upon the arrival of an embassy from the injured to demand satisfaction, Romulus decided that those who had done the injury should be delivered up for punishment to those they had wronged. Tatius, however, espousing the cause of his friends, would not consent that any persons should be taken into custody by their enemies before trial, and particularly Roman citizens by outsiders, but ordered those who complained that they had been injured to come to Rome and proceed against the others according to law. The ambassadors, accordingly, having failed to obtain any satisfaction, went away full of resentment; and some of the Sabines, incensed at their action, followed them and set upon them while they were asleep in their tents, which they had pitched near the road when evening overtook them, and not only robbed them of their money, but cut the throats of all they found still in their beds; those, however, who perceived the plot promptly and were able to make their escape got back to their city. After this ambassadors came both from Lavinium and from many other cities, complaining of this lawless deed and threatening war if they should not obtain justice.

LII. This violence committed against the ambassadors appeared to Romulus, as indeed it was, a terrible crime and one calling for speedy expiation, since it had been in violation of a sacred law; and finding that Tatius was making light of it, he himself, without further delay, caused those who had been guilty of the outrage to be seized and delivered up in chains to the ambassadors to be led away. But Tatius not only was angered at the indignity which he complained he had received from his colleague in the delivering up of the men, but was also moved with compassion for those who were being led away (for one of the guilty persons was actually a relation of his); and immediately, taking his soldiers with him, he went in haste to their assistance, and overtaking the ambassadors on the road, he took the prisoners from them. But not long afterwards, as some say, when he had gone with Romulus to Lavinium in order to perform a sacrifice which it was necessary for the kings to offer to the ancestral gods for the prosperity of the city, the friends and relations of the ambassadors who had been murdered, having conspired against him, slew him at the altar with the knives and spits used in cutting up and roasting the oxen. But Licinius writes that he did not go with Romulus nor, indeed, on account of any sacrifices, but that he went alone, with the intention of persuading those who had received the injuries to forgive the authors of them, and that when the people became angry because the men were not delivered up to them in accordance with the decision both of Romulus and of the Roman senate, and the relations of the slain men rushed upon him in great numbers, he was no longer able to escape summary justice and was stoned to death by them. Such was the end to which Titius came, after he had warred against Romulus for three years and had been his colleague for five. His body was brought to Rome, where it was given honourable burial; and the city offers public libations to him every year.

We shall postpone until later the burial of Titus Tatius and the annual libations in his honour, and proceed to Plutarch's version. In the fifth year of this joint reign, some ambassadors from Laurentum who were going to Rome were attacked and robbed on the way by relations and friends of the king, Titus Tatius. Because they resisted they were killed. Romulus wanted to punish the guilty at once, while Tatius hesitated and took his time. Unable to take revenge by legal means, the people of Lavinium then 'fell upon him as he was sacrificing with Romulus at Lavinium, and killed him, but they escorted Romulus on his way with loud praises of his justice'. So not only did Romulus not try the assassins, according to 'some historians' he let them go, 'saying that murder had been requited with murder'. This raised the suspicion that he had not in the least regretted the murder of his colleague.[19]

Rather than wonder which of the three versions is the most ancient (they are obviously closely related, albeit with numerous variants), it is perhaps preferable to look at individual elements within each account. For Livy, the episode originated in the blows with which Titus Tatius' relations assaulted the envoys of the Laurentians, thus violating the 'law of nations'. Therefore, when Titus Tatius went to Lavinium for the 'annual sacrifice', he was killed, in a way which was not made clear, by a mob evidently enraged by the fact that he had not responded to the envoys' protests and had not punished the offenders. In Dionysius, the reason behind the embassy from Laurentium was the fact that friends of Titus Tatius with their bands, in raiding territory that was not their own, had plundered goods and animals belonging to the Lavinians, wounding and killing, moreover, all who dared to resist. When the ambassadors reached Rome to express their legitimate complaints, Titus Tatius opposed Romulus' sentence, whereby the guilty were to be delivered up, and demanded that the accusers return to Rome in person to ask for justice. Yet when, having done this, the ambassadors left Rome, they were set upon on their return journey by some of the Sabines and many were killed as they slept. Romulus arrested those guilty of this second, more serious violation of the 'law of nations' and handed them over to the ambassadors to be taken away and duly punished. Titus Tatius, however, with his soldiers, followed them and freed the culprits. For this, not long afterwards, he was murdered at Lavinium, where he had gone for 'a sacrifice which it was necessary for the kings to offer . . . for the prosperity of their city'. The friends and relations of the ambassadors plotted against Titus Tatius and killed him at the altar 'with the knives and spits used in cutting up and roasting the oxen' (oxen that were evidently destined for sacrifice and the following banquet). According to Licinius Macer, however, Titus Tatius was stoned to death by the Lavinians. Romulus, for his part, did not punish those guilty of the murder, but simply took the body of his colleague back to Rome to give it a fitting and honourable burial.

Plutarch, in turn, records that friends and relations of Titus Tatius attacked, robbed and killed some ambassadors from Laurentum who were on their way to Rome (like Livy, he does not explain the purpose of the mission). Romulus wanted to punish the guilty immediately but Titus Tatius hesitated, so relations of the victims killed him while he was making a sacrifice with Romulus, who then buried his colleague in Rome 'near the so-called Armilustrium'. Following a plague and other portents which affected Rome as well as Laurentum, both the murderers of the ambassadors and those of Titus Tatius were punished. Romulus, for his part, purified the city with expiatory rites.[20]

The fact that the two kings had to go to Lavinium for a sacrifice (according to Livy), that was to take place in honour of the *dei patrii* (according to Dionysius of Halicarnassus), inevitably brings us to the annual sacrifices which, even in the republican period, the priests and magistrates of the Roman people had to perform every year at Lavinium in honour of Vesta and the Penates. This was because, by a circular process, Lavinium was a metropolis of Alba, Alba in turn was a metropolis of Rome, and from Alba came both the goddess Vesta and the Penates of the Roman people.[21] The type of death reserved by the Lavinians for Titus Tatius is far more interesting. According to Livy he was simply killed by an angry mob, while Licinius Macer, on the other hand, says that the people of Lavinium stoned him to death – an act of collective revenge by a civic body that had seen its ambassadors attacked and killed.[22] It seems that quite unexpectedly we are brought back to the time of the twins' youth, when Romulus and Remus fought with cattle thieves or Alban shepherds over grazing, and revenge was expressed in ways that were as bitter as they were immediate, although stoning – as is well known – is an eminently ritualised way of putting someone to death.[23]

The kind of death reserved for Titus Tatius by Dionysius of Halicarnassus, however, may seem much more 'characteristic'. He is stabbed by the relations and friends of the murdered ambassadors at the altar where he is preparing to perform the sacrifice with 'the knives and spits used in cutting up and roasting the oxen'. For the people of Lavinium, Titus Tatius, in as much as he assumed the role of 'tyrant' and almost lost every human characteristic, has, as it were, taken the place of the animal destined for sacrifice. This image will be read into the killing of 'tyrants' in Rome in a much later period. Indeed, starting with Caligula for example, their end is not a simple assassination but a ritualised death. As John Scheid has pointed out, with regard to the killing of 'tyrants', 'these are ritual deaths that produce a picture for a broader perspective, proclaiming symbolically their role of tyrants in relation to the social system'.[24] It is not by chance that a famous line of verse by Ennius has been traced to the episode described by Dionysius and an exclamation by Romulus: 'O Tite, tute, Tati, tibi tanta, tyranne, tulisti.'[25]

By not punishing those guilty of the death of the Lavinian ambassadors, Titus Tatius, who made a pilgrimage with Romulus to Lavinium to sacrifice to the Penates of that city and to Vesta, not only violated the 'law of nations' (in itself an extremely grave offence), but he, a Sabine, also completely upset the relationship (*syngeneia*) which existed between motherland and colony, and which through Alba (a powerful conjunction) united Lavinium and Rome. They were ties so indissoluble that even in Claudius' time there was still a 'pater patratus populi Laurentis foederis / ex libris Sibullinis percutiendi cum populo Romano'.[26] The two origins (Sabine of Titus Tatius, and Alban of Romulus) explain clearly the different attitudes of the kings with regard to the episode of the ambassadors. In the same way these origins explain how the revenge of the Lavinians brought down only the 'outsider' Titus Tatius, a Sabine king of Rome who changed into a 'tyrant' and consequently, having become like an animal, became a sacrificial victim to Vesta and the Penates of Lavinium.

Romulus buried his colleague Titus Tatius with honour in either Laurentum or Armilustrium (an adjoining locality situated on the Aventine), and every year the Sabine king was entitled to public funeral *parentationes*, like Acca Larentia and Tarpeia before him.[27] These posthumous honours, at least according to the tradition, satisfied the Sabine component of Rome, which did not impose on Romulus a working relationship with another Sabine monarch after the tragic 'disappearance' of his 'colleague'. The annual 'public libations' in Tatius' honour mentioned by Dionysius of Halicarnassus, like those for Acca Larentia and Tarpeia, evidently could not be dismissed in the republican era. Only thus do the public funeral *parentationes*, to which the 'heroicised' *filii* of Augustus (Gaius Caesar and Lucius Caesar) and later those of Tiberius (Germanicus and Drusus Caesar) were entitled, make sense within a religious system like the polytheistic Roman one, which shows large elements of continuity in rituals.[28]

4. ROMULUS' WARS

Dionysius of Halicarnassus attributed the conquest of Cameria and its reduction to the status of a colony to the joint reign of Romulus and Titus Tatius. However, he says that when Rome was afflicted by a serious plague after the death of the Sabine king, the Camerini rebelled and expelled the Roman colonists. While Livy makes no mention of Cameria, Plutarch does refer to it after the death of the Sabine king. After the conquest of Cameria, 'among other spoils [Romulus] brought also a bronze four-horse chariot from Cameria, and dedicated it in the temple of Vulcan. For it he had a statue made of himself, with a figure of Victory crowning him'.[29] According to Dionysius, as a result of this victory Romulus celebrated a second triumph (the first had been celebrated after he slew Acron, king of Caenina, and the consequent consecration of the *spolia opima* in the temple of Jupiter Feretrius). From the explicit information given by Plutarch, it has been suggested that the site of the temple dedicated by Romulus was the place where the Vulcanalia were later held. Evidently Plutarch, who identified this building as the seat of the senate, designed to accommodate one hundred and fifty or two hundred senators, could not imagine that in reality the sanctuary beneath the Lapis Niger was too small to hold the senate assembly, or even a bronze four-horse chariot.[30]

Plutarch dated an early victory by Romulus over 'Sabine' Fidenae to just after the rape of the Sabine women and set a subsequent conquest in the same period. Later he wrote of one of Romulus' conquests after the death of Titus Tatius. Livy and Dionysius of Halicarnassus, however, acknowledge a war against Fidenae only when Romulus was sole king. The people of Crustumerium had sent food supplies to famine-stricken Rome, but the men of Fidenae attacked the boats and seized their cargo. Romulus then invaded their country, captured the city, and reduced Fidenae to the status of colony.[31]

The war against Veii, one of the most important Etruscan cities across the Tiber, followed the war against Fidenae. According to

Livy the Veientes, after the defeat of the Fidenati (who, as Etruscans, were their blood relations), 'made an incursion into Roman territory which more resembled a marauding expedition than a regular campaign'. Romulus overpowered the Veientes who left their city to defend it, but he did not attempt to take the city. The Veientes sent ambassadors to Rome to sue for peace, and Romulus granted them a hundred years' truce. According to Dionysius and Plutarch, however, the facts were markedly different: the Veientes used their own conquest of Fidenae, the city of their 'blood relations', as a pretext for war and sent to Rome a regular mission which obtained no satisfaction. The military campaign took place near Fidenae, and the Veientes were soundly defeated. Romulus celebrated his third triumph. Following the defeat of Veii the Romans acquired the country of the *Septem pagi* and the salt-works near the mouth of the Tiber.[32]

Obviously it was not difficult to call seriously into question these 'Romulean' conquests. Ettore Pais and Gaetano De Sanctis in the past, and Tim Cornell more recently, have reconstructed the wars against Fidenae and Veii in the fifth century BC. Gaetano De Sanctis, more particularly, considered that the 'Romulean' conquest of Fidenae was 'an anticipation of the real conquest that occurred at the end of the fifth century, when the real victories over the Veii began'.[33] Dominique Briquel interpreted Romulus' victories according to the triple schema proposed by Georges Dumézil for the three Indo-European functions. Thus, the victory over Acron, the king of Caenina, belonged to the first function (the 'regal'), because Romulus had dedicated the *spolia opima* then in the temple of Jupiter Feretrius; the easy victory over Cameria related to the second function (exclusively 'warrior'); and the victory over Fidenae and Veii belonged to the third (eminently 'economic') function, because of the richness of the booty taken from them.[34] Here we shall simply point out that, according to tradition, Romulus waged many more than three wars: against the Crustumerians, Antemnates and Caeninenses; then against Titus Tatius' Sabines; and then, following the death of the Sabine king, against Fidenae, Cameria and Veii. Taken together these constitute evidence that we should dismiss a simple 'ternary' schema.

Instead, it must be emphasised that Romulus' victories should be considered for all practical purposes 'founding' elements in the context of the age of kings. The victory over and slaying of Acron, the king of Caenina, establishes the institution of the *spolia opima* and the triumph; the victory over Cameria gives Romulus the opportunity for his second triumph; the victory over Veii provides his third. The prudent Livy, for his part, disregarded these 'Romulean' triumphs, attributing the first triumph celebrated 'in town' to Lucius Tarquinius Priscus after his victory over Collatia ('triumphans Romam redit').[35] The establishment of Roman colonies by Romulus in Antemnae, Crustumerium, Fidenae and Cameria was another characteristic feature: the model of the Roman colonial policy was already projected onto the founder. It would provide the later model of Roman colonisation, which was taken as an example by Philip of Macedon when, in a letter, he reproved the people of Larissa, who were very jealous of their citizenship, inviting them to follow the Roman model and – in order to increase the strength of their city – admit all the *metoikoi* who resided there.[36]

Romulus' conquests north of Rome clarify the impression the ancients had of the *ager Romanus* at the death of the founder, a territory that extended on the right bank of the Tiber as far as Antemnae, Crustumerium and Fidenae, across from Veii. It was a markedly extended territory that corresponded to the expansion of the city, whose population had progressively increased thanks to the conquests which also brought new citizens. As the founder, Romulus clearly had to provide the city not only with political, economic and social structures, but also with a territory that allowed Rome at least the promise of later conquests. They were conquests which, after the interval provided by the reign of the peaceful Numa, would be undertaken by an eminently warrior king, Tullus Hostilius, the king whom Ettore Pais called even a 'double' – today we would say a clone – of Romulus.[37]

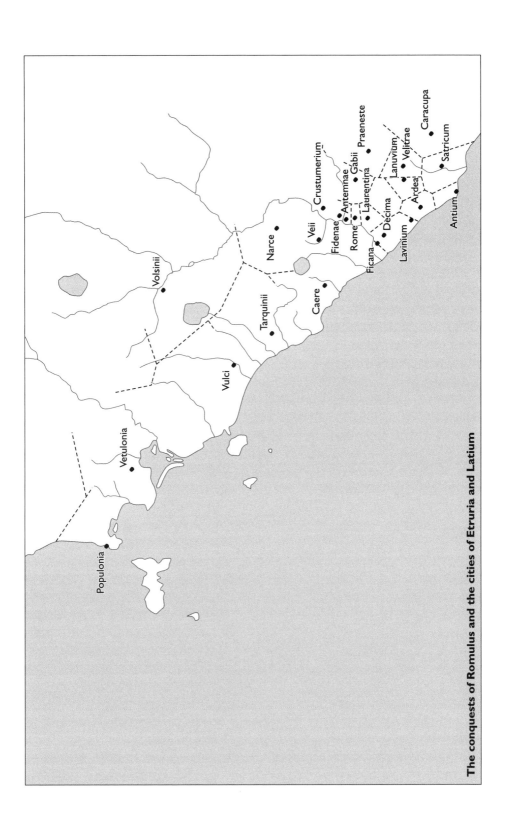

The conquests of Romulus and the cities of Etruria and Latium

CHAPTER 4

The disappearance of the founder: Romulus 'cut into pieces' or his apotheosis

I. THE FOUNDER'S DISAPPEARANCE: TWO TRADITIONS

In the last century of the republic and later in the Augustan period, the death of the first king, Romulus the founder, constituted a problem on many levels for the Romans. Dionysius of Halicarnassus spoke of 'many different stories', various accounts on which there was evidently no agreement. According to one of these – a version Dionysius considered 'rather fabulous' – Romulus disappeared during a review of the army 'in the camp'. Suddenly there occurred supernatural phenomena which obscured the light, or somehow removed Romulus from everyone's sight, and when these phenomena ceased the throne was empty. After searching in vain, the people finally understood – or were made to understand – that the king had ascended to heaven to be among the gods, or better, that he had been swept up into heaven by his father Mars, and therefore was numbered among them. In the second account – held by Dionysius to be 'more plausible' – Romulus died at the hands of his 'own people'; more precisely, at the hands of the senators, because he had changed from a good king to a tyrant. He had distributed land captured from the Veientes without consulting the people, given privileges to the longest-standing citizens ahead of those who had enrolled more recently, and punished criminals with excessive cruelty.

> For these reasons, they say, the patricians formed a conspiracy against him and resolved to slay him; and having carried out the deed in the senate-house, they divided his body into several pieces, that it might not be seen, and then

came out, each one hiding his part of the body under his robes, and afterwards burying it in secret.

A third version, whose credibility Dionysius does not judge, holds that while Romulus was addressing the people he was killed by 'the new citizens', the ones he treated less well. They had taken advantage of a storm and nightfall, when the crowd had dispersed, and the king was without the protection of his bodyguards. That day (5 July) was later called the *Poplifugia* ('the flight of the people') on calendars in memory of the event.[1]

While Livy also discussed the day of Romulus' death or disappearance, his more concise account seems to ignore both the parabola of Romulus' transformation from a good king into a tyrant and the difference in his attitude towards 'new' and 'old' citizens. The recollection that he was held dearer by the people than the senators ('Multitudini tamen gratior fuit quam patribus') remains constant, though. The king's miraculous disappearance is set on the Campus Martius at the Goat's Marsh, while he was holding an assembly 'to review his troops'. Livy then describes the storm and the cloud that hid Romulus from view, and the fear above all of the young Romans ('Romani pubes') – those young men with whom Romulus had always had a privileged relationship – when they saw the throne suddenly empty. 'Then, when a few men had taken the initiative, they all with one accord hailed Romulus as a god and a god's son, the King and Father of the Roman City', and they begged his favour for the protection of their descendants. Yet Livy also records, 'there were some, I believe, even then who secretly asserted that the king had been rent in pieces by the hands of the senators'. In each case admiration for the dead man and alarm at the moment – a moment of power vacuum while the citizens were 'distracted with the loss of their king' and 'in no friendly mood towards the senate' – give more weight to the first version, which is definitively confirmed by the testimony of Proculus Julius, a descendant of one of the Trojan clans that had moved to Rome from Alba. Proculus Julius vowed during an assembly that Romulus had appeared to him early one morning, 'descended suddenly from the sky', to announce both his immortality and the future greatness of Rome.[2] Livy was surprised that in a case like this such faith was placed in the testimony of one man, and ascribed this to the need to ease the sense of loss among the plebeians and soldiers. Evidently – as is at once clear – his first book was not only written, but also published, before the death of Augustus, whose ascent into heaven was testified to by a senator called Numerius Atticus, with explicit reference to the preceding testimony of Proculus Julius on the ascent of Romulus.[3]

Plutarch, like Dionysius of Halicarnassus, did not fail to emphasise the transformation of Romulus from a good king into a tyrant, advancing as evidence his assumption of a new ostentation in style of dress (the scarlet tunic and toga bordered with purple), the creation of a bodyguard of young men called *celeres*, and his escort of lictors 'to bind at once those whom he ordered to be bound.' By this time the patricians met in the senate 'more from custom than for giving advice'. The king had disappeared on the Nones of July (7 July), and Plutarch also gave two totally conflicting versions of his disappearance. According to the first, because of his tyrannical behaviour, the senators murdered him in the temple of Vulcan, dismembered his body, and then each carried away a piece of it hidden beneath his robe. In the second version, Romulus' disappearance occurred 'neither in the temple of Vulcan nor when the senators alone were present', but 'near the so-called Goat's Marsh', under the same unusual circumstances described by Dionysius and Livy. When the people, who had dispersed during the storm, reassembled near the Goat's Marsh after it had abated and 'anxiously sought for their king', the 'nobles', who had not fled during the storm but preferred to huddle together, exhorted them to venerate Romulus as a god, 'since he had been caught up into heaven'. From a good king he had become their beneficent god. But since 'some' accused the 'nobles' of imposing a silly story on the people and being themselves the murderers, Plutarch's account contains the testimony of Proculus Julius, to whom Romulus had miraculously appeared to announce that the Romans should now pray to him by the name of Quirinus. Therefore, as a result of this announcement, and now that he was numbered among the gods, a temple was built to the new god on the Quirinal.

After reviewing the most important evidence regarding the disappearance of Romulus the king, one overriding point must be made immediately: the two versions (that of the apotheosis and that of the murder) are not alike in any respect; in fact, they must be kept rigorously separate. Romulus' ascent to heaven took place at Goat's Marsh while all the people – including the senators, naturally – were assembled. The murder and dismemberment of the body occurred instead where the senate met, or more precisely – according to Plutarch – in the Vulcanal, which was depicted as the meeting place of the senate, and in the presence of the *patres* alone. Most importantly, in the case of the death of a Roman king or later an emperor, ascent into heaven or assassination are not only diametrically opposite, they also of necessity imply completely opposite representations of the king himself, both in life (more particularly, in the case of Romulus, in the last phase of his life) and after death. Romulus can be venerated on earth as a god thanks to his ascent into heaven. In turn, this assumption into heaven, an indispensable element for his 'divinity after death' ('divinitas post mortem'), at least from the time of Ennius, implies and presupposes at Rome a good king or, better still, a well-deserving king *par excellence*. There is a further point that is perhaps too often neglected: if and when Romulus, after his death, is identified with the god Quirinus, this identification at the same time introduces to Rome the cult of that god, to whom, as a result – we shall return later to this – a temple was erected there for the first time.[4]

The version according to which the founder was assassinated by the senators soon projected eminently tyrannical characteristics on to the final phase of Romulus' life, to the extent that – as we shall see – according to the tradition found in Appian, in 44 BC the conspirators chose the senate ('to bouleuterion') for the murder of Caesar in an attempt to appeal to the other senators. In choosing the venue for the murder of the tyrant of their time, they wanted explicitly to imitate the more ancient senators when they killed Romulus, who changed from a good king to a tyrant ('ho kai peri Rhomylon tyrannikon ek basilikou genomenon elegeto symbenai'). For their part, and in close connection with Romulus' death, Dionysius of Halicarnassus and Plutarch illustrated at length the activities and characteristics of the founder's 'tyranny' in the last phase of his life: the exclusion of patricians from effective government of the city (Plutarch); the restitution of land and hostages to the people of Veii, without consulting beforehand either the people (Dionysius of Halicarnassus) or the senate (Plutarch); and excessive severity in punishing offenders: 'For instance, he had ordered a group of Romans who were accused of brigandage against the neighbouring peoples to be hurled down the precipice after he had sat alone in judgement upon them, although they were neither of mean birth nor few in number.'[5]

Finally, one more point of major importance may be made concerning the discrepancies between the two accounts and their different outcomes. If – as Plutarch had already observed – the dismemberment of the corpse caused a real disappearance (*aphanismos*) of the founder's body (it was taken away by the senators who concealed the pieces under their togas), this macabre and shocking *aphanismos* seems, in the documents we have, to exclude in principle, at least at first, any hypothesis of his 'divinity after death'. The two versions – the dismemberment and the ascent into heaven – are 'combined' only in narrative complexes which we can term 'mixed'; in other words, in those typical narrative complexes in which the theory of assassination is judged more probable and reliable, and where the apotheosis version is presented as an expedient necessarily adopted by the guilty senators to divert any suspicion from themselves while at the same time accounting for the disappearance of the founder's body. In this case the role of Proculus Julius (note that he was an ancestor of both Caesar and Augustus) seems not only important but also fundamental. Thanks to his testimony, Romulus' followers, distressed and by then almost rebellious, calmed down. Harmony finally returned to the city, and they worshipped a new god.[6]

2. THE ASCENT INTO HEAVEN: THE HIGHLY AMBIGUOUS CHARACTERISTICS OF A TRADITION

There has been much debate about the time when the tradition of Romulus' ascent into heaven and his transformation into the god Quirinus emerged. It is a question, at least in my opinion, of two problems which must be kept rigorously separate. It was possible for Ennius to refer to Romulus, in the invocations of the Romans after his disappearance, as 'Romulus divus' without this epithet already implying his identification with Quirinus. It is very likely that Quirinus had previously been invoked by Hersilia at the time

of the definitive encounter between the Romans and the Sabines.[7]
Kurt Latte considered that the assimilation of Romulus with
Quirinus occurred a century later, but prior to the construction
of the temple on the Quirinal in 293 BC. Georg Wissowa had pre-
viously dated it much later, in Sulla's time, while C. Joachim
Classen believed that such an assimilation should be attributed to
Caesar, and traced it back, with greater accuracy, directly to the
years 54 to 51 BC.[8]

For our part, taking our lead from certain hints in Cicero, we
shall change considerably the more general approach to the
problem. In 52 BC Cicero showed great reluctance to identify
Romulus with Quirinus in *De legibus*. In this work he discusses
with his friend Atticus the actual undertakings of Marius (to
which Cicero had recently dedicated a poem). When Atticus asks
whether the facts had been as Cicero described them, he replies:

> I will answer you, Atticus, but not until you have yourself
> answered a question. Is it a fact that Romulus, after his death,
> while wandering about near the place where your house now
> stands, met Proculus Julius, told him that he was a god, and
> was called Quirinus, and ordered that a temple be dedicated
> to him on that spot? And is it true that at Athens, likewise
> not far from your old home, Aquilo carried off Orithyia? For
> that is what tradition tells us.

To Atticus' puzzled query about the purpose of his questions,
Cicero adds, 'to keep you from inquiring too critically into traditions which are handed down in that way'. While Cicero in *De offi-
ciis* and in *De natura deorum* (in 45 to 44 BC) can still hint at the
identification of Romulus with Quirinus, albeit with reservations,
in one of his letters to Atticus in 45 he reveals – rather paradoxically at the very moment he seems to accept (perhaps ironically)
this identification – that he also knows the tradition of the murder
of the founder by the senators: 'I put that in about your neighbour
Caesar because I had learned of it from your letter. I'd rather have
him sharing a temple with Quirinus than with Salus.'[9]

The temple of Quirinus, like that of Salus, arose on the Quirinal
not far from the house of Atticus. Therefore, if, according to
Cicero, it was preferable that Caesar, thanks to one of his statues,

shared the temple of Quirinus rather than that of the goddess Salus,[10] this wording (which evidently must not have been too cryptic for Atticus) certainly alluded to the death of Romulus, murdered and dismembered by the senators, because only his death – not the goddess Salus ('Safety', 'Salvation') – would have allowed Romulus to be assimilated to the god Quirinus after his body's disappearance (his *aphanismos*, as Plutarch said). Much later, in AD 449, the learned Polemius Silvius emphasised this in his calendar.[11] It is an assimilation which should not be surprising in a polytheistic system like the Roman. Only consider the traditions of the assimilation after death of King Latinus to Jupiter Latiaris, or the assimilation of Aeneas – after his disappearance – to Jupiter Indiges (or Pater Indiges).[12] In any case, we must note that in this religious system the cult and the ritual practices were meant to be rendered exclusively to the gods (in order Quirinus, Jupiter Latiaris, and Jupiter or Pater Indiges), with the rider that whoever did not accept the identification of Romulus with Quirinus within the ambit of that system could claim legitimately that the founder's body had completely vanished, since the senators, having cut the corpse into pieces, had taken possession of it by burying its 'parts' in different places.

At any rate, even if taken bodily into heaven and thus deprived of a burial, Romulus and Aeneas were assimilated to gods only on the level of beliefs – as Cicero said, there were some who believed Romulus 'to be the same as Quirinus' ('quem quidem eundem esse Quirinum putant'). These beliefs were also open to debate, even more in the case of the founder, who – in Varro's opinion – had a tomb located in the Comitium, 'behind' or 'in front of' the *rostra*, the orator's tribune. It is a note that is clearly very important in the present context. Horace's commentators in fact recorded Varro's note concerning the 'Quirinal bones' ('*nefas videre!*'), those bones that were, as Horace says, 'sheltered from the wind and sun', until a barbarian, taking advantage of the weakness of Rome after the civil wars, impiously scattered them with his horse's 'clattering hoof'.[13]

As we shall see, Varro was very consistent as regards the Greek model he adopted as a paradigm, setting the tomb of the *oikistes* (founder) in the Forum (behind or in front of the *rostra*). In an attempt to determine the position of Romulus and Aeneas in

Rome after their deaths, we turn once again to highly characteristic ritual practices. We know that in the Augustan-Tiberian epoch the images of Aeneas and Romulus, differently from those of the *divi* (Divus Julius and later Divus Augustus), were paraded in funeral processions among the images of ancestors. Certainly the image of Romulus was carried at the funeral of Augustus, and the images of Romulus and Aeneas were carried at the funeral of Drusus Caesar, where images of the Alban kings – naturally starting with Ascanius – made appearances as well.[14] There is another extremely important point: the *divi* after their *consecratio* cannot take part in funerals with the *imagines* that represent them, even those of their own relatives. Among the many images that escorted the coffin at Augustus' funeral, that of Caesar, who was by then Divus Julius in the city, was missing. The reason for this absence becomes clear when we remember that after the *consecratio* of Augustus it was also decreed by *senatus consultus* that the image of the dead emperor, who was also a *divus* by then, could never be paraded at funerals, not even at those of his relations. Such an interdiction makes sense, since the spheres of *funus* and *divinitas* were not only antithetical but absolutely incompatible in Rome.[15]

The tradition on Romulus' tomb, coming from an historian and 'antiquarian' like Varro, must be carefully assessed. From this perspective, as we shall see, the location of this tomb, decorated with two lions and 'behind' or 'in front' of the orator's tribune (therefore in the Comitium), clearly proves to be very significant. It is highly unlikely, however, that this tomb can be identified with the monument discovered by Giacomo Boni at the end of the nineteenth century beneath the Lapis Niger (facing the *curia* and near the arch of Septimius Severus). This tomb Ettore Pais had already proposed be identified as the temple of Vulcan (the Vulcanal), whose origins, he thought, must be dated back to the second quarter of the sixth century BC.[16] At least two details are at odds with such an identification. According to the explicit evidence of Verrius Flaccus the Lapis Niger must be located 'in the Comitium' ('Niger lapis in Comitio locum funestum significat'). And yet, also according to Verrius Flaccus, the temple of Vulcan arose 'supra Comitium', as is specified for the bones which, 'ex prodigiis, oraculorumque responsis', were transferred by senate decree from the Janiculum into the city and buried precisely in the temple of Vulcan 'quod est supra Comitium'.[17] Moreover, at least in the description given by Plutarch, the temple of Vulcan, as a meeting place of the senate, must be understood as a place which was closed ('synedrion kai bouleuterion aporreton'), erected by Romulus for the purpose of consulting the senators – together with Titus Tatius – 'without being disturbed' ('aneu tou pareno-cleisthai').[18] The sanctuary beneath the Lapis Niger was instead clearly in the open, as is shown not only by its remains (the altar, the stone column which very probably supported a statue, and the inscription itself with the 'lex sacra'), but also by the presence inside it in ancient times of a 'lotos aequaeva urbi' and a 'cupressus aequalis' (impressive trees, if their roots could reach as far as Caesar's Forum).[19] The temple of Vulcan, moreover, must have arisen 'supra Comitium', in an elevated place and with a balustrade from which it was possible to address the people.[20]

Beyond any precise identification of the sanctuary beneath the Lapis Niger (according to some the 'place . . . for the tomb of Romulus', but in fact never used as his burial place; according to others, the tomb of his *nutricius* Faustulus; or else the tomb of Hostus Hostilius, an ancestor of King Tullus Hostilius),[21] it is, however, evident that Varro – and, according to an annotator of Horace, many others – did not accept either the tradition that Romulus ascended to heaven, or the tradition of the dismemberment of his body by the senators. According to Varro, Romulus (however he had died) had a tomb, and this tomb, in accordance with his position of founder, was in the Comitium, just as the tombs of founders in Greek cities, beginning with that of Theseus at Athens, were located in the centre of the *agorai*.[22] After our observations on the Vestal Tarpeia, it will come as no surprise that Varro used Hellenic models for the most ancient history of Rome and its monuments. As a city could not exist from its foundation without a 'common hearth', so, according to Varro – once the version according to which Romulus was 'simply' dead had been accepted – his tomb could not be anywhere but in the Comitium.[23]

3. ROMULUS AND THE GOD QUIRINUS

The assimilation of Romulus to the god Quirinus after his ascent to heaven was already current in the Augustan period to the point that Ovid, as we shall see, set the ascent not on the day on which it had occurred (the Poplifugia on 5 July) but on the feast day of the god Quirinus (the Quirinalia on 17 February). Note, however, that Livy, although he reported the version of Romulus' apotheosis, carefully avoided recording a possible assimilation of the founder to that particular deity, an assimilation which was accepted by Dionysius of Halicarnassus and Plutarch. As for his reticence (the Romans did no more than acclaim Romulus as 'a god and a god's son, the King and Father of the Roman City'), it is not very surprising. In Augustus' time, when the image of Romulus was still paraded among those of the ancestors of the *domus Augusta* at funerals, that assimilation did not constitute a 'dogma', but rather a simple belief.

From this viewpoint, moreover, we can see something that is very typical. In Dionysius of Halicarnassus and Plutarch, Quirinus is a completely new god, whose cult had been established in Rome only after the disappearance of the founder and as a result of the testimony of Proculus Julius. Varro, however, had previously counted Quirinus among the gods to whom an altar had been dedicated following a vow by King Titus Tatius; besides, he was a god whose name, together with those of many other deities, had a Sabine 'flavour'.[24] From this we can infer that if Varro's hypothesis was not completely isolated, and a cult of Quirinus already existed in Rome before the disappearance of Romulus, this would explain the reluctance, first of Ennius – who restricted himself to numbering Romulus among the 'dii genitales' – and later of Livy, to identify the vanished founder with this particular deity, who must have been honoured already in Rome before Romulus' miraculous disappearance.

In fact, the great antiquity of the cult of Quirinus – which predates the construction of his temple on the Quirinal in 293 BC by Lucius Papirius Cursor, son of the Papirius who had vowed to do this in 325 after one of his victories over the Samnites – is supported not only by the presence of the 'flamen Quirinalis' among the most important flamens of the city, but also by the existence – again on the Quirinal – of a 'Quirini sacellum', which Pliny the Elder counted 'among the most ancient temples of Rome'.[25] It was not difficult for André Magdelain to contradict and almost overturn the hypothesis advanced by Georges Dumézil of an

'agrarian' Quirinus as a deity of the 'third Indo-European function', and instead emphasise his characteristics of a god of the
community of the Quirites, basing this on the name (*Covirino*),
which was undoubtedly connected with *co-viria*, the *curia*.[26] A
strong pointer in this direction, although it has never been considered in this context, is also the coincidence of the Quirinalia
with the 'festival of fools' (the *feriae stultorum*) on 17 February.

As is well known, the Romans celebrated with special rites the
festival of the *curiae* on the day of the Fornacalia (a movable feast
established, according to tradition, by Numa Pompilius), the date
of which was announced in advance every year by the *curio
maximus*, the leader of all the *curiae*. Romans who had forgotten
their own *curia* could still perform the 'sacred ceremonies' prescribed for the *curia* to which they belonged on the day of the
Quirinalia. Georges Dumézil and Angelo Brelich, along with
others who have seen in Quirinus an 'agrarian' god, have stressed
the coincidence of the 'festival of fools' with the Quirinalia, while
almost ignoring that the Fornacalia were meant to be celebrated
in Rome not in honour of Quirinus but in honour of the goddess
Fornax, a deity who was – as André Magdelain has pointed out –
'represented' in a way that was both appropriate and necessary.[27]
The fact that 'fools', who by then were ignorant of the *curia* to
which they individually belonged, celebrated their forgotten
original *curia* on the day of the Quirinalia makes sense, if
Quirinus is understood much more simply as the god of all the
Quirites, the Roman citizens who, after the foundation of the city,
had been divided into the thirty *curiae* established by Romulus.

Thus we can understand the identification of Romulus, who
ascended into heaven, with the god Quirinus, as he is defined by
Ennius: 'father and custodian of the homeland', he who cast the
Romans 'into the territories of light'.[28] Romulus, who established
the thirty *curiae* into which he divided the citizens, could not but
be transformed, as a result, into the god Quirinus, a Mars 'who
presides over peace', a 'tranquil Mars', without ties to the 'agricultural' sphere, who fitted legitimately, by his very nature, into
the original divisions of the body civic, divisions that Romulus
had established. Such a view may also explain the exact correspondence of the Roman precapitoline triad (Jupiter, Mars,
Quirinus) with the triad depicted in the Gubbio Tables in

Umbria, where *Iou-*, *Mart-* and *Vofonio-* are represented, and where *Vofonio-* was quickly recognised as the exact equivalent of *Covirino (Quirinus).[29]

4. THE DISMEMBERMENT OF THE BODY: COMPARATIVIST PERSPECTIVES

Having examined at length the legend of the apotheosis of Romulus and the long process of his identification with Quirinus, we must observe, however, that this very uncertain identification had not fully occurred even in the Augustan-Tiberian epoch, when – as has already been seen – the image of Romulus was paraded at the funeral of Augustus and then later, in AD 23, in the funeral procession of Drusus Caesar.

We therefore turn now to the legend which has it that the body of the founder was cut into pieces by the senators inside the senate. Walter Burkert, in particular, has been credited with having thrown light on the profound political and ideological importance of the problems relating to the 'disappearance' of the body of Romulus in the last century of the republic (his *aphanismos*, according to Plutarch). It is not improbable that certain features of the 'tyranny' of Romulus 'at the end', when he is again sole king after the death of Titus Tatius (as we have seen, a death that was also obscure and violent), echo themes of anti-Caesarian polemics; in particular, polemics against the 'tyranny' of Caesar 'at the end'. As the conspirators – according to Appian – chose the senate for the assassination of the dictator, because they wished to imitate the example of the ancient senators who had murdered Romulus when 'he changed from a king to a tyrant', so the episode of the historical tyrannicide, in a sort of circular process, seems in some respects to have had its own effects on the representation of the causes and motives of the tyrannicide of legend. And not only on the representation of causes and motives, but, highly significantly, also on particular features of the representation of events that followed this legendary tyrannicide. In John of Antioch's account – a typical example of the narrative complexes that we have termed 'mixed' – it is, importantly, 'primarily the plebeians and the soldiers' ('to plethos kai hoi stratiotai malista') who look anxiously for Romulus after his disappearance (achieved in this case by dis-

memberment at the hands of the senators), and who provoke disorder and plan uprisings, just as the urban plebeians and veterans,
who had joined forces before in Rome, were the main protagonists
immediately after the Ides of March in the disorder and riots following the death of Caesar, especially at his funeral.[30]

With regard to the cult of the king, Burkert claims that at least
on certain levels 'destruction' (obviously of the body) and divin-
isation coincide, and he suggests comparing the legend of the
assassination of Romulus by the senators with the ritual sacrifice
of the bull and the banquet that followed it in the *feriae Latinae*,
celebrated annually on the Alban Hill. In this example the bull
'represented' King Latinus, who, having miraculously disappeared in the war against Mezentius, was identified with Jupiter
Latiaris, in whose honour the *feriae* were held. However, the
comparison poses problems when two particular details are considered. In the dismemberment legend, Romulus' body was
simply buried; the senators did not prepare a banquet with it. As
we have already pointed out with regard to the feast 'manqué' of
the prototypical *luperci*, the sharing of meat during the banquet
in the *feriae Latinae* was evidently intended to confirm, by means
of the fair distribution of the flesh of the sacrificial bull each year,
the 'equality' of the peoples who comprised the Latin league,
whose names were recorded on a famous list provided by Pliny
the Elder.[31]

Marie Delcourt has already drawn attention to the antiquity of
the legend of Romulus' dismemberment in comparison with that
of his ascent to heaven. This was very important, and it led
Delcourt to compare the tradition of Romulus, who was cut into
pieces by the senators, with the legend of Mettius Fufetius, dictator of Alba, who was torn apart by chariots on the order of King
Tullus Hostilius. The dismemberment of Romulus corresponded
to that of Mettius Fufetius, while the legend of Romulus' apotheosis matched that of the fate of Tullus Hostilius, who, while performing sacrifices to Elicius, was struck dead and burnt, together
with his entire household, by a lightning bolt from Jupiter (the
god had been enraged and 'exasperated' by the non-ritual ('non
rite', 'prava religione') performance of those sacrifices).[32] At least
two considerable objections should be made to this construction.
The death of Mettius Fufetius, who was not a king but a dictator,

cannot be compared with that of Romulus, since the kind of torture reserved for the Alban Mettius Fufetius is simply determined by his sin. After his treachery in the battle against the Veientes and the Fidenates, his body, by order of King Tullus, was tied to two four-horse chariots (or two horses), which, spurred 'in opposite directions', served 'to rend' his body, just as Mettius Fufetius with his treachery had 'rent' the *fides* and the pacts (*foedera*) previously established with Tullus Hostilius and the Romans. (Note the absence from the legend of any suggestion of a quartering of the body, even though Livy commented: 'Such was the first and last punishment among the Romans of a kind that disregards the laws of humanity.') Furthermore, it must be observed that it is difficult to compare Romulus' ascent to heaven (in which tradition he was not torn apart) with Tullus Hostilius' final punishment, which, though cruel and ruthless, nevertheless was intended to punish Mettius Fufetius in an exemplary way for his sin of *perfidia*.[33]

Later comparativist perspectives focused more closely on comparisons drawn from the Indo-European world. It seems to me that they too should be put aside, not only because of the absence of really significant comparisons inferred from that context (the Vedic Asvins, the Dioscuri, Pelias and Neleus),[34] but also – perhaps above all – because it is somewhat arbitrary to link Remus with the ox and Romulus with the horse and connect their different destinies after death with these animals; namely, death for the twin associated with the ox (Remus), and immortality for the twin associated with the horse (Romulus). In point of fact, Romulus appears in a relationship that can be termed 'solid' with the world of cattle (ox and cow) at the very moment of foundation of his city, when the two animals drive the ploughshare that traced the primitive furrow. Remus, however, according to the tradition found in Ovid regarding the origin of the festival of the Lupercalia, was restricted – as we have seen – to recovering the *iuvenci* that the robbers had tried to steal.[35] Finally, with regard to the parallel between the death of Romulus, murdered by the senators, and that of Titus Tatius, murdered at Lavinium by relatives and friends of the Laurentian ambassadors who had been attacked, here – as we have seen – it applies solely to the assassination. Titus Tatius is connected to the world of oxen only very indirectly, in that he did not punish his friends and relatives who, with bands of robbers, had raided the Laurentians' territory and plundered, among 'many goods', their herds as well.[36]

5. ROMULUS IN THE SOUTH SEAS

In an attempt to explain the legend of Romulus' dismemberment, Angelo Brelich, returning to a suggestion already advanced by James Frazer, drew attention – with explicit reference to Jensen's earlier research – to people 'in a state of nature', whom Jensen defines as figures of the type *dema*. 'The *Dema* are beings who lived in the mythic primal past, who, after having founded the principal institutions of a people, were slain.' Afterwards, 'from their bodies – from the parts of their bodies, often buried – sprang useful plants for the sustenance of the people'.[37]

Starting from a fundamental and, in his opinion, original identicalness of Romulus and Quirinus, Brelich linked Romulus' death by dismemberment with agrarian fertility rites. His reconstruction, however, confused and almost combined two completely antithetical versions (whereas Ennius counted Romulus among the 'dii genitales', Cicero doubted his identification with the god Quirinus). We have seen that only by a physical ascent to heaven – which precludes being cut into pieces by the senators – could Romulus be transformed into Quirinus and worshipped as him.

Moreover, even if according to Dionysius of Halicarnassus the parts of Romulus' body were buried by the senators with the intention, as shrewd as it was obvious, of making them disappear, in order to avoid being accused of homicide, the ancient records make no claim that any plant grew from these pieces of his body. (The different link between the Quirinalia and the 'festival of fools' has been examined.) Furthermore, whilst the tubers that were 'cut into pieces before being planted in order to produce new food plants' by 'primitive cultivators' were well suited to the diet of the people to whom Jensen – and after him Brelich – refers, they do not seem very appropriate to the rural landscape of the ancient Roman *ager*, where 'man's cultivation of the soil of *Latium vetus* seems to have been limited, until the end of the eighth century, to growing cereals and a few legumes'.[38]

In the wake of Georges Dumézil – and implicitly accepting the hypothesis that Quirinus was an 'agrarian' god – Marshall Sahlins has been quick to compare the fate of Romulus with that of Captain Cook, whom the Hawaiians immediately identified on his arrival in Hawaii as 'their lost god/king', the 'Year God, Lono, known especially as the patron of agricultural fertility', who returned every year to renew the fertility of the soil. Nevertheless, Sahlins – paradoxically, considering his purpose – seems not to know the dismemberment version (he ignores Brelich's research based on this version), but only that of the founder's ascent to heaven, as well as another version according to which Romulus is 'the victim of the sacrifice he himself offers at the altar of (his father) Mars'.[39] As we have seen, it is impossible to connect Romulus-Quirinus to the agricultural sphere. Regarding the other version, we shall merely note here that it was simply never documented in antiquity.

6. A ROMAN VIEW: THE DISAPPEARANCE OF ROMULUS AND THE FOUNDATION OF THE *COMITIA*

In more recent times, credit goes above all to Filippo Coarelli for having brought together the two traditions of Romulus' disappearance in the much firmer context of typical Roman institutions. In so doing, he abandoned the very faint, more vaguely comparativist tracks. According to Coarelli, the assassination of Romulus by the senators in the Comitium – specifically in the sanctuary of Vulcan – gave rise to the foundation 'myth' of the *comitia curiata*, while his disappearance on the Campus Martius – specifically at the Goat's Marsh – established that of the *comitia centuriata*. There is thus a doubling 'of the foundation myth of the *comitia* in relation to both of the places in which they were subsequently held'.[40] However, we have shown that the temple of Vulcan was not situated precisely in the Comitium, where the *comitia curiata* were held in ancient times, but rather – however this should be understood – 'above the Comitium' and therefore, much more simply, in its immediate vicinity.[41]

Besides problems of precise topographical identification, however, if the two traditions of the disappearance of Romulus are interpreted as foundation legends of the two types of *comitia* (*comitia curiata* and *comitia centuriata*), an essential difficulty lies in two details. On the one hand, the Roman traditions never link the *comitia centuriata* with the founder; rather, they are in complete agreement that those *comitia* considerably postdated Romulus, because they were established by the 'good' king Servius Tullius.[42] On the other hand, one of the traditions – as we have seen – placed the dismemberment of Romulus' body not in the open, where the *comitia* were held, but indoors, more specifically in the seat of the senate.

7. THE BODY OF ROMULUS AND THE ORIGINS OF THE PATRICIATE

Let us take a different track, yet one which, like that proposed by Filippo Coarelli, is also eminently 'Roman'. Instead of isolating the saga of the founder's disappearance – as has happened too often – we shall instead link it to the events that followed. If the purpose of Romulus' ascent to heaven was to transform him into a god, then the dismemberment of his body – as we shall see – also had a special 'function'. On an institutional level, the episodes following the king's death are highly relevant: for the first time the interregnum and the 'authority of the *patres*' ('auctoritas patrum') appear. After the disappearance of Romulus, the city had been open to disorder and discord: on the one hand, discord between Roman and Sabine senators; on the other, discord between patricians and plebeians. The Sabine senators, who after Titus Tatius' death gladly accepted the government of Romulus alone, now wanted the new king to come from their own ranks, while at first the Roman senators feared an 'alien' king could somehow limit their powers. Since the city, in the absence of someone who held *imperium*, was in grave danger after Romulus' disappearance, the senate resorted to the stratagem of the interregnum. Livy describes how this worked in detail:

> And so the hundred senators shared the power among themselves, establishing ten decuries and appointing one man for each decury to preside over the administration. Ten men exercised authority; only one had its insignia and lictors. Five days was the period of his power, which passed in rotation to all; and for a year the monarchy lapsed.[43]

However, it was a rather turbulent interregnum. Not only was it the first, but it lasted a year and was, according to the tradition relating to the monarchic period, by far the longest.[44] While the clashes between Latins and Sabines over the choice of a new king explained its unusually long duration, it may be seen that, in this particular instance, the period allowed the great majority of the patricians (or rather, all of them), divided into decuries, to exercise the interregnum. According to Livy, then, the patricians concerned numbered one hundred, while Dionysius says there were two hundred or else one hundred and fifty, the figure reported by Plutarch. Plutarch added that they exercised power without being divided into decuries, but in turn ('en merei'), and that their office lasted not five days but, continually taking turns, scarcely twelve hours (six by day and six at night):

> This distribution of times seemed well adapted to secure equality between the two factions, and the transfer of power likely to remove all jealousy on the part of the people, when they saw the same man, in the course of a single day and night, become king and then a private citizen again.[45]

Ignoring any calculations (which for that matter are not very difficult) of the number of *patres* involved and the process of their rotation, we see that this first interregnum, besides being collective (in some traditions unequivocally shared by all the *patres*) is, at least in the beginning, pre-eminently collegial, thanks to the system of division into decuries. Without doubt possession of the auspices was joint and collegial. In the course of this first interregnum the patricians appear for the first time as the holders of the auspices, and, during various interregnums in the historical period down to the end of the republic, they always hold them jointly and collegially. According to the famous Ciceronian adage, in the absence of consuls or higher ranking magistrates, 'the auspices return to the patricians' ('auspicia ad patres redeunt').[46] Similar comments can be made with regard to the 'authority of the patricians'. This extraordinary power of 'growth' was also joint and collective – much later it was a simple power of ratifying decisions of the people's *comitia* – and it too appeared for the first time in the selection of Numa, Romulus' successor. Having held the auspices during the interregnum, now the patricians become holders of *auctoritas* as well. As Santo Mazzarino pointed out, 'the *auctoritas* is covered by the *auspicia*: the higher *auctoritas patrum* is linked to their power in the *interregnum*'.[47]

After examining the institutional consequences of the disappearance – in Plutarch the *aphanismos* – of the founder, we now turn to the version of his death which Livy said was 'little known'. According to this version the patricians not only murdered Romulus, but they also tore apart his corpse, each of them taking away a piece of his body. As Plutarch relates in *Romulus*, '[they] cut his body in pieces, put each a portion into the folds of his robe, and so carried it away'. According to Plutarch, then, it was simply carried away, without any mention of the burial of the pieces, while in *Numa* he recalled that the senators, by then tired of being governed by a king, had killed Romulus because they 'desired to transfer the power to themselves'. At this point in Dionysius' version of the story, the purpose (as shrewd as it is obvious) of the interment of the parts was to make the body disappear, so that the senators could make more credible the founder's miraculous disappearance and calm the resentment of the plebeians, who were extremely suspicious of them.[48]

Apart from the anti-tyrannical reasons or any moralistic attitudes, the strangest element of this version is not the assassination, certainly. It is clearly the dividing up of the corpse, its division and distribution in 'parts' (a distribution that would involve all of the patricians together). The vast range of possible comparisons deduced from the mythic theme of the death of the founder or 'cultural hero' has generally furnished a useful frame of reference. At the same time, the infinite valencies assumed by this theme from time to time in different cultures – as we have seen at length – reveal the objective impossibility of really meaningful illuminating comparisons with respect to the legendary episode of the dismemberment of Romulus' body.

Yet Romulus, the *rex* whose augur's rod (the *lituus*) remained in the *curia* of the Salii, was also the natural holder of the auspices, which he took for the first time – as Ennius recorded[49] – together with his brother Remus at the moment of the foundation. He himself performed the rite of reading the auspices on his investiture. No 'patricians' authority' had been exercised on his selection, nor, evidently, could it have been, because the patricians, prior to being established by Romulus, simply did not exist. As for his *imperium*, Romulus, like Numa after him, did not take care to present a 'lex curiata' to the people, once again because the *curiae*, before Romulus established them, clearly did not exist and were therefore never able to gather in *comitia*. After his death the patricians became *interrex* and held the auspices. When it was necessary to choose a new king they appeared beforehand as *auctores*, co-holders of the auspices, with greater 'authority' over the decisions of the people when Numa was selected.[50] We therefore ask how and when this change occurred, how and when the auspices and the *auctoritas* were able to transfer materially from Romulus to the patricians. At this point we must infer that if – according to Cicero – it was Romulus who created the two fundamental institutions on which the government of the city of Rome rested (the auspices and the senate),[51] and the senators in turn created the interregnum, then thanks to the dismemberment of the founder's body, the patricians could be *interrex*, collectively and in perpetuity. They possessed what was most precious in that body; namely, the auspices, since these are essential in the legitimate government of the city, allowing whoever holds them to contact the gods and know their will, in order to act according to their wishes and keep their 'peace'.

Clearly we are looking at the sphere of the sacred here, since the auspices and originally the *auctoritas* belong to this sphere. Both are elements that passed from the *patres* by means of heredity to their descendants, the *patricii*. Later they would distinguish the *patricii* – organised into a closed class and structured according to their *gentes* – from the rest of the population. It is precisely the uniqueness of the patricians' possession of the auspices, on which they insisted during the conflict of the orders, that prevented plebeians in the high republican period from entering the magistratures that provided for the imperial management. It also prevented the contracting of 'mixed' marriages between patricians and plebeians. The patricians did not want the 'gentilitial rights' to be confused, as the consuls of 445 BC maintained they would be in their response to a bill from the plebeians' tribune, Gaius Canuleius, which aimed to abolish this prohibition.[52]

Now the episode of the division by the patricians of the first king's body has a meaning and a function. In dismembering Romulus' corpse they had meant to 'dismember' in fact both the auspices and *auctoritas* of which Romulus was the sole repository and the first holder. By each taking possession of a part of his body, they entered into possession, collectively and severally, of those auspices and that *auctoritas*, as if the body of the founder had been their custodian from the very beginning. As often happens in Rome, it is a matter of a code that was evidently very poor on the level of the abstract, but – as should be clear by now – evidently very rich on the level of 'ideology', more particularly political 'ideology'. Recently the origins of the Roman patriciate have been discussed – or, to be more precise, the era in which the Roman patriciate was constituted as a closed class. Our considerations allow us to conclude that, according to a legend that is very ancient, at least two distinctive and hereditary attributes of this class (possession of the auspices and possession of *auctoritas*) were traced back almost to the origins of the republic, and they arose from a type of death (the dismemberment of Romulus' body) that is midway between assassination and ritual homicide.

In this context a comparison emerges – even if at first glance it appears rather a paradoxical comparison – with the fate of the debtor who owed money to a number of creditors, according to one of the statutes of the Twelve Tables. While the fate of the debtor who was in debt to a single creditor was at least temporary imprisonment in the latter's house, in chains and fetters, the debtor who was in debt to several creditors could, according to the statute, after three market days had passed, and once he had been definitively sentenced, be cut into pieces. The 'size' of the part of the corpse taken by each creditor did not necessarily have to correspond to the size of the debt. It was a terrible punishment which did not fail to excite repugnance in some of the ancient annotators of this legal provision.[53]

In actual fact, if the debtor had broken the *fides* (in this specific case, in a private contract) and was stained with the crime of *perfidia*, his body – like that of Mettius Fufetius earlier – could be 'rent' into grisly pieces, into *partes*. An addition was suggested by the legal decemvirs whereby the 'part' of the body of the debtor taken by the creditor was not in relation to the size of the debt. It was as if by taking possession of these pieces the creditors could feel that they were regaining a part of their lost debt which until then had been 'contained' only in the debtor's body and consequently could be reappropriated only by possessing a 'part' of that body. If the creditors chose not to sell the debtor into slavery 'across the Tiber', but instead to cut up his body, the fact that this choice was economically utterly irrational must be an indication of the deep meaning attached to the punishment.[54]

As for the legend of the dismemberment of Romulus' body by the *patres* and hence their taking possession of the auspices, we cannot help drawing attention here to what Gaetano De Sanctis, in another connection, termed the 'patrician lock-out'. The patricians had based on legal precedent their prerogative of becoming the only higher-ranking magistrates in the city through the fundamental circumstance that they alone were legitimate holders of the auspices. However, an additional factor is also well known: gentilitial plebeians were present among the titled consuls at festivals in the historical period. This occurred consistently from the time of Junius Brutus (who became one of the founding fathers of the republic in 509, the traditional date of the first consular elections) down to 483, and then, more sporadically, from 482 to 428. Various attempts have been made to explain the presence of these plebeian nobles in the context of an exclusively patrician administration of the consular colleges until the laws of Licinius Sextius of 366 BC. However, we must accept the more obvious and 'economic' conclusion that the plebeians were not excluded from the supreme magistrature (whatever it was called) from the beginning of the republic.[55] Their exclusion, then, occurred slowly and progressively only in the course of the first half of the fifth century, and ended – at least apparently – in 428. While the conflict of the orders explains such an exclusion, the explanation that was given for it later by the patricians is fundamental, at least from our point of view. This was that the plebeians were deprived of the auspices 'by their very nature', and therefore it was impossible for them to make contact with the world of the gods and consult them on the outcomes of their actions as eventual magistrates and holders of 'imperium'. Only the patricians claimed to possess the auspices and imperium from the beginning. It is not unlikely, then, that the legend of the dismemberment of the founder's body by the ancient *patres*, who – as we have seen – had thus taken possession of the auspices originally held only by Romulus in the 'material-ness' of his body, should also be traced back to this period. After the expulsion of the last of the Tarquins, which occurred thanks also to the support of the plebeians, the patricians had also proudly arrogated to themselves the assassination of the first king (which occurred when he, a good king, changed into a 'tyrant'). They traced to that legendary tyrannicide their exclusive posses-sion of those auspices which qualified them alone to hold higher ranking magistracies.

While the patricians' claim of responsibility for the 'primordial tyrannicide' of that Romulus whom the plebeians had always held dear makes good sense during the first half of the fifth century at very bitter moments in the conflict of the orders, the fortune of the founder figure in later centuries clearly would have helped to reduce such a claim to that 'very obscure voice' of which Livy spoke. However, as we shall now see, that 'very obscure voice' was vital enough to be transformed even at the end of the republic into a real threat.

8. THE DEATH OF ROMULUS AND THE DESTINY OF CAESAR

The death of Romulus at the hands of the senators, when he had appeared to change from a good king into a 'tyrant', became a real threat in Rome again much later. The threat was advanced by one of the consuls in the senate against Pompey before the *lex Gabinia* against the pirates was carried. There were fears that, by infesting the seas and at the same time blocking the passage of food supplies, the pirates would cause severe famine in the city. The law was received 'extraordinarily favourably' by the people, since it was aimed at avoiding food shortages. However, it was opposed by 'the most influential and authoritative members of the senate', who feared the emergency powers that it conferred on Pompey, who was charged with 'reclaiming' – using extraordi-nary means – the whole Mediterranean from the pirates. According to Plutarch, one of the two consuls then said to Pompey 'that, if he wanted to imitate Romulus, he would not escape Romulus' fate'. Pompey, in effect, thanks to the *lex Gabinia*, obtained powers so extreme that they almost made him appear a 'tyrant', but, according to one of the consuls of that year, he would not escape the fate of the founder, who had been assassinated by the senators when he changed from a good king into a 'tyrant'.[56] The consul's threat in 67 BC demonstrates convincingly – if there were any further need of demonstration – that in those years the tradition of Romulus' ascent into heaven and his transformation at the same time into the god Quirinus was still not definitively formulated. We note, however, Cicero's later reference in 45, when he maintained that he preferred Caesar (thanks to the presence of one of his statues) to share the temple of Quirinus rather than that of the goddess Salus. This proves – as we have seen – that, even if Cicero seemed not to accept entirely this identification, or seemed to accept it in a very occasional, 'wavering' way, the identification did not cancel out the tradition of the founder's assassination by the ancient *patres*.[57]

Regarding the death of Caesar, we have a tradition that was still present in Appian (and therefore probably also in the historian Asinius Pollio, a contemporary of Caesar). The conspirators, Brutus and Cassius,

> chose the Senate as the place (*to bouleuterion*), believing that, even though the senators did not know of it beforehand, they would join heartily (*prothymos*) when they saw the deed; and it was said that this happened in the case of Romulus when he changed from a king to a tyrant. They thought that this deed, like that one of old, taking place in open Senate, would seem to be not in the way of a private conspiracy (*kat'epiboulen*), but in behalf of the country (*huper tes poleos*).

For Brutus, killing Caesar meant acquiring the title of tyrannicide, 'because that would be the killing of a king' ('hos basilea aphainontes'). To kill the friends of Caesar would transform them into the bearers of civil war, into 'partisans' ('stasiotai'); in this case, into partisans of the dead Pompey.[58]

In the very long speech which the 'Thucydidean' Cassius Dio attributed to the consular Fufius Calenus in defence of Mark Antony, to whom Cassius Dio was notoriously very close, Fufius Calenus refuted, one by one, the arguments used by Cicero against the consul of that year. Cicero had strongly inveighed against Mark Antony, claiming that, at the Lupercalia of 44, having broken away from the other *luperci* with whom he had been running, he had attempted to place a diadem on Caesar's head, hailing him king in the name of the Roman people. His behaviour was given a completely different interpretation in the speech attributed by Cassius Dio to Fufius Calenus. It was portrayed as an astute expedient by Mark Antony to dissuade Caesar from accepting the kingdom. According to Fufius Calenus, the episode had occurred in the Forum, since the Forum had been the source of 'many deliberations for freedom'. It occurred, more particularly, on the orator's platform, the *rostra*, from which had been sent forth 'thousands upon thousands of measures on behalf of the republic'. It took place at the festival of the Lupercalia, in order that the dictator might remember Romulus, and would be reminded implicitly of his pitiful death. The acclamation came from the mouth of a consul (Mark Antony), so that Caesar would call to mind the deeds of the consuls of ancient times. And it came from one who spoke in the name of the people, so that Caesar would reflect that he was seeking to establish his own tyranny (*tyrannein*) 'not over Africans or Gauls or Egyptians, but over very Romans'. Thus, on that day, Mark Antony had 'by his cleverness and consummate skill' prevented 'the tyranny of Caesar', by inducing the dictator to give up his original plans.[59]

Stephan Weinstock has discussed at length the 'Romulean' characteristics of Caesar the dictator, especially in the years of the dictatorship for life.[60] On what precisely took place on the Ides of March in 44 BC, the day of the tyrannicide, it is natural to repeat what Alex Home, 'R. N., of Buskenburn, Berwickshire, while with Captain Cook on his Last Voyage', wrote in his log of 1779 about Cook's death:

> What I have here said I do not Aver to be the Real Truth in Every particul although in General it may be pretty Nigh the Matter. I have carefully Assorted such Relations as had the greatest appearance of Truth. But indeed they were so Exceedingly perplexed in their Accounts that it was a hard matter to Colect Certainty, in particular cases, or indeed to write any Account at all.[61]

On that day the men of the Royal Navy did not understand either the concatenation of events or the Hawaiian 'reasons' for the ritual killing of Captain Cook. In the Severan Period, however, the historian Cassius Dio at a distance of more than two and a half centuries was much more peremptory, both about the unfolding of events and about the causes that determined them: 'It happened as follows, and his death was due to the cause now to be given.' Examining the many accounts of the tyrannicide, we mention here only that, even according to Suetonius, when the conspirators, who had explored various possible ways to kill Caesar, learned that the senate was convened for the Ides of March in Pompey's *curia*, they 'easily chose the date and the place'. In the Roman calendar the date was exactly a month after the Lupercalia of February, on which day Mark Antony had sought to place the diadem on the head of the 'dictator for life'. The place – Pompey's *curia* on the Campus Martius – could not but strongly evoke the name of the man who in the past had been the dictator's most important opponent.[62]

Let us now examine the inevitable parallels – which evidently did not escape contemporaries – between the position of Romulus and that of Caesar, the dictator for life. First, by a senate decree, from the beginning of 44 BC the person of Caesar was declared sacrosanct or, more accurately, Caesar's body was declared 'sacred and inviolable', like those of the tribunes of the plebeians on whose benches he had the right to sit during spectacles. Second, again by senate decree, he enjoyed another most unusual privilege: that of being buried, when he died, 'inside the pomerium' ('entos tou pomeriou'). Even though it was a corpse, the body of Caesar – like that of a Vestal – would never have been a source of contamination for the city, and for this reason alone his tomb could be within the sacred boundary of Rome, like the tomb of Romulus, which Horace's commentaries, following Varro's lead, placed in the Comitium 'in front of' or 'behind' the orator's tribune.[63] According to Plutarch, from the time when Romulus, towards the end of his reign, had begun to act like an absolute monarch, 'he dressed in a scarlet tunic, and wore over it a toga bordered with purple, and sat on a recumbent throne when he gave audience. And he had always about him some young men called Celeres, from their *swiftness* in doing service.' In Caesar's case too, the senate decreed not only that he 'should always ride, even in the city itself, wearing the triumphal dress', but he was also granted 'a gilded chair . . . and a garb that the kings had once used'. While the *celeres* provided Romulus' body-guard, Caesar was assigned 'a body-guard of knights and senators'. And while Romulus, after the murder of Acron, dedicated *spolia opima* in the temple of Jupiter Feretrius, Caesar was also permitted to place *spolia opima* in the temple of Jupiter Feretrius, 'as if he had slain some hostile general with his own hand'.[64]

In 45 BC the title *Imperator* was added to the privileges of always wearing triumphal garments in the city and at sacrifices, and of dedicating *spolia opima* in the temple of Jupiter Feretrius. This was intended to fix permanently in an onomastic formula the imperial acclamations he had received.[65] It was a privilege that was followed by a second, equally characteristic: 'a special thanksgiving whenever any victory should occur and sacrifices should be offered for it, even if he had not been on the campaign or had any hand at all in the achievements'. In fact Caesar, as dictator and by then dictator for life, possessed 'supreme power', not only with respect to other magistrates, but more generally compared to all other holders of *imperium* who led armies, and this 'special thanksgiving whenever any victory should occur' compares with similarly problematical developments in the Augustan era when every military campaign, even if it had been conducted (*ductu*) by someone else, was understood to have been accomplished 'under the auspices' of the emperor.

Between Romulus and Caesar there is a final – and probably definitive – comparison to make. Starting in 45 or 44 BC, the *cognomen* 'Father of the Country' ('pater patriae') is an integral part, to all intents and purposes, of the title 'Caesar'. It would be wrong to trivialise the tremendous potentiality implicit in such an attribute by looking at its later consequences as if they were somehow 'crystallised' in the imperial period. Thanks to this designation Caesar became a true father for all the citizens, and in return all the citizens were bound to him by true filial ties, to the extent that, after his death, by senate decree the Ides of March were marked *parricidium* on calendars, since on that day the father of all the citizens had been murdered by some of his impious and wicked sons. Romulus – as is well known – is also a *pater* for the

Romans within a heritage of knowledge that can be traced back to Ennius. In Livy he appears not only as 'father of the city' (*pater urbis*) but also as 'father of the country' (*pater patriae*), and as such is compared with Camillus, the 'second founder' of Rome, who liberated the city from the Gauls.[66]

After the parallels that have been pointed out between the 'lifestyles' of Romulus, in the last phase of his reign, and Caesar, the dictator for life, in the first months of 44, it becomes clear why Caesar's assassins chose the seat of the senate – as already emphasised by Appian – for the murder, even if it is probable that it can be attributed only to a chance that on the senate's agenda was a matter related to the *auspices*.[67] Similarities between the legendary assassination and the one that really occurred appear more interesting, however. Just as the senators of antiquity, all together, had killed Romulus, 'surrounding him' ('periechontes'), so the conspirators encircled Caesar ('en kykloi periechomenos'), and they, too, all took part in the murder, with some wounding others in the confusion, 'for all had to take part in the sacrifice and taste of the slaughter'. Finally, just as following the death of Romulus there was a disorderly and confused flight (which began the celebration of the Poplifugia), so it was said that everyone fled *en masse* after Caesar's death and 'alarmed those who met them by saying nothing intelligible, but merely shouting out the words: "Run! Bolt doors! Bolt doors!"', provoking a disorderly and seemingly mad flight of the other citizens.[68] If Brutus, Cassius and the other conspirators intended to imitate the senators of the Romulean epoch, they very probably achieved their aim.

Epilogue

The first to deny any historicity to the figure of Romulus, the founder of Rome, was Barthold Georg Niebuhr, in the first volume of his *Storia romana*, published in 1813. In his opinion at least, the figure, from his miraculous birth to his equally miraculous ascent to heaven, was an ensemble of legends, formed from the most varied elements: the sagas that circulated in ancient Latium and which could have been transmitted orally, and those spread by Greek historians, who, from at least the fourth century, were interested in Rome and its most ancient history. There were violent attacks on Niebuhr, who was in those years the Prussian ambassador in Rome, chiefly from spheres closely connected to the Curia. Since by denying the historicity of Romulus he was also denying the passing of the legitimacy of the empire from Romulus through Augustus and Constantine to the Roman pontiffs, so Abbot Don Carlo Fea, the curator of the Capitoline Museums, could reject Niebuhr's arguments in one of his libellous pamphlets that was full of horror at the outrage to the reigning pope and of acrimony towards suppositions that Fea himself held to be contemptible and ill-founded.[1]

In the first volume of *The History of Rome*, published in 1854, Theodor Mommsen was even more impatient and dismissive:

> The story of the foundation of Rome by refugees from Alba under the leadership of the sons of an Alban prince, Romulus and Remus, is nothing but a naïve attempt of primitive quasi-history to explain the singular circumstance of the place having arisen on a site so unfavourable, and to connect at the same time the origin of Rome with the general metropolis of Latium. Such tales, which profess to be historical but are merely improvised explanations of no

very ingenious character, it is the first duty of history to dismiss.

However, we must not forget either the flourishing of a historiography linked to the names Bachofen and Gerlach, which can be defined euphemistically as 'reactionary'. Gerlach in particular defended the historical existence of Romulus; to him it seemed that whoever denied his existence was stained with horrible and execrable *Liberalismus*.[2]

It would perhaps take too long to draw up a list of all the modern historians, of the most diverse tendencies, who have denied the real existence of Romulus in the twentieth century. Gaetano De Sanctis, in the first volume of his monumental *Storia dei Romani*, merely considered Romulus the legendary eponym of Rome, producing analogous examples drawn from the Greek world. In his turn Ettore Pais, referring to Theodor Mommsen, traced the entire legend of Romulus and Remus back to the fourth century BC, 'with the aim of legitimising the two-fold consular magistrature', which Pais himself traced to this period, in the context of his reductionist view of the monarchic and high republican eras as a whole.[3]

Anglo-Saxon historiography has always shown great scepticism with regard to the supposed 'historicity' of a founder by the name of Romulus. Suffice it to say that in a standard work like the *Cambridge Ancient History* this possibility is excluded very simply: 'The version which makes the two founders twins cannot be shown to have existed before the end of the fourth century.' It is natural to note here that by dating the legend of the twins to the fourth century BC Hugh Last was following not only Gaetano De Sanctis, whom he did not fail to cite, but also Ettore Pais, who – as we have seen – had already opted for that date. Some decades later, Tim Cornell also wrote in exactly the same terms with regard to the historicity of Romulus, concluding after a long examination of the most ancient legends of Latium:

In general the narrative accounts of the origins of Rome, from Aeneas to Romulus, cannot be considered historical. They represent a complex mixture of popular legend, folk-tale, and learned conjecture, and are important for the study of Roman historiography and the development of Roman self-consciousness.[4]

Dominique Briquel, drawing inspiration from the famous hypothesis of a tripartition of functions common to all Indo-European peoples that was first enunciated by Georges Dumézil, has in numerous studies considered the figure and the legend of Romulus a wholly typical element of the first function (kingliness in its warrior aspect), sufficiently typical to be contrasted with his successor, the good king Numa, who was completely devoted to the rites and religious practices which he established. More recently A. Meurant has followed in the wake of Briquel, still in the perspective opened by Dumézil; however, he has had to acknowledge 'a Roman variant of the Indo-European theme'. And Jacques Poucet has also repeatedly lashed out against the historicity of a founder by the name of Romulus, considering the entire tradition of the history of Rome before the Etruscan kings to be nothing more than legend.

Notwithstanding the complete unanimity of the historians with regard to the legendary character of the founder Romulus, an excavation conducted by Andrea Carandini and his team in the 1990s at the foot of the Palatine Hill revealed a wall, which, in their view, can be dated round the mid-eighth century BC. This wall, whose exact nature and precise purpose we do not know, is said to be not only proof that the foundation of Rome should be set on the canonical date attributed to it by the ancient historians (754 BC), but also proof of the existence of its founder Romulus. All of this is in the framework of a broader, more elaborate reconstruction of the Roman society and religion of ancient times.[5]

To these hypotheses one can very easily object that even in Caesar's time Sallust attributed the foundation of Rome to Aeneas; that the Greek historian Timaeus in the fourth century BC, establishing a synchronicity between the foundation of Rome and that of Carthage, determined that Rome had been founded in 814 BC; and that historians of that same fourth century, like Callias and Alcimus, acknowledged Rhomos alone without giving him a twin.[6] Reactions were not lacking from historians either: Emilio Gabba and Jacques Poucet in particular criticised the archaeologists for their objective irresponsibility in interpreting this fragment of a wall, which it is not even certain belonged to a gate. Added to this was their substantial and indisputable irresponsibility in dealing with the entire literary tradition, which also has a 'stratification' to which close attention should be paid. T. P. Wiseman, therefore, reviewing both the Rome and Romulus exhibition mounted in the Terme Museum in 2000 and Andrea Carandini's *Giornale di scavo*, could not avoid a very definite conclusion:

> Carandini neither explains nor attempts to fill the mysterious lacuna in the mythical memory that creates, for him, a dark age between the two heroic ages of Latinus and Romulus; nor does he give any reason for why it should correspond chronologically with the Alban king-list, which he agrees is a complete invention.[7]

This brief – perhaps too brief – historiographical excursus should go some way towards justifying this book, which is perhaps the only book to feature Romulus as the founder. We have tried to point out the defining moments in his life from his birth to his death that became the nuclei of legend. Clearly the exposure of the twins calls to mind other famous exposures; however, it is essential to note that while elsewhere we are talking about single infants (Moses and Cyrus, for example), in Rome we have a story of twins designed to give shape to the life of both (Romulus and Remus) until Remus' death at the moment of the city's foundation. Hence the primary, unavoidable need to piece together the inner coherence of the twins' youth, a youth set in the wild world of nature, under the sign of their ancestor Faunus.

It is highly significant that, after Rhea Silvia, who has been made pregnant by the god Mars, gives birth to them, the wicked Amulius, king of Alba, orders his servants to drown them in the Tiber, and that here, after they are miraculously saved, it is a she-wolf – clearly a totem animal – that suckles them. Then, as in many societies studied by ethnologists and anthropologists, the twins spend their youth far from centres of habitation, joining other groups of youths and spending their time stealing livestock and defending their own plunder. From this perspective, attention is focused on one of the *aitia* of the festival of the Lupercalia in Ovid, in which the *luperci*, 'naked' and wild under the guidance of Remus and his companions, retrieve the stolen beasts first, while Romulus, when he arrives with his companions, sees that his brother has already eaten the half-raw meat of a she-goat sacrificed to Faunus.[8]

Following the various 'segments' of the legend, it should now be clear that when the good Numitor, having been restored to the throne of Alba, invites the twins to found a new colony, Remus must make an exit. Thus far both the twins have possessed 'wild' capabilities. At the moment of foundation at least, Romulus seems to have abandoned them. Both take the auspices. Those of Romulus are superior, and while the founder traces the pomerium, Remus, in arms, crosses it and is killed by either his twin or Celer, who was Romulus' assistant at the time. We emphasise one point: Remus, who has never abandoned his state of nature, cannot enter the neat and tidy world formed by the city, a city which is, moreover, delimited by a pomerium.[9]

One element which cannot be passed over in silence is the profoundly ambiguous nature of Romulus. Even after founding Rome, Romulus seems to not lose any of the characteristics that had marked a large part of his youth. We shall include in his dossier both the setting up of the Asylum in a valley of the Capitoline Hill, where men of all kinds and social states (including slaves) gathered, and the rape of the Sabine women, contrived by the astute founder in order to end the shortage of women. The Sabines responded to this abduction with a war which sees other legendary figures in turn appear, such as Tarpeia and Mettius Fufetius. In fact, while the war against the Sabines led to the 'doubled city', the joint reign of Romulus and the Sabine king, Titus Tatius, was very brief and ended with the murder of Titus Tatius in Lavinium: a death as tragic as it was obscure.[10]

If we wish to follow the schema elaborated by Georges Dumézil, it must be said that Romulus constantly appears in the garb of a king who loves and pursues conquests: conquests of other cities and territories. The cities conquered to the north of Rome are Antemnae, Crustumerium, Fidenae and Cameria. However, we are not dealing with simple conquests, since in all of these cities Romulus the 'demagogue' establishes colonies of Roman citizens who will have their own fields to plough or cultivate in those lands. Romulus then fought against the very strong

Etruscan city of Veii, which was defeated, and the Romans gained the salt-works at the mouth of the Tiber, a resource of great importance for the city of Rome.[11]

Romulus' great love of war contributes to making even the senate suspicious of him, since now he has adopted tyrannical practices and no longer consults the senators even on matters of the highest importance, such as the fate of the lands taken from the Veientes. Here, on his death, the tradition divides completely. Either Romulus dies, killed by the senators, who, having dismembered him, take possession each of a piece of his body – and above all of the most precious element that his body by nature possesses: the auspices – or else he ascends to heaven while he is presiding over an assembly at the Goat's Marsh (a storm breaks and when it abates he is no longer to be seen on his throne). The testimony of Julius Proculus on this point will be the definitive one: he will testify before the senate that Romulus has appeared to him more handsome and more magnificent than any human being, instructing the Romans to worship him now as the god Quirinus.[12]

As I pointed out in the preface, this study of Romulus is not a book about ancient history; rather it aims to be a book of historical anthropology on the ancient world. As we have seen in our historiographical excursus, the historians (even the most eminent historians) have attempted with great skill and philological acumen to identify in the figure of the founder Romulus clues and pointers which together might lead to a history of Rome that is more 'true', projecting to the fifth or the fourth century BC elements that the ancient tradition attributed to Romulus. In reality the problem is more complex. It is this: not to examine separately the 'segments' of the legend of Romulus and Remus, and then those of Romulus alone, but instead to treat these as a unified whole.

We are dealing with a unified whole which possesses its own inner coherence, from the birth of the twins to the death of Remus, and then from the reign of Romulus to his mysterious disappearance. In this legendary whole each 'segment' has its own function: the suckling by a totem animal; the unhappy fate of Remus, the 'savage' destined to be excluded from the world of the city; the ambiguous warrior status of Romulus, who seems irresistibly drawn to wars of conquest (so much that his successor

Numa is known for the peace that distinguishes his reign and the religious institutions he introduced); and finally, the double tradition of the death of the founder, who – at least according to Dionysius of Halicarnassus – can more truly be said to have been cut into pieces by the senators.[13]

In the light of what we have seen, then, the saga of Romulus the founder becomes fully intelligible, with one proviso: that we do not attempt to consider historical a figure who never was historical, but was invented by the Romans themselves to account not only for the birth of their city, but also – thanks to his gifts – for Rome's imperial destiny, which took it from a small centre in Latium to a dominant city of the Mediterranean basin and beyond, and for a provincial system which, to a large extent, even as early as Augustus' time, seemed chaotic.

Appendix I. The ambiguous status of Tarpeia

When, in regard to the foundation of the city, the question of the common hearth has been examined,[1] it has also been pointed out that Dionysius of Halicarnassus discussed at length the view held by some that its institution should be attributed to Romulus. He preferred instead that the construction in Rome of a temple to Vesta – and therefore the institution of the college of Vestal Virgins – be attributed to Numa Pompilius, the second king. We shall confine ourselves here to the observation that the tradition which attributed the cult of Vesta to Romulus was not an isolated one: it dated back – if our arguments are correct – at least to Varro, and spanned a major part of the ancient tradition, from Propertius to Plutarch and down to the *Chronographer of 354*.[2]

Here we shall not dwell on the features of the 'character' Tarpeia, who was – according to a very long tradition of studies – a local divinity of the 'mons Tarpeius', later 'downgraded' to a simple heroine,[3] or on the features of her tomb, in which some have claimed to see an ancient trophy that was later mistaken for a tomb.[4] The comparisons with legends drawn from the Greek world offer nothing that might lead us to consider Tarpeia as anything other than an eminently Roman 'character'.[5] Much more eminently Roman, if the legend of her act of betrayal could later be easily shifted (by Varro) from the Sabine siege to the Gallic siege of 390 BC. According to this tradition, which is evident in the obscure poet Simylos, a maiden named Tarpeia opened the gates of the citadel not to Titus Tatius' Sabines but to Brenno's Gauls.[6] We simply point out that, starting with Livy, that part of the ancient tradition which attributed to Numa the establishment of the Temple of Vesta and the priesthood of the Vestals also retained unmistakeable traces of the ambiguous status of Tarpeia.[7] Livy records that Tarpeia, the daughter of

Spurius Tarpeius, commander of the citadel, was corrupted by Titus Tatius' gold when she went outside the walls to fetch water for a sacrifice ('aquam forte ea tum sacris extra moenia petitum ierat').[8] According to Valerius Maximus, Suetonius and Servius, the *virgo* Tarpeia encountered Titus Tatius and negotiated the betrayal when – as in Livy – she went outside the walls to fetch water for sacrificial purposes.[9] Since the girl is *virgo*, these sacrificial purposes cannot but lead us to the cult of Vesta and the Vestals' specific task of fetching water for the sacred ceremonies to honour the goddess.

Let us pause on these two elements (the virginity and the fetching of water for sacrificial purposes: a necessary condition and a characteristic task – as is well known – of the Vestal Virgins). We infer that even in the then 'canonical' tradition, which attributed to Numa the building of the Temple of Vesta and the institution of the priesthood of the Vestals, implicit signs remained of an 'ambiguous' Vestal Tarpeia; the more so if one of the first four Vestals consecrated by Numa really was called Tarpeia.[10] For my part, however, I prefer a Tarpeia 'virgo Vestalis ante litteram' in the sense proposed by M. C. Martini.[11] Another factor that points to her having been a Vestal was her interment alive. As the *Chronographer of 354* records, 'Hic (sc. Tatius) arma defodit, eo quod secreta Romuli ei propalare noluisset'.[12] We could infer from this that the characteristics of Tarpeia's death – *virgo* buried alive beneath shields – also allude, in Roman descriptions, to the type of punishment reserved for the Vestal guilty of incest.[13]

If we then turn to the iconographic material (two coins and a panel from the frieze in the Basilica Aemilia),[14] we find that on the Lucius Titurius Sabinus denarius of 89 BC Tarpeia is depicted menaced by two Sabines who hurl their shields at her.[15] Above them stand a crescent moon and a star, signs of the eternal night that awaits her. Note, however, that the star is also an intimation that she will be heroised;[16] so Lucius Titurius Sabinus had perhaps followed a tradition similar to that which appeared several decades before in Calpurnius Piso.[17] Years later, a Lucius Petronius Turpilianus denarius of 19 BC depicts Tarpeia standing alone while shields begin to pile up around her legs.[18]

On the Basilica Aemilia frieze, which dates from the late Republic or early Augustan period, Tarpeia, with a full veil to her shoulders, appears partially buried, not only by the Sabines' shields, but also by real rocks. Two other characters are in the scene; very probably one is Titus Tatius and the other Mars, who is evidently angry at the betrayal that brought harm to his son.[19] Naturally, if Tarpeia was not only covered by shields but there were also real rocks at the bottom, this would strengthen – in the frieze as well – her status of 'ambiguous' Vestal.

Appendix II. A wall at the foot of the Palatine Hill

The recent book – which can now be considered definitive – on the excavations conducted at the foot of the Palatine Hill by the team led by Andrea Carandini[1] makes it possible to get to the heart of the problem posed by the discovery of a wall, which is datable to *c.*725 BC and is linked by Carandini to the Romulean foundation.[2] From the first accounts of this discovery there has been no lack of criticism, some of it severe, of its interpretation as evidence of the truth of the ancient tradition of the foundation of Rome by Romulus.[3] There has also been enthusiastic acceptance of this interpretation.[4]

What I am interested in is the frankly excessive importance attributed to this discovery. The ancients also discussed the date of the foundation of Rome. Sallust, we saw,[5] attributed the foundation directly to Aeneas, Timaeus made it coincide with that of Carthage, and Varro – we have already noted this – dated it to 754/753. Other historians put it later: either not much later (for example, Fabius Pictor suggests 748/747) or several decades later (Cincius Alimentus maintains it was in 729/728).[6] Under these circumstances it is therefore admissible to highlight the great discrepancy between literary documents and archaeological finds without being labelled either a masochist or a hypocrite for doing so.[7]

As we proceed along our trail we shall observe, moreover, that it is merely a matter of a wall, and that therefore the historical conclusions drawn from it by Carandini, beginning with the real existence of a founder who was perhaps called Romulus, may seem extreme. A wall at the foot of the Palatine could simply be identified as a defensive wall, or a boundary wall around the hill, unless it is a case of a simple *agger*. Paraphrasing Gertrude Stein ('a rose is a rose is a rose is a rose . . .'), we would suggest that 'a wall is a wall is a wall is a wall . . .', a simple wall. Besides, it seems very difficult to identify the five graves discovered in the walled complex as 'burials' of 'sacrificial remains',[8] since there is no indication they should be interpreted in this way. The cases of the pairs of Gauls and Greeks buried alive in the Forum Boarium 'sub terram . . . in loco saxo consaeptum' are clearly very different,[9] as is that of the Vestals found guilty of incest.[10]

It is, however, interesting to note how the problem of the 'character' of Romulus seems to refer, at the historiographical level, to important thematic nodes that were much discussed in the nineteenth century after the publication of the first volume of *Römische Geschichte* by Barthold Georg Niebuhr. In fact, 'on the evening of 21 April 1832' Carlo Fea, an authentic 'antiquarian' very closely connected to the Curia and for many decades Commissioner of Roman Antiquities and President of the Capitoline Museum, delivered a long address entitled *Of the praises of Romulus and Rome* in the Sabine Academy. However, taking advantage of that 'usual occasion', Abbot Fea did not confine himself to talking about one of the most important archaeological discoveries to occur in Rome or its immediate suburbs, as was customary. Instead, having chosen, very appropriately, the theme of Romulus and Rome, he entered a field which to him, an 'antiquarian,' scholar, and illustrator of monuments from the late republican and especially the imperial periods, was certainly not usual. From there he criticised and scornfully rebutted

> the man who attempts with critical antiquarian subtleties to call into doubt the first centuries of Roman history and *Romulus*, founder of the same, as subjects of fable rather than true history. The man who, in Rome itself, accuses that illustrious figure of being a *brigand*, and the leader of assassins, rather than the legitimate Sovereign according to the common right of the people, not knowing his benevolent intentions, much less those sublime intentions of God, who guided him. The man who exaggerates and distorts the *liberty* of that people to the extent that he makes it the Sovereign.[11]

The one who, according to Fea, had 'accuse[d] that illustrious figure of being a *brigand*' was Alessandro Verri in his *Notti romane*. In this work Tullius, speaking about the Asylum, turns to the shade of Romulus and exclaims: 'Here is the asylum in which assembled those pernicious rogues who, later subjugated by your magnanimous imperium, founded the – as you see – eternal city.' However, in this work, first published in 1792, Verri absolutely did not question the historicity of the founder. Rather, emphasising the tradition of the originally very motley nature of the Asylum and, in particular, the tradition of the murder of Romulus by the *patres*, the Milanese scholar – at least according to Fea – transformed Romulus into a 'leader of assassins'. Since Alessandro Verri also asserted the superiority of Christian Rome over pagan Rome, opening the way – as Piero Treves has claimed – 'to that exaltation of the uninterrupted historical continuity of the Urbe which was peculiar to restorative antiquarianism', it is highly likely that what vexed Abbot Fea in the *Notti romane* were the constant appeals, attributed to the founder, to 'love of liberty' and his reference to the 'illustrious Republic, marvellous among all that were in the world', 'worthy of immortal life, extinguished in brief', when the Romans 'bowed to the yoke of tyrants' (an allusion to Augustus, whose providential function Fea exalted, and – we shall see – not just in the *Lodi*).[12]

The author who carried greater authority than the 'critical antiquarian subtleties' was Bartold Georg Niebuhr (explicitly cited together with Michelet), whom Fea had doubtless known during the time of his residence in Rome as Minister for Prussia. After the publication of his *Römische Geschichte* (I–II, 1811–12; III, 1832), Niebuhr's influence, was – at least in the strictly historical area – notably superior to that of the younger Michelet.[13] As a matter of fact, Michelet, in the first volume of *Histoire romaine. République*, which was conceived in Rome in 1830 and published shortly thereafter, made much use of the *Römische Geschichte*, especially with regard to the Roman institutions of the ancient epoch, warmly praising Niebuhr, just as he praised, in even more enthusiastic tones, Giambattista Vico, his predecessor in 'criticism'.[14]

As for the 'critical antiquarian subtleties', it soon becomes clear that they must be detected in the *Quellenforschung*, that long, meticulous examination of the literary tradition. However, with regard to criticism of the sources, the clashes between Carlo Fea and Niebuhr are not limited solely to Romulus; in his *Storia dei vasi fittili*, Rome, 1832 (the same year as the *Lodi*), Fea also attacks the historicity of the immigration of the Lydians from Asia Minor into Italy, about which Niebuhr had shown himself at least sceptical.[15]

At this point it is crucial to note how the insistence on the historicity of Romulus – and consequently on the historical legitimacy of his power – had the aim of showing, through the unbroken line of holders of that same power (from Romulus to Augustus and then Constantine), the legitimacy of the successors of Romulus, Augustus and Constantine in what Fea calls the 'Administration' of the empire. These legitimate successors in the 'Administration' were then embodied in the Roman pontiffs, Peter's successors, in a time of attacks and challenges (especially after the Romagna uprisings) to the temporal dominion of the Holy See. This explains Fea's overriding, declared intention, in an absolutely 'continuistic' perspective, to propose in the *Lodi* 'a *compendium* of a *new Roman History*; an overview from *Romulus* to our time'.

Carlo Fea died, 'after being chronically ill for several months' – as the prince, Don Agostino Chigi, noted in his diary.[16] The abbot had been his librarian for thirty-six years. Fea died on 18 March 1836 and therefore was unable to attend the celebration of the anniversary of the foundation of Rome held by Angelo Mai on 21 April 1837 in the Papal Roman Academy of Archaeology, an academy which, because it was 'Papal', was far more authoritative and prestigious than the Sabine Academy. But if he had heard the Vatican Library's Prefect's *Ragionamento*, the Commissioner of Roman Antiquities would surely have been saddened. Mai, who by then was very famous, especially after his edition of Cicero's *De republica*, not only passed over in silence any possible transfer of power from Romulus, Augustus and Constantine to the 'sovereign pontiff' Gregory XVI, but also, in order to celebrate 'with due praises the common home of all peoples', put forward as the 'postulate' of his *Ragionamento* 'that the authority of present Rome not only is not inferior to, but even exceeds that of Ancient Rome, which merited the most noble epic of the great Virgil'. He continued:

So I ask that Gentile Rome be turned into Christian Rome. I demand that Saint Peter the Apostle be substituted for the Trojan Aeneas, the papal tiara for the laurels of the Caesars, and that in place of the Capitoline eagles the wholesome banner of the Redeemer's Cross be flown. Lastly I demand that no longer are we guided by the consular legions in the conquest of the world, but by the evangelical platoons of the missions.[17]

As for the founder, whose historicity he evidently did not publicly call into question, Angelo Mai merely observed that in the Rome of Gregory XVI there existed

a college, almost an asylum (certainly better than the one that was established by Romulus in the Palatine wood), which was open to any nation for the training of apostles, that is, conquerors of new peoples and kingdoms for the Vatican See. (This was the College of Propaganda Fide.)[18]

We shall forgive Mai's scant precision in locating Romulus' Asylum in the 'Palatine wood', rather than the Capitol. On the other hand, it is important to note here the approach of that *Ragionamento*. While the problem of the full legitimacy of temporal power due to the successors of St Peter was not even touched on, the Vatican Prefect (who was also the secretary of the 'Sacred Congregation of Propaganda Fide'), in the wake of Pope Leo (explicitly mentioned), emphasised the positive work of the conversions carried out by a church which, radiating from Rome, had overcome the 'narrow' confines of its ancient empire to reach into Africa as far – as he said – as 'Cafreria', and into the two Americas and even Oceania.

In a rather small environment like that of Rome in those years it is impossible that the Vatican Library's Prefect, still a friend of Pietro Giordani and 'immune to any sectarian closure in religious and political ideas', did not know the pamphlet published by the Commissioner of Roman Antiquities only a few years before. The choice of a very different way of celebrating the anniversary of the foundation of Rome must therefore have been part of his attitude of 'sympathiser in his heart' – as Sebastiano Timpanaro expressed it – 'to ideas of renewal': 'ideas' that led him to prefer the positive and enormous work of conversion to Christianity performed by the church to emphasis on its small temporal dominion.[19]

Nevertheless, it is useful to observe that while Fea was the first to oppose Niebuhr on Romulus, similar criticisms of him were revived more than fifteen years later by Franz Dorotheus Gerlach and Johann Jacob Bachofen in their *Geschichte der Römer* (1851). Later again Gerlach alone, in his *Vorgeschichte, Gründung und Entwicklung des römischen Staats*, criticised not only Niebuhr but also Schwegler and Mommsen. As Santo Mazzarino observed: 'In defending . . . the historical existence of Romulus, Gerlach believed he was defending . . . the principle of authority', which, in his view, had been 'shaken' 'in the State as in the field of science'. Gerlach's words would evidently not have displeased Abbot Fea, who – like him – had been convinced that criticism of Romulus was coming not only from the new German historiography but also from Michelet, who, at least implicitly – according to Gerlach – was one of those 'philosophers' saturated with horrible and execrable *Liberalismus* 'from across the Seine'.[20]

Notes

NOTES TO CHAPTER I

1. On Fabius Pictor's account see *FGrHist 809* F 4a = *HRR* 1², fr. 5a, which according to Plutarch, *Rom.* 3.1, 'in the majority of cases' followed Diocles of Peparethus (*FGrHist* 820 F 2). On the much debated relations between Diocles and Fabius see B. W. Frier, *'Libri Annales Pontificum Maximorum': The Origins of the Annalistic Tradition* (Rome: 1979), pp. 260–1; L. Moretti, 'Chio e la lupa Capitolina', *RFIC*, 108, 1980, pp. 50ff.; Ampolo and Manfredini 1988, pp. 276–8; Wiseman 1995, p. 57.

2. On Romulus and Remus the sons of Aeneas or of a daughter of Aeneas, see the legend reported by Dionysius of Halicarnassus I.73.2; on the connection between Aeneas and Romulus and Remus, see above all T. Cornell, 'Aeneas and the Twins: The Development of the Roman Foundation Legend', *ProcCambrPhilolSoc*, 21, 1975, pp. 1ff. I leave aside, however, the much less specific information in Lycophron, *Alexandra* 1231–5, while on *hamnoi* in line 1227 I share the interpretation of E. Ciaceri, *La Alessandra di Licofrone* (Catania: 1901), p. 315; on Callias see *FGrHist* 564 F 5; on Aemilia the mother of Romulus, see Plutarch, *Rom.* 2.3. For more detail on this question see Wiseman 1995, pp. 52ff. See Fraschetti 1981, pp. 103–5, for the ideological meanings which such genealogies could assume (e.g. in Alcimus, *FGrHist* 560 F 4, in which Romulus is said to have been the son of Aeneas and *Tyrrhenia*, Alba the daughter of Romulus, and Rhomus, who – it is claimed – founded Rome, the son of Alba); on the possible relations between Alcimus and the Syracuse of Dionysius II, see A. C. Cassio, 'Two Studies on Epicharmus and His Influence', *HSCPh*, 99, 1985, pp. 43ff. On Sallust and the supposed foundation of Rome by Aeneas, see *Cat.* 6.1: 'Urbem Romam, sicuti ego accepi, condidere atque habuere initio Troiani, qui, Aenea duce profugi sedibus in certis vagabantur'. More generally, on the tradition of Aeneas and his relations with the peoples of ancient Italy, see L. Braccesi, 'Il mito di Enea in Occidente', in Carandini and Cappelli 2000, pp. 58ff.

3. The 'canonical' tradition is the one set down by Livy I.3.11; Dionysius of Halicarnassus I.77–8; Plutarch, *Rom.* 3.2–4; *OGR* 19, 4. For further documentation see Rosenberg 1914, cols 341–54; also M. Hauer-Prost, *LIMC*, VII.1, 1994, pp. 615ff.

4. On the way Mars is presented, see Dionysius of Halicarnassus I.77.1–2; Livy I.4.2; Plutarch, *Rom.* 3.4 (but without reference to Mars); see *OGR* 19.5, which records the legends attributed to Marcus Octavius and Licinius Macer, in which it was Amulius himself who violated Rhea in the manner related by Dionysius of Halicarnassus I.77.1. For the version recorded by Promathion in his *Historia Italike* see *FGrHist* 817 F 1.

5. See above all S. Mazzarino, 'Antiche leggende sulle origini di Roma', *StRom*, 8, 1960, pp. 385ff.; also Mazzarino 1966, II, 1, pp. 188ff.; J. Heurgon, *La vie quotidienne chez les Étrusques* (Paris: 1961), pp. 312–14; G. D'Anna, *Problemi di letteratura latina arcaica* (Rome: 1976), pp. 46ff.; Ampolo and Manfredini 1988, pp. 272–6; Wiseman 1995, pp. 57–61.

6. See Dionysius of Halicarnassus I.79.1–4; Livy I.4.3; Plutarch, *Rom.* 3.4–5; *OGR* 20.2.

7. On the Ogulnian monument see Livy X.23.11; also C. Dulière, *Lupa Romana: recherches d'iconographie et essai d'interprétation*, vol. 1 (Brussels, Rome: 1979), pp. 58–62; also, though on very shaky ground, A. W. J. Holleman, 'Encore la Louve Capitoline', *Latomus*, 46, 1987, pp. 180–1; G.-Ch. Picard, 'La louve romaine, du mythe au symbole', *RA*, 1987, pp. 251ff.; Wiseman 1995, pp. 72ff.; on the Ficus Ruminalis on the slopes of the Palatine see Ampolo and Manfredini 1988, pp. 282–3; F. Coarelli, *LTUR*, II, 1995, p. 249.

8. See Dionysius of Halicarnassus I.79.6–10; Livy I.4.6–8; Plutarch, *Rom.* 4.1–4; *OGR* 20.3–4 and 21.5. On the rationalist interpretation of Acca Larentia as *lupa* – prostitute, see Licinius Macer, *HRR* 1², fr. 1; also Ampolo and Manfredini 1988, p. 284, and Coarelli 1988, pp. 129ff., on the other Acca Larentia, 'nobilissimum scortum', who was active at the future site of Rome at the time when Hercules arrived in Italy. On *lupa* 'prostitute', see some notes which I have great difficulty in following in A. W. J. Holleman, 'Lupus, Lupercalia, lupa', *Latomus*, 44, 1985, pp. 609ff. On Acca Larentia see also n. 29 below.

9. On Theseus as 'founding hero' see above all C. Calame, *Thésée et l'imaginaire athénien. Légende et culte en Grèce antique* (Lausanne: 1990); on his special relations with young people, see P. Vidal-Naquet, 'Le chasseur noir et l'origine de l'éphébie athénienne', in Vidal-Naquet 1981, pp. 151ff.

10. Herodotus I.107–28.

11. On Pompeius Trogus see Justin I.4–6, also D. Fehling, *Die Quellenangaben bei Herodot, Studien zur Erzählungskunst Herodot* (Berlin: 1971), pp. 83–4. For the significance of the dog in the Persian world see the commentary by D. Asheri on Herodotus, *Le storie, libro I, La Lidia e la Persia* (Milan: 1988), p. 336. For the Hirpi Sorani see Servius *ad Aen.* XI.786, with notes by Briquel 1980, pp. 274–5. On wolves as totem animals in ancient Italy see De Sanctis 1980, I, p. 220; also Alföldi 1974, pp. 68ff.; also S. Cataldi, 'Popoli e città del lupo e del cane in Italia meridionale e in Sicilia', in M. Sordi (ed.), 'Autocoscienza e rappresentazione dei popoli dell'antichità', *ContrIstStAnt*, XVIII (Milan: 1992), pp. 55ff. For further eth-

nological comparisons, for example, with the Nootka Indians, see J. Frazer, *The Golden Bough* (London: 1913), vol. VII, 2, pp. 270–1.

12. See Wiseman 1995, pp. 18ff., on the following: J. R. Harris, *The Cult of the Heavenly Twins* (Cambridge: 1906), *passim*; J. R. Harris, *Was Rome a Twin-Town?* (Cambridge: 1927); J. Puhvel, 'Remus et frater', *History of Religions*, 15, 1975, pp. 146ff.; J. Puhvel, *Comparative Mythology* (Baltimore: 1987); and G. Dumézil (trans. P. Krapp), 1966, pp. 241ff. See also A. Meurant, 'L'idée de gémellité aux origines de Rome', *EMC*, 67, 1999, pp. 199ff.; A. Meurant, 'Romolo e Remo gemelli primordiali: aspetti di un tratto leggendario di grande rilevanza', in Carandini and Cappelli 2000, pp. 33ff., where he is obliged to admit the existence, within a 'general universal scheme', of an 'Indo-European version of the theme of twinship' and of a 'Roman variation on the Indo-European theme', a 'variation' significant enough and in some respects 'anomalous' enough with regard to the 'Indo-European version' to constitute to all intents a *unicum*, as recognised earlier by D. Briquel, 'La triple fondation de Rome', *RHR*, 189, 1976, pp. 145ff., who referred (p. 149) to 'une transformation complète du thème'. On the theme of twinship in Rome see also E. Pellizer, 'Miti di fondazione e infanti abbandonati', in M. Guglielmo and G. F. Gianotti (eds), *Filosofia, storia, immaginario mitologico* (Turin: 1997), pp. 81ff.

13. See B. G. Niebuhr, *Römische Geschichte*, vol. 1, 3rd edn, ed. by M. Isler (Berlin: 1873), pp. 170ff.; Wiseman 1995, pp. 138ff.; T. Mommsen, 'Die Remuslegende', *Hermes*, 16, 1881, pp. 1ff., reprinted in T. Mommsen, *Gesammelte Schriften*, vol. IV (Berlin: 1908), pp. 1ff.; J. Carcopino, *La Louve du Capitole* (Paris: 1925).

14. See above all J. Assmann, *Das kulturelle Gedächtnis: Schrift, Erinnerung und politische Identität in frühen Hochkulturen* (Munich: 1997), pp. 37ff.; also more generally A. Hahn, *Konstruktionen des Selbst, der Welt und der Geschichte* (Frankfurt: 2000).

15. Cornell 1995, p. 60.

16. Here it is essential to refer to J. Vansina, *Oral Tradition and History* (Madison, WI: 1985); for other aspects of these problems see also E. J. Hobsbawm and T. Ranger (eds), *The Invention of Tradition* (New York: 1983).

17. On the role attributed by Niebuhr to the *carmina convivalia* see A. Momigliano, 'Perizonius, Niebuhr, and the Character of Early Roman Tradition', *JRS*, 47, 1957, pp. 104ff.; A. Momigliano, *Contributo alla storia degli studi classici [e del mondo antico]*, vol. 2 (Rome: 1960), pp. 69ff.; N. M. Horsfall, 'Myth and Mythography at Rome', in Bremmer and Horsfall 1987, p. 10, and the more general observations by T. P. Wiseman, 'Roman Legend and Oral Tradition', *JRS*, 79, 1989, pp. 129ff.; T. P. Wiseman, *Historiography and Imagination* (Exeter: 1994), pp. 23ff.; Wiseman 1995, pp. 129ff.

18. Wiseman 1995, pp. 133ff.

19. See Wiseman 1995, pp. 125ff., where the repetition of the prudent 'let us

suppose' makes plain the extremely hypothetical nature of the solutions proposed. It seems to me that, in taking Remus as 'the first sacrificial victim', one can hardly cite Propertius III.9.5 ('caeso moenia firma Remo') or Florus I.1.8 ('prima certe victima fuit munitionemque urbis novae sanguine suo consecravit'), because in both cases (despite Florus' use of terms such as *victima* and *consecravit*) the purpose of the statements is once more to confirm, using an episode which could serve as an example from the very beginning, the invulnerability of the walls of Rome, which Remus had attempted to cross (see Livy I.7.2: 'inde ab irato Romulo, cum verbis quoque increpitans adiecisset, "Sic deinde quicumque alius transiliet moenia mea", interfectum'; and Dionysius I.87.4). See also F. Schwenn, *Die Menschenopfer bei den Griechen und Römern* (Giessen: 1915) (facsimile reproduction, Berlin: 1975), pp. 140ff.; P. Arnold, 'Les sacrifices humaines et la "devotio" à Rome', *Ogam*, 9, 1957, pp. 27ff. Finally one may see some significance in the fact that no Roman examples were considered among the many instances adduced by A. Brelich, *Presupposti dal sacrificio umano* (Rome: 1966–7), pp. 44–8, with regard to 'human sacrifices in foundation rites'; on this see also pp. 67ff.

20. See R. Adam and D. Briquel, 'Le miroir prénestin de l'Antiquario Comunale de Rome et la légende des jumeaux divins en milieu latin à la fin du IVe siècle av. J.C.', *MEFR(A)*, 94, 1982, p. 44, with the proviso, however, that the figure possesses certain characteristics of Mercury 'mais pas l'ensemble des caractéristiques du dieu'; T. P. Wiseman, 'Democracy and Myth: The Life and Death of Remus', *LCM*, 16, 8, 1991, pp. 115ff.; R. Weigel, 'Lupa Romana', *LIMC*, VI, 1 1992, pp. 293–6; F.-H. Pairault Massa, 'Aspetti e problemi della società prenestina tra IV e III secolo a.C.', in *La necropoli di Preneste: periodo orientalizzante e medio-repubblicano* (Atti del II Convegno di Studi archeologici) (Palestrina: 1992), pp. 141–4; F.-H. Pairault Massa, *Iconologia e politica nell'Italia antica* (Milan: 1992), pp. 178–9.

21. On Rhea Silvia see K. Klugmann, 'Due specchi di Bolsena e di Talamone', *AnnInst*, 51, 1879, p. 41; Rosenberg 1914, col. 1183; Weigel, p. 293; Wiseman, 'Democracy and Myth', pp. 115ff. On Acca Larentia, see Pairault Massa, 'Aspetti e problemi', pp. 141–4; Pairault Massa, *Iconologia e politica*, p. 179. On Lara-Tacita, T. P. Wiseman, 'The She-Wolf Mirror: An Interpretation', *Papers of the British School at Rome*, 61, 1993, pp. 1–6.: cf. T. P. Wiseman, 'Reading Carandini', *JRS*, 91, 2001, pp. 182ff.

22. On Faunus see Wiseman, 'Democracy and Myth', pp. 115ff.; on the *lupercus*, see Rosenberg 1914, col. 1183, Wiseman, 'Democracy and Myth', pp. 115ff.; on Pan see Wiseman, 'The She-Wolf Mirror'; T. P. Wiseman, *Remus. A Roman Myth* (Cambridge: 1995), p. 70; Wiseman, 'The God of the Lupercal', *JRS*, 85, 1995, pp. 5–6.

23. On the equation with Faustulus, see Klugmann, 'Due specchi', pp. 42–3; R. Peter, in Roscher, *Ausführliches Lexikon der griechischen und römischen Mythologie*, I, 5, 1886; Adam and Briquel, 'Le miroir prénestin', pp. 42–3;

Weigel, p. 293; on the Tiber, see Pairault Massa, 'Aspetti e problemi', p. 143; Pairault Massa, *Iconologia e politica*, p. 179; on the god Quirinus, see Wiseman, 'The She-Wolf Mirror'.

24. See Wiseman 1995, pp. 70–1.

25. See Ovid, *Fasti* II.583ff., more particularly, concerning the sons of Lara, 615–16 ('fitque gravis geminosque parit, qui compita servant / et vigilant nostra semper in urbe, Lares'); on the Lares Praestites, who had a single altar in Rome, see Ovid, *Fasti* V.129–30 ('praestitibus Maiae Laribus videre Kalendae / aram constitui parvaque signa deum'); on these problems see Fraschetti 1990, pp. 260ff.; in Rome only one shrine was built to the Lares Praestites, very probably close to the Forum; lastly see F. Coarelli, *LTUR*, III, 1996, p. 175).

26. See Chapter 2, n. 44.

27. See Dionysius of Halicarnassus I.76.3. It may be noted that in Greece and Rome the broad-brimmed hat characterised not only Mercury but also those defined more broadly as 'travelling heroes', like Bellerophon, Perseus, Oedipus and Theseus. This type of hat was the typical headgear worn in the country and on journeys; see R. Paris, *DAGR*, IV, 1, pp. 421–2, and E. Schuppe, *RE*, XIX, I, 1937, cols 1119–24.

28. Concerning the identification of the naked man with the stick as Pan, see Wiseman (works cited in n. 22 above). On the iconography of Pan, see J. Boardman, *LIMC*, VIII, 1, 1997, pp. 923ff.

29. See A. Momigliano, 'Tre figure mitiche: Tanaquilla, Gaia Caecilia, Acca Larentia', *Miscellanea della Facoltà di Lettere e Filosofia dell'Università di Torino*, series II, 1968, pp. 3ff.; A. Momigliano, *Contributo alla storia degli studi classici e del mondo antico*, vol. 4 (Rome: 1969), pp. 455ff.; Coarelli 1988, pp. 129ff.; J. Scheid, *Romulus et ses frères. Le collège des frères Arvales modèle du culte public dans la Rome des empereurs* (Rome: 1990), pp. 18–24, with pp. 590–3, especially on G. Radke, 'Acca Larentia und die fratres Arvales. Ein Stück römisch-sabinischer Frühgeschichte', *ANRW*, I, 2, 1972, pp. 421ff. Lastly, on the annual *parentationes* for Acca Larentia, see A. Fraschetti, 'L'eroizzazione di Germanico', in A. Fraschetti (ed.), *La commemorazione di Germanico nella documentazione epigrafica: 'Tabula Hebana' e 'Tabula Siarensis'* (Rome: 2000), p. 158.

30. Cornell, 'Aeneas and the Twins', pp. 1ff.; R. A. Laroche, 'The Alban King-List in Dionysius I.70–1: A Numerical Analysis', *Historia*, 31, 1982, pp. 112ff.; R. A. Laroche, 'Early Roman Chronology: Its Schematic Nature', in Carl Deroux, *Studies in Latin Literature and Roman History* (Brussels: 1983), pp. 5ff.; G. Brugnoli, 'Reges Albanorum', in *Atti del Convegno Virgiliano di Brindisi nel bimillenario della morte* (Perugia: 1983), pp. 157ff.; G. Brugnoli, 'I "reges albani" di Ovidio', in A. Pasqualini (ed.), *Alba Longa. Mito, storia, archeologia* (Rome: 1996), pp. 127ff.

31. In Lavinium Aeneas was venerated as *Pater Indiges*; see Sextus Pompeius Festus, *De Verborum Significatu Quae Supersunt Cum Pavli Epitome*, ed. by Wallace M. Lindsay (Leipzig: 1913, reprinted Hildesheim: 1965), p. 94;

also Aulus Gellius II.16.9 and Servius Dan., *ad Aen.* I.259 and XII.794; the eulogy of the Forum of Pompey (*CIL* X, p. 8348 = *I.It* XIII.3 no. 85) and that of the Forum of Augustus (*CIL* I, p. 189). See J. L. De La Barrera and W. Trillmich, 'Eine Wiederholung der Aeneas-Gruppe vom Forum Augustum samt ihrer Inschrift in Mérida (Spanien)', *MDAI(RA)*, 103, 1996, pp. 119ff. On the *heroon* of Aeneas at Lavinium, see P. Sommella, '"Heroon" di Enea a Lavinio. Recenti scavi a Pratica di Mare', *RPAA*, 44, 1971–2, pp. 47ff., in particular pp. 72ff.; cf. an earlier work, G. K. Galinsky, *Aeneas, Sicily and Rome* (Princeton, NJ: 1969), p. 158; F. Zevi, 'Il mito di Enea nella documentazione archeologica: nuove considerazioni', in *L'èpos greco in Occidente, Atti del XIX Convegno di Studi sulla Magna Grecia* (Taranto: 1979), pp. 247ff.; F. Zevi, 'Note sulla leggenda di Enea in Italia', in *Gli Etruschi e Roma. Incontro di studi in onore di M. Pallottino* (Rome: 1981), pp. 145ff.; Carandini 1997, pp. 539ff.; F. Fulminante, 'La morte e la divinizzazione di Enea', in Carandini and Cappelli 2000, pp. 213–15 (with further references). On the Latin king identified with Jupiter Latiaris on the Monte Cavo near Alba, see Festus p. 212, 15ff.; *Scholia Bobiensia* to Cicero, *Pro Plancio*, p. 218, 25ff. Hildebrandt; see also A. Alföldi, *Early Rome and the Latins* (Ann Arbor: [no date, but 1964]), pp. 29ff.; more generally in A. Pasqualini, 'I miti albani e l'origine delle "feriae Latinae"', in A. Pasqualini, *Alba Longa*, pp. 217ff.

32. Brelich 1976, pp. 57ff. On the '*Saturnia regna*' the essential reference for the ancient documentation remains E. Panofsky, 'Preistoria umana in due cicli di Piero di Cosimo', in *Studi di iconologia. I temi umanistici nell'arte del Rinascimento* (Turin: 1975), pp. 39ff.

33. See Hesiod, *Theogony*, 1011–16. For a high dating of these lines see Zevi, 'Il mito di Enea', p. 233; N. Valenza-Mele, 'Hera e Apollo a Cuma e la mantica sibillina', *RIASA*, 14–15, 1991–2, p. 8; C. Ampolo, 'La ricezione dei miti greci nel Lazio: l'esempio di Elpenore ed Ulisse al Circeo', *PdP*, 49, 1994, pp. 271ff. For the equation of Agrius with Silvius, see M. Durante, 'Agrion ede Latinon', *PdP*, 6, 1951, pp. 216–17; A. Alföldi, *Die troianischen Urahnen der Römer* (Basel: 1957), pp. 24ff., with the review by S. Weinstock, *JRS*, 49, 1959, pp. 170–1, and Alföldi's reply, *Early Rome*, p. 239, n. 1. For the equation with Faunus, J. Gagé, 'Énée, Faunus et le culte du Silvain Pélasge', *MEFR*, 72, 1961, pp. 101ff.; Carandini 1997, p. 77. On the archaic 'woodland kings', see Mazzarino II, 1, 1966, p. 194. For a general treatment see also P. Dräger, 'Waren Graikos und Latinos Brüder? Hesiod F 5 (MW) und der Name der Griechen', *Gymnasium*, 99, 1992, pp. 409ff.

34. Virgil, *Aeneid* VII.170–2 ('Tectum augustum, ingens, centum sublime columnis, / urbi fuit summa. Laurentis regia Pici, / horrendum silvis et religione parentum'), and the notes by V. I. Rovicac, 'Latinus Genealogy and the Palace of Picus (*Aeneid* 7.45–9, 170–91)', *CQ*, 30, 1980, pp. 140ff. On Latinus, see, for example, R. Lesueur, 'Latinus ou la paternité manquée (*Enéide*, VII–XII)', *REL*, 57, 1979, pp. 231ff.; A. Grandazzi, 'Le roi

Latinus. Analyse d'une figure légendaire', *CRAI*, 1988, pp. 481ff. On situating the shrine of Solfatara Laurentina, see F. Della Corte, *La mappa dell'Eneide* (Florence: 1972), pp. 188–9; of earlier works, note above all H. Boas, *Aeneas' Arrival in Latium* (Amsterdam: 1938), pp. 195ff. For an attempt to 'systematise' the chronology of Picus, Latinus and Faunus, see A. Carandini, 'Il sito di Roma nell'età preurbana. Introduzione al problema', in *StMisc*, 30 (Rome: 1998), pp. 171ff.

35. On the 'wild' features of Faunus see above all Brelich 1976, pp. 66ff., with the ancient documentation therein adopted. On Faunus *Silvicola*: Virgil, *Aeneid* X.551; *semicaper*: Ovid, *Fasti* V.101. For further epithets see G. Wissowa in Roscher, *Ausführliches Lexikon der griechischen und römischen Mythologie* I, 2, 1886–90, cols 1454ff. On laurel in the palace of Latinus: Virgil, *Aeneid* VII.59ff. From this standpoint the difficulties of the commentators on Virgil in trying to situate and identify the city of King Latinus are easily understood. As noted by F. Castagnoli (in *Enea nel Lazio. Archeologia e mito. Catalogo della mostra* (Rome: 1981), p. 157; see also F. Castagnoli, *Lavinium*, vol. 1, *Topografia generale. Fonti e storia delle ricerche* (Rome: 1972), pp. 85ff.), this was 'an imaginary city, without a name', which in Livy and Dionysius of Halicarnassus could be referred to only by periphrasis. On Alba see below, n. 62.

36. See Varro, *Ling.* VII.36; Dionysius of Halicarnassus V.16.3; Livy II.7.2; Plutarch, *Numitor* 15.3–7 (see also Ovid, *Fasti* III.291ff.), and the observations of J. Scheid, 'Numa et Jupiter ou les dieux citoyens de Rome', *Archives de Sciences Sociales de Religion*, 59, 1985, pp. 41ff.

37. See Virgil, *Aeneid* VII.85–91: 'Hinc Italae gentes omnisque Oenotria tellus / in dubiis responsa petunt; huc dona sacerdos / Cum tulit et caesarum ovium sub nocte silenti / pellibus incubuit stratis somnosque petivit, / multa modis simulacra videt volitantia miris / et varias audit voces fruiturque deorum / conloquio atque imis Acheronta adfatur Avernis'; see also Servius, *ad Aen.* VII.81: 'FAVNI Faunus *apo tes phones* dictus, quod voce, non signis, ostendit futura'. On these matters see J.-P. Vernant (ed.), *Divinazione e razionalità* (Turin: 1982) and for more detail E. Benveniste, 'Il vocabolario latino dei segni e dei presagi', in *Il vocabolario delle istituzioni indoeuropee*, vol. II (Turin: 1976), pp. 477ff.

38. See Mommsen 1887, vol. I, p. 77, n. 1; also more generally P. Catalano, *Contributi alla storia del diritto augurale* (Turin: 1960), vol. I, pp. 49ff. See also R. Bloch, *La divination dans l'antiquité* (Paris: 1984), pp. 56ff.; from an earlier date, R. Bloch, *Les prodiges dans l'antiquité classique* (Paris: 1963), pp. 77ff. Also, for example, C. Guittard, 'La tradition oraculaire étrusco-latine dans ses rapports avec le vers "saturnien" et le "carmen" primitif', in *La divination dans le monde étrusco-italique*, suppl. no. 52 to *Caesarodunum*, 1986, pp. 33ff.

39. Livy I.4.8. On the first Silvius 'born by some accident in the forest', see Livy I.3.6; also Dionysius of Halicarnassus I.70.1–3.

40. A. Giardina, 'Allevamento ed economia della selva in Italia meridionale', in

Società romana e produzione schiavistica, vol. I; A. Giardina and A. Schiavone (eds), *L'Italia: insediamenti e forme economiche* (Rome, Bari: 1981), p. 98; A. Giardina, *L'Italia romana: storie di un'identità incompiuta* (Rome, Bari: 1997), p. 152; more generally, see G. Traina, *Ambienti e paesaggi di Roma antica* (Rome: 1990), *passim*.

41. Sallust, *Cat.* 6.1: 'Aborigines, genus hominum agreste, sine legibus, sine imperio, liberum atque solutum'; see also J.-C. Richard, 'Varron, l' "Origo gentis Romanae" et les Aborigenes', *RPh*, 57, 1983, pp. 29ff.; N. Golvers, 'The Latin Name "Aborigines". Some Historiographical and Linguistic Observations', *AncSoc*, 20, 1989, pp. 193ff.; G. D'Anna's commentary on *OGR*, *Origine del popolo romano* (Milan: 1992), pp. 74–5; D. Briquel, '"Pastores Aboriginum" (Justin 38.6–7). A la recherche d'une historiographie grecque anti-romaine disparue', *REL*, 73, 1995, pp. 44ff.; D. Briquel, *Le regard des autres. Les origines de Rome vues par ses ennemis* (Besançon: 1997), pp. 32ff. On the *Chronographer of 354*, see *MGH*, Autores Antiquissimi IX 1, p. 143.

42. On the education of the twins at Gabii, see Dionysius of Halicarnassus I.8.5; Plutarch, *Rom.* 6.2 (see *De fortuna Romanorum* 320 E); *OGR* 21.1, according to which it was Numitor who 'secretly arranged everything'; E. Peruzzi placed much stress on this in *Origini di Roma* (Florence: 1970), vol. II, pp. 10ff., but note the well founded reservations of J. Poucet, *Les origines de Rome : Tradition et histoire* (Brussels: 1985), pp. 235–6, n. 9. On the tradition of the twins being educated at Gabii in Plutarch, see above all D. Musti, 'Varrone nell'insieme delle tradizioni su Roma Quadrata', in *Gli storiografi latini tramandati in frammenti. Atti Conv. Urbino, 9–11 maggio 1974* (Urbino: 1975), pp. 301–3.

43. Plutarch, *Rom.* 6.5; see Dionysius of Halicarnassus I.79.11, with an explicit reference to 'the hut of Romulus', on which see A. Balland, 'La "casa Romuli" au Palatin et au Capitole', *REL*, 62, 1984, pp. 57ff.; P. Pensabene, 'La "casa Romuli" sul Palatino', *RPAA*, 63, 1990–1, pp. 115ff.; F. Coarelli, *LTUR*, I, 1993, pp. 241–2.

44. See Dionysius of Halicarnassus I.32.3–5. On the Lupercal, Ulf 1982, pp. 29ff.; more recently F. Coarelli, *LTUR*, III, 1996, pp. 198–9. On the Augustan restorations see *RG* 19.

45. G. Dumézil, *Archaic Roman Religion*, trans. by Philip Krapp (Chicago, London: 1966), vol. 1, p. 340.

46. Plutarch, *Rom.* 21.6. On the two groups of *luperci*, M. Corsaro, '"Sodalitas" et gentilité dans l'ensemble lupercal', *RHR*, 91, 1977, pp. 137ff.; also R. Fiori, ' "Sodales". "Gefolgschaften" e diritto di associazione in Roma arcaica (VIII–V sec. a.C.)', in *'Societa et ius'. 'Munuscula' degli allievi a F. Serrao* (Naples: 1999), pp. 114ff. On their transformation into *creppi*, see Festus (see n. 31 above), p. 49: 'Crep[p]os, id est lupercos, dicebant a crepitu pellicularum, quem faciunt verberantes'. See e.g. K. Kerényi, 'Lupo e capra nella festa dei Lupercalia', in *Miti e misteri* (Turin: 1979), pp. 357ff., which also considers the etymological connection between *lupercus*

and *lupus*, discussed, as is well known, by J. Frazer, *Publii Ovidii Nasonis Fastorum libri sex* (London: 1928), vol. II, pp. 337ff., where, however, they are transformed into he-goats. If there is no doubt about the etymological connection between *lupercus* and *lupus* (see also Ulf 1982, pp. 14ff.), it should nevertheless be noted that the *luperci* in the late Republican and Augustan ages could have been assimilated into *hirci*, as shown not only by Festus (see n. 31 above), p. 42 ('Caprae dictae, quod omne virgultum carpant, sive a crepitu crurum. Unde et crepas eas prisci dixerunt'), but also one of the *aitia* of the institution of the feast in Ovid, *Fasti* II.425ff., where the institution was linked with the barrenness of the ravished Sabine women, in response to Juno Lucina in her grove on the Esquiline Hill ('Italicas matres, . . . sacer hircus inito'), and with the interpretation then given by the Etruscan haruspex, sacrificing a goat and compelling the women to submit to the blows with thongs made from the skin of the animal. See also Varro, *Ling.* VI.34 (and on Varro also n. 50 below).

47. On the use of *nudus* with reference to Cincinnatus in this scene, see Pliny, *Natural History* XVIII.20; on the Senate emissaries' invitation to put on the toga, Livy III.26.9. On the relation between the toga and citizenship, see *Dig.* 49.14.32; also *CTh* XIV.10.1. On the exiles, a reference to Pliny, *Ep.* IV.11.3, is sufficient, with the commentary by A. N. Sherwin-White, *The Letters of Pliny* (Oxford: 1966), p. 281. The critical comments of D. Porte, 'Note sur les Luperci nudi', in *Mélanges J. Heurgon. L'Italie préromaine et la Rome républicaine*, vol. II (Rome: 1976), pp. 817ff., on the thesis of A. W. J. Holleman, 'Ovid and the Lupercalia', *Historia*, 27, 1973, pp. 260ff., are severe but justified. See also D. Porte, 'An Enigmatic Function of the Flamen Dialis (Ovid, *Fasti* 2.282) and the Augustan Reform', *Numen*, 20, 1973, pp. 222ff. In this account Augustus, wishing to sanitise the Lupercalia, made the *luperci* put on a sort of loin-cloth. On the representation of the toga in Rome see most recently C. Vout, 'The Myth of the Toga: Understanding the History of Roman Dress', *G&R*, 43, 1996, pp. 204ff.

48. G. Dumézil, *Mitra-Varuna. Essai sur deux réprésentations indo-euro-péennes de la souveraineté* (Paris: 5th edn, 1948), pp. 38ff.; on *gravitas* see G. Dumézil, *Idées romaines* (Paris: 2nd edn, 1969), pp. 142ff.

49. Plautus, *Poen.* 522–3 ('liberos homines per urbem modico magis pari est gradu ire; / servile esse duco festinantem currere'); *Historia Augusta*, Alexander Severus 42.2 ('cursorem numquam nisi servum suum, dicens ingenuum currere nisi in sacro certamine non debere, . . . habuit'). On the race of the *luperci* see G. Piccaluga, 'L'aspetto agonistico dei Lupercalia', *SMSR*, 33, 1962, pp. 51ff.

50. In spite of the extensive efforts of A. Kirsopp Michels, 'The Topography and Interpretation of the Lupercalia', *TAPhA*, 84, 1953, pp. 35ff. (for a similar interpretation see also A. W. J. Holleman), it seems to me very difficult to dismiss the extremely precise evidence of Varro, *Ling.* VI.34: 'Lupercis nudis lustratur antiquum oppidum Palatinum gregibus humanis

cinctum'. On the route followed by the *luperci* during their race, see most recently the discussion by A. Ziolkowski, 'Ritual Cleaning-up of the City: from the Lupercalia to the Argei', *AncSoc*, 29, 1998–9, pp. 191ff. On the marginal space reserved for the young men at the moment of their initiation, see the seminal work by A. Van Gennep, *I riti di passaggio* (Turin: 1981), pp. 97ff.; on Rome see A. Fraschetti, 'Il mondo romano', in G. Levi and J.-C. Schmitt (eds), *Storia dei giovani*, vol. I, *Dall'antichità all'età moderna* (Rome, Bari: 1993), pp. 61ff.

51. Valerius Maximus, II.2.9. The reliefs relating to the *luperci* and the young men on horseback in the *transvectio equitum* were collected by P. Veyne, 'Iconographie de la *transvectio equitum* et des Lupercales', *REA*, 62, 1960, pp. 100ff. See also E. Wrade, 'Statuae lupercorum habitu', *MDAI(RA)*, 90, 1983, pp. 187ff.; most recently S. Tortorella, 'L'adolescenza dei gemelli, la festa dei "Lupercalia" e l'uccisione di Amulio', in Carandini and Cappelli 2000, pp. 244ff. (in particular p. 251), on the interpretation of a Campanian slab in the wake of Pietro Rosa; see in particular M. A. Tomei, *Scavi francesi sul Palatino. Le indagini di Pietro Rosa per Napoleone III* (Rome: 1999), p. 438.

52. See G. Dumézil, *Le problème des Centaures* (Paris: 1929), *passim*; Alföldi 1974, *passim*; P. Vidal-Naquet, 'Le chasseur noir', in Vidal-Naquet 1981 (see n. 9 above), pp. 151ff. On the Roman twins see also D. Briquel 1980, pp. 271ff., D. Briquel, 'Les enfances de Romulus et Rémus', in *Hommages à R. Schilling* (Paris: 1983), pp. 53ff.

53. Cicero, *Pro Caelio* XI.26 ('Fera quaedam sodalitas et plane pastoricia atque agrestis germanorum Lupercorum, quorum coitio illa silvestris ante est instituta quam humanitas atque leges, si quidem non modo nomina deferunt inter se sodales, sed etiam commemorant sodalitatem in accusando, ut ne quis id forte nesciat timere videatur!'); see A. W. J. Holleman, 'Cicero on the Luperci (*Cael.* 26)', *AntClass*, 44, 1975, pp. 198ff.

54. See R. Schilling, 'Romulus l'élu et Rémus le réprouvé', *REL*, 38, 1960, pp. 182ff.; also R. Schilling, *Rites, cultes et dieux de Rome* (Paris: 1979), pp. 103ff. On *exta*, clearly in the sense 'meat', see Plautus, *Miles gloriosus* 712; *Poen.* 491, 804; *Stichus* 251; Virgil, *Georgics* II.396; *Aeneid* VIII.183; cf. the further examples which may be drawn from *ThLL* V.2, col. 1965. For the Greek definition of *splanchna*, corresponding to *exta*, see M. Detienne, *Dionysos mis à mort* (Paris: 1977), pp. 174ff.; for Roman customs see J. Scheid, 'La spartizione a Roma', *StStor*, 25, 1984, pp. 945ff.; also J. Scheid, 'La spartizione sacrificale a Roma', in C. Grottanelli and N. Parise (eds), *Sacrificio e società nel mondo antico* (Rome, Bari: 1988), pp. 267ff.; most recently Scheid, *La religion des Romains* (Paris: 1998), pp. 75ff.

55. For Octavius see Suetonius, *Augustus* 1.1; for Camillus, Livy V.21.8 and Plutarch, *Camillus* 5.6, with commentary by L. Piccirilli on Plutarch *Le Vite di Temistocle e Camillo* (Milan: 1983), pp. 304–5. For the case of Sulla (a case in which interpretations were delivered ecstatically), see Augustine, *De Civitate Dei* II.24, with the observations of R. Schilling, 'A propos des

"exta": l'extispicine étrusque et la "litatio" romaine', in *Hommages à A. Grenier*, vol. III (Brussels: 1962), pp. 1371–8. On the *exta* as an earnest of victory, J. Hubaux, *Rome et Véies* (Paris: 1958), pp. 221–39, 279–85; Briquel 1980, pp. 271ff.

56. See above all P. Vidal-Naquet, 'Une civilisation de la parole politique', in Vidal-Naquet 1981, pp. 22–3.

57. On the cult of Hercules at the *ara maxima*, see Livy I.7.12; Dionysius of Halicarnassus I.40.3–4; Servius, *ad Aen.* VIII.269; *OGR* 8, 1–3 (with commentary by J.-C. Richard on Pseudus-Aurelius Victor, *Les origines du peuple romain* (Paris: 1983), pp. 132–4, and by G. D'Anna on *OGR*, *Origine del popolo romano*, pp. 83–4); also essential is J. Bayet, *Les origines de l'Hercule romain* (Paris: 1926), pp. 248ff. As is well known, the theory of the Phoenician origin of the cult has been upheld by R. Rebuffat, 'Les Phéniciens à Rome, *MEFR(A)*, 78, 1966, pp. 7ff.; see also D. Van Berchem, 'Sanctuaires d'Hercule-Melqart. III. Rome', *Syria*, 44, 1967, pp. 307ff. On the *ara maxima* of Hercules, Coarelli 1988, pp. 61ff., and F. Coarelli, *LTUR*, III, 1996, pp. 15ff.

58. Livy I.5.1–3; Dionysius of Halicarnassus I.79.12–14; Plutarch, *Rom.* 7.1–2.

59. Dionysius of Halicarnassus I.80.3.

60. The dependence of Dionysius of Halicarnassus on Fabius Pictor has been questioned by J. Poucet, 'Fabius Pictor et Denys d'Halicarnasse: Les enfances de Romulus et de Rémus', *Historia*, 25, 1976, pp. 201ff., in a debate with D. Timpe, 'Fabius Pictor und die Anfänge der römischen Historiografie', *ANRW*, I, 2, 1972, pp. 928ff. See also G. P. Verbrugghe, 'Fabius Pictor's "Romulus and Remus" ', *Historia*, 30, 1981, pp. 236–8.

61. See Livy I.6.3; Dionysius of Halicarnassus I.85.1–3; Plutarch, *Rom.* 9.1–2.

62. On Alba Longa, where archaeology seems to indicate 'a topography of independent villages and associated necropolises which can be dated to a pre-urban age', see L. Crescenzi and E. Tortorici in *Enea nel Lazio*, pp. 18–19; S. Quilici Gigli, 'A proposito delle ricerche sull'ubicazione di Alba Longa', *PdP*, 38, 1983, pp. 140ff.; see also A. Grandazzi, *The Foundation of Rome*, trans. J. M. Todd (Ithaca, NY, London: 1997), pp. 129ff; and recently P. Chiarucci, 'La documentazione archeologica pre-protostorica nell'area urbana e le più recenti scoperte', in *Alba Longa*, pp. 1ff. However, the existence of 'dependent inhabited points linked together as villages and recognising a principal centre of habitation' (Carandini 1997, p. 533) should not lead us to speak of Alba Longa as a 'city'. In the ancient representations it is a city solely by virtue of being founded by Ascanius and destroyed by Tullus Hostilius.

63. See above all P. Kretschmer, 'Remus und Romulus', *Glotta*, 1, 1909, pp. 288ff.; W. Schulze, *Zur Geschichte lateinischer Eigennamen* (2nd edn, Berlin: 1933), p. 219 and pp. 579ff.; E. Peruzzi, *Origini di Roma* (Florence: 1970), vol. 1, pp. 20ff.; also C. De Simone, 'Etruskischer Literaturbericht; neuveröffentliche Inschriften', *Glotta*, 53, 1975, p. 135; see also C. De Simone, 'Il nome di Romolo', in Carandini and Cappelli 2000, pp. 30–1.

64. Festus (see n. 31 above), pp. 6–7: 'Altellus Romulus dicebatur . . . Sicut enim fit diminutive a macro macellus, a vafro vafellus, ita ab alterno altellus.' For the derivation of the name Altellus from *alter* rather than *alternus*, see F. Mencacci, *I fratelli amici. La rappresentazione dei gemelli nella cultura romana* (Venice: 1996), p. 176. On their shared etymon see Festus, p. 327: 'Romulus et Remus a virtute, hoc est robore, appellati sunt', and note the different assertion in *OGR* 21.5: 'Alterum Remum dictum videlicet a tarditate, quippe talis naturae homines ab antiquis remores dicti'; see Skutsch 1985, pp. 226–7.

65. For the appraisal of the twins see Plutarch, *Rom.* 6.3. On Romulus' introduction of the *manipulares*, see Plutarch, *Rom.* 8.7, with commentary by Ampolo and Manfredini 1988, pp. 291–2.

NOTES TO CHAPTER 2

1. Dionysius of Halicarnassus I.85.1–2; Livy I.6.3; Plutarch, *Rom.* 9.1–3.

2. See Livy I.6.4; Dionysius of Halicarnassus I.85.4–6; Plutarch, *Rom.* 9.4. On Remoria, see the discussion in Wiseman 1995, pp. 110ff. and J. Aaronen, *LTUR*, IV, 1999, pp. 204–6. Ennius, as we know, fixed the taking of the auspices by Romulus on the Aventine (I^2 fr. 80 Vahlen = I 75 Skutsch), while it remains very uncertain where Remus took the auspices. If with Skutsch 1985, p. 224, we revise *in monte* to *in Murco*, it would also refer to a part of the Aventine, if it could be proved (see *Sextus Pompeius Festus*, ed. by Wallace M. Lindsay (Leipzig: 1913, reprinted Hildesheim: 1965), p. 135) that the Aventine was previously called *mons Murcus*: see F. Coarelli, *LTUR*, III, 1996, pp. 289–90. On the expression *auspicium auguriumque* in Ennius, see A. Magdelain, 'L'inauguration de l' "Urbs" et l' "imperium"', *MEFR(A)*, 89, 1977, pp. 17–22, and Magdelain 1990, pp. 217–22.

3. Livy I.7.2–3; Dionysius of Halicarnassus I.87.2–4; Plutarch, *Rom.* 10.1–2; *OGR* 23.6.

4. See *OGR* 23.6; John Malalas VII, p. 170 Dindorf.

5. For the expression *ad inaugurandum templa*, referring to both the twins, see Livy I.6.4. On the two *auguracula* of Rome see above all Coarelli 1983, pp. 177ff., and F. Coarelli, *LTUR*, I, 1993, pp. 142–3. On the distinction between *auspicia maxima* and *auspicia minora*, see Mommsen 1887, vol. I, pp. 91ff., and P. Catalano, *Contributi alla storia del diritto augurale* (Turin: 1960), vol. I, pp. 44ff.

6. On this see J. N. Bremmer, 'Romulus, Remus and the Foundation of Rome', in Bremmer and Horsfall 1987, pp. 38, 47.

7. On the idea of original sin, see T. Zielinski, 'Le messianisme d'Horace', *AntClass*, 8, 1939, pp. 171ff.; also H. Wagenvoort, 'The Crime of Fratricide (Hor., *Epod.* 7.18). The Figure of Romulus Quirinus in the Political Struggle of the 1st Century BC', in *Studies in Roman Literature, Culture and Religion* (Leiden: 1956), pp. 169ff.; P. Jal, *La guerre civile à Rome*

(Paris: 1963), p. 406; M. Benabou, 'Rémus, le mur et la mort', *AION ArchStAnt*, 6, 1984, pp. 103ff.; A. Johner, 'Rome, la violence et le sacré: les doubles fondateurs', *Euphrosyne*, 19, 1991, pp. 291ff.

8. On the foundation rites of Antioch and Alexandria, see John Malalas VIII, pp. 200–1 Dindorf; also Wiseman 1995, pp. 124ff.; A. Carandini 1997, p. 197; and Carandini, 'Variazioni sul tema di Romulus', in Carandini and Cappelli 2000, pp. 134–41 (with some very sensitive shifts of perspective); also M. Di Fazio, 'Sacrifici umani e uccisioni rituali nel mondo etrusco', *RAL*, series IX, XII, 2001, pp. 482–3.

9. From a similar perspective, see J. Bayet, 'La croyance romaine aux présages déterminants: aspects littéraires et chronologiques', in *Hommages Bidez-Cumont* (Brussels: 1949), pp. 21–3; in his *Croyances et rites dans la Rome antique* (Paris: 1971), pp. 81–2, Bayet was able to date the birth of the legend surrounding the death of Romulus: 'non seulement après la surprise gauloise (*circa* 390 *a. C.*), mais une fois reçu le mensonge de l'arrivée soudaine de Camille et de l'extermination, *sur place*, des bandes celtiques'.

10. On Altellus, see Chapter 1, n. 64; on the race round the *antiquum oppidum*, see Chapter 1, n. 50.

11. On the feasts in the *curiae*, see p. 47 ff. See Ennius, p. 79, line 109.

12. On the death of Remus at the time of the Palilia, see Ovid, *Fasti* IV, 837ff., with annotation by P. Drossart, 'La mort de Rémus chez Ovide', *REL*, 50, 1972, pp. 187ff.; on the establishment of the Lemuria, see Ovid, *Fasti* V, 451ff. Naturally the shifting of the funeral date from the Palilia or the days immediately after it to the Lemuria, which began on 9 May, explained the reasons for the celebration and the very name of the festival.

13. Scheid 1984, pp. 135–6.

14. Virgil, *Aeneid* I.291–3: 'Aspera tum positis mitescent saecula bellis; / cana Fides et Vesta, Remo cum fratre Quirinus iura dabunt'; see also Servius, *ad Aen.* I.292: 'vera tamen hoc habet ratio, Quirinum Augustum esse, Remum vero pro Agrippa positum, qui filiam Augusti duxit uxorem, et cum eo pariter bella tractavit', with notes by J.-M. Roddaz, *Marcus Agrippa* (Rome: 1984), pp. 205–6.

15. Livy I.7.3; Plutarch, *Rom.* 9.4 and 11.3 (for the extension to the Comitium). On this see above all, F. Castagnoli, 'Roma quadrata', in *Studies Presented to D. Moore Robinson* (St Louis: 1951), pp. 389ff.; also Castagnoli 1993, pp. 179ff., and A. Magdelain, 'Le pomerium archaïque et le *mundus*', *REL*, 59, 1971, pp. 103ff.; Magdelain 1990, pp. 155ff.; D. Musti, 'Varrone nell'insieme delle tradizioni', pp. 297ff.; A. Grandazzi, 'La "Roma quadrata": mythe ou réalité?', *MEFR(A)*, 105, 1993, pp. 493ff.; A. Mastrocinque, 'Roma quadrata', *MEFR(A)*, 110, 1998, pp. 681ff.; F. Coarelli, *LTUR*, IV, 1999, pp. 207–9.

16. Dionysius of Halicarnassus I.88.2. For the foundation ditch in Ovid, see *Fasti* IV.821–4: 'Fossa fit ad solidum, fruges iaciuntur in ima / et de vicino terra petita solo; / fossa repletur humo plenaeque imponitur ara / et novus accenso fungitur igne focus'. On the impossibility of identifying

this ditch with the *mundus* of Ceres in the Comitium, see Castagnoli,
'Roma quadrata', pp. 389ff.; Castagnoli 1993, pp. 181ff.; Magdelain, 'Le
pomerium archaïque et le *mundus*', pp. 99ff.; also Magdelain 1990,
pp. 82ff.

17. Compare Festus (see n. 2 above), pp. 310–12: 'Quadrata Roma <locus> in
Palatio ante templum Apollinis dicitur, ubi reposita sunt, quae solent boni
ominis gratia in urbe condenda adhiberi, quia saxo m<i>nitus est initio in
speciem quadratam', with the following quotation from Ennius, III fr. 10
Vahlen = IV fr. 150 Skutsch. On the *auguratorium* of the Palatine later
incorporated into the house of Augustus, see F. Coarelli, *Roma sepolta*
(Rome: 1984), p. 142, and F. Coarelli, *LTUR*, I, 1993, pp. 143; L. Chioffi,
'"Fertur Resius" tra l'"augurium" di Romolo e il "pomerium" di Claudio',
RPAA, 65, 1992–3, pp. 137ff. However, it seems to me very difficult to
identify as 'Roma Quadrata', as R. Cappelli has recently suggested
('Questioni di iconografia', in Carandini and Cappelli 2000, especially p.
169), the 'sacred preparations, with altar' depicted in the Pompeian group
of frescos in the triclinium of the house of Marcus Fabius Secundus, since
'Roma Quadrata', in the evidence available to us, was not 'surmounted by
a fire lit by Romulus at the moment of the foundation of the Palatine city'.
It is equally difficult to see the strictly toga-clad figures depicted in the
scene as the Salii Palatini, since these figures do not bear the iconographic
markers intended to denote the Salii, above all the bucklers and 'purple
tunics', as Plutarch explains, *Numa* 13.4. On the dress of the Salii, see M.
Torelli, *Lavinio e Roma. Riti iniziatici e matrimonio tra archeologia e storia*
(Rome: 1984), p. 109.

18. Castagnoli had already followed this path in 'Roma quadrata', pp. 397–9;
also Castagnoli 1993, pp. 186–97, and Grandazzi, 'La "Roma quadrata"',
pp. 523ff. On Servius' 'regions' as simple designations for the tribal territories of the city, see Fraschetti 1990, pp. 181ff., and A. Fraschetti, *LTUR*,
IV, 1999, pp. 194–6. Besides, the somewhat tortuous and irregular distribution of the four urban tribes could hardly have been at the origin of the
myth of 'Roma Quadrata': see D. Palombi, *LTUR*, IV, 1999, pp. 196–7,
with fig. 83.

19. On this question see above all A. Magdelain, 'L'inauguration de l' "Urbs"
et l' "imperium" ', pp. 11ff.; Magdelain 1990, pp. 209ff., also 'Le pomerium
archaïque et le *mundus*', pp. 103ff., and Magdelain 1990, pp. 155ff. See also
B. Liou-Gille, 'Le pomerium', *MH*, 50, 1993, pp. 94ff.

20. On Romulus' pomerium, see Magdelain, 'L'inauguration'; Coarelli 1983,
pp. 262ff.; F. Castagnoli, 'Su alcuni problemi topografici del Palatino',
RAL, series VIII, 34, 1979, pp. 344ff.; Castagnoli 1993, pp. 326ff. As for the
text of Tacitus (*Annals* XII.24.1–2), I welcome the emendation by E.
Koestermann, *Corneli Taciti Annales libri qui supersunt* (Leipzig: 1965), p.
236: 'ad sacellum Larum. Forumque Romanum et Capitolium', instead of
the vulgate 'ad sacellum Larum, inde forum Romanum. Forumque et
Capitolium', because it is clear that if the Roman Forum was added to the

city only by Titus Tatius it could not have been included within Romulus' pomerium.

21. On the 'disconcerting nature of the documentation' relating to the pomerium, see A. Giardina, *L'Italia romana. Storie di un'identità incompiuta* (Rome, Bari: 1997), pp. 117ff.; A. Giardina in A. Giardina (ed.), *Storia di Roma dall'antichità a oggi*, vol. I (Rome, Bari: 2000), pp. 23ff.

22. See Livy I.3–15 and 8.5–8. For Cicero's definition, see *Rep.* I.32.49: 'Quid est enim civitas nisi iuris societas civium?' with notes by C. Ampolo, 'Le origini di Roma e la "cité antique" ', *MEFR(A)*, 92, 1980, pp. 567ff. On Romulus' asylum, see T. P. Wiseman, *LTUR*, I, 1993, p. 130; D. van Berchem, 'Trois cas d'asylie archaïque', *MH*, 17, 1960, pp. 29ff.; Y. Toutscheu, 'La fondation de Rome et l'asile de Romulus. L'asile de Romulus et son interprétation en France de Bossuet à Fustel de Coulanges', in *Da Roma alla terza Roma (XVII Seminario di Studi storici), 'Initia urbis'. Le fondazioni di Roma, Constantinopoli, Mosca* (Naples: forthcoming).

23. Livy I.8.7, 9.11 ('quasdam forma excellentes, primoribus patrum destinatas, ex plebe homines quibus datum negotium erat, domos deferebant') and I.10.6–7 (see also below, n. 31). On the abduction of the Sabine women, see B. Liou-Gille, 'L'enlèvement des Sabines', *Latomus*, 50, 1991, pp. 342ff.; J. R. Jannot, 'Enquête sur l'enlèvement des Sabines', in *La Rome des premiers siècles* (Florence: 1992), pp. 131ff.

24. Livy I.13.8 (see also Livy X.6.7: 'ut tres antiquae tribus, Ramnes, Titienses, Luceres, suum quaeque augurem habeant'); Plutarch, *Rom.* 10.1. On Lucumo, Dionysius of Halicarnassus II.37.2 and 5; Cicero, *Rep.* II.14; on the Luceres, see Poucet 1967, pp. 338ff. On the institution of the tribes and the curia by Romulus alone at the moment of foundation, see Dionysius of Halicarnassus II.7.

25. On the ethnic basis of the subdivisions, see B. G. Niebuhr, *Römische Geschichte*, vol. 1, 3rd edn, ed. by M. Isler (Berlin: 1873), pp. 189ff.; A. Piganiol, *Essai sur les origines de Rome* (Paris: 1917), pp. 244ff. On the Indo-European tripartition, Dumézil 1974, pp. 175–6. On tribes and *curiae* as artificial creations, C. Ampolo, 'La nascita della città', in A. Momigliano and A. Schiavone (eds), *Storia di Roma, I, Roma in Italia* (Turin: 1988), pp. 169ff.; Cornell 1995, pp. 114ff. On the tribes as subdivisions of the *ager*, see Varro, *Ling.* V.55; Dionysius of Halicarnassus II.7.4 on the allocation of plots of land by Romulus to the thirty *curiae*. On connections between the *curiae* and the organisation of the army, see J. Martínez-Pinna Nieto, *Los orígenes del ejército romano* (Madrid: 1981), pp. 264ff.

26. Richard 1978, pp. 198ff., esp. p. 199, for debate with T. Mommsen, P. De Francisci, F. De Martino and R. Orestano.

27. On parity of votes among citizens in the *comitia curiata*, see Livy I.43.10: 'Non enim, ut ab Romulo traditum ceteri servaverant reges, viritim suffragium eadem vi eodemque iure promisce omnibus datum est, sed gradus facti, ut neque exclusus quisquam suffragio videretur et vis omnis penes primores civitatis esset'; see also Dionysius of Halicarnassus IV.20.1–3. On

this see A. Fraschetti, 'Servio Tullio e la partizione del corpo civico', *Metis*, 9–10, 1994–5, pp. 129ff., in particular p. 131. On the *curiae* and the *comitia curiata*, see R. E. A. Palmer, *The Archaic Community of the Romans* (Cambridge: 1970); M. Torelli, 'Tre studi di storia etrusca', *DdA*, 8, 1974–5, pp. 29ff.; Richard 1978, pp. 211ff.; L. Capogrossi Colognesi, *Dalla tribù allo Stato. Le istituzioni dello Stato cittadino* (Rome: 1990), pp. 91ff.; Cornell 1995, pp. 116ff.; C. Panella, 'Meta Sudans', *LTUR*, pp. 70ff. (with further references).

28. For the cult of Hercules at the high altar see above p. 37.
29. R. Martin, 'Essai d'interprétation économico-sociale de la légende de Romulus', *Latomus*, 26, 1967, pp. 297ff.
30. Livy I.9; Dionysius of Halicarnassus II.30; Plutarch, *Rom.*14, with commentary by Ampolo and Manfredini 1988, pp. 305–8.
31. Livy I.11.5–13.5; Dionysius of Halicarnassus II.37–45; Plutarch, *Rom.* 17–19. On the variants of the legend see especially Poucet 1967, pp. 187ff.
32. On Hostus Hostilius and his burial in the Forum see F. Coarelli, *LTUR*, IV, 1999, pp. 295–6 (with additional sources). The three versions of the Mettius Curtius episode are reported in Varro, *Ling.* V 148. For the Sabine version see Livy I.12.9–10; Dionysius of Halicarnassus II.42.2–6; Plutarch, Rom. 18.5–6. Regarding these see Å. Åkerström, 'Lacus Curtius und Seine Sagen', *Corolla Archaeologica principi hereditario regni Sueciae Gustavo Adolpho dedicata* (Lund: 1932), pp. 72ff.; Poucet 1967, pp. 241ff. On the monuments marking the 'Lacus Curtius', see C. F. Giuliani, *LTUR*, III, 1996, pp. 166–7. As noted, the site of the temple of Jupiter Stator has been much debated: see F. Castagnoli, 'Aedes deum Penatium in Velia', *RFIC*, 110, 1982, pp. 495ff.; Castagnoli, 1993, pp. 377ff.; F. Castagnoli, '"Ibam forte via Sacra" (*Hor., Sat.* I.9.1)', *Quaderni di topografia antica*, 10, 1988, pp. 99ff.; Castagnoli 1993, pp. 381 ff.; Coarelli 1983, pp. 26ff.; F. Coarelli, *LTUR*, III, 1996, pp. 155–7; A. Ziolkowski, 'The "Sacra via" and the Temple of Iupiter Stator', *OpRom*, 17, 1989, pp. 225ff.; Ziolkowski 1992, pp. 87ff.; J. Arce, 'Juppiter Stator en Roma', *Actes del XIV Congrès Internacional d'Arqueologia* (Tarragona: 1994), pp. 79ff.; J. J. Carerols Pérez, *'Sacra via' (I a.C.-I d.C.). Estudios des las fuentes escritas* (Madrid: 1995), pp. 109ff.
33. See Varro, *Ling.* V 47: 'Carinae pote a caeri<m>onia, quod hinc oritur caput Sacrae Viae ab Streniae sacello quae pertinet in arce<m>, qua sacra quotquot mensibus feruntur in arcem et per quam augures ex arce profecti solent inaugurare. Huius Sacrae Viae pars haec sola vulgo nota, quae est a Foro eunti primore clivo.' On the route of the Via Sacra see especially D. Palombi, 'Contributo alla topografia della via Sacra, dagli appunti di G. Boni', *Quaderni di topografia antica*, 10, 1988, pp. 97ff.; Ziolkowski, 'The "Sacra via"', pp. 225ff.; for a recent summary of this discussion, F. Coarelli, *LTUR*, III, 1999, pp. 223ff.
34. Dionysius II.50.2; for the Comitium, Plutarch, *Rom.* 19.10.
35. See L. Gernet, 'Sur le symbolisme politique: le Foyer commun', *Cahiers*

internationaux de Sociologie, 1952, pp. 22ff.; L. Gernet, *Anthropologie de la Grèce antique* (Paris: 1976), pp. 382ff.; for the role of Fustel de Coulanges and recent developments, see C. Ampolo in his introduction C. Ampolo (ed.), to *La città antica. Guida storica e critica* (Rome, Bari: 1980), pp. xiiiff.; and more generally see F. Hartog, *Le XIXe. siècle et l'histoire. Le cas Fustel de Coulanges* (Paris: 1988), pp. 23ff.

36. On this see the review by G. Giannelli, *Il sacerdozio delle Vestali romane* (Florence: 1913), pp. 12ff. (with bibliography).

37. See Varro, *Ling.* V.41: 'Hic mons ante Tarpeius dictus a virgine Vestale Tarpeia, quae ibi ab Sabinis necata armis et sepulta'; Varro, *Ant. rer. div.* fr. 282 Cardauns: ' Vestam [. . .] ignem pertinentem ad focis, sine quibus civitas esse non potest'. For a Vestal called Tarpeia who was already 'consecrated' by Numa see Plutarch, *Num.* 10.1. See Appendix I, p. 121ff.

38. For Calpurnius Piso, *HRR* I² F 5; Fabius Pictor and Cincius Alimentus, respectively FF 8 and 5.

39. For Tarpeia's death see Livy I.11.7; Dionysius of Halicarnassus II.44.1; Plutarch, *Rom.* 17.4; *Parall. Min.* 15.

40. See Plutarch, *Rom.* 22.1. Alban Vestals are referred to in *CIL* VI 2172 = *ILS* 5011 and *CIL* XIV 2410 = *ILS* 6190. There were still active Vestals at Alba in AD 382 when Primigenia, an Alban Vestal, committed incest with a certain Maximus (Simmaco, *Ep.* IX.147, p. 274 Seeck). On Primigenia see W. Ensslin, *RE*, XXII, 2, 1954, col. 1974; *PLRE*, I, p. 725.

41. For these see C. Ampolo, 'Analogie e rapporti tra Atene e Roma arcaica. Osservazioni sulla "Regia", sul "rex sacrorum" e sul culto di Vesta', *PdP*, 26, 1971, pp. 443ff.; lastly, with regard to the circumstance that 'this model of Fustel's' may be 'difficult to apply to the Italic cities', see A. Ziolkowski, *Storia di Roma* (Milan: 2000), pp. 20–1.

42. Dionysius II.65 and 66.1.

43. See De Sanctis, I, 1980, p. 201, with reference to Servius, *ad Aen.* VIII.190, where it may be observed that Virgil's commentator refers to only one shrine, which is not and cannot be located on the Palatine, 'in quo ei per virgines Vestae sacrificabatur'. Lastly, similar suggestions in Carandini 1997, p. 52. Note, with regard to a goddess called Caca, the irrefutable observation of Dumézil 1974, p. 60 n. 1: 'Si il y a eu une déesse *Caca*, ce qui n'est pas établi, *Cacus* est seulement un personnage de légende'. See Wissowa in Roscher, *Lex.* I, 1, 1886, cols 842–3.

44. See Livy I.20.3; observe, however, that according to Dionysius of Halicarnassus II.50.3, Titus Tatius had already sacrificed to Vesta; see Varro, *Ling.* V.74.

45. For evidence see C. Ampolo, 'La formazione della città nel Lazio, Periodo IVB (640/630–580 a.C.)', *DdA*, 2, 1980, pp. 165–92; C. Ampolo, 'Die endgültige Stadtwerdung Roms im 7. und 6. Jhr. V. Chr. Wenn Rom entstand die "civitas"', in *Palast und Hütte. Symposium der A. von Humboldt-Stiftung* (Berlin: 1979; Mainz: 1981), pp. 319ff.; C. Ampolo, 'Sulla formazione della città di Roma', *Opus*, 2, 1983, pp. 425ff. (in

response to A. Guidi, 'Sulle prime fasi dell'urbanizzazione nel Lazio pro-tostorico', *Opus*, 1, 1982, pp. 279ff.); Ampolo, 'La nascita della città', pp. 156ff. For the *regia*, see F. E. Brown, 'New Soundings in the Regia', in *Les origines de la république romaine (Entretiens Hardt XIII)* (Vandoeuvre, Geneva: 1966), pp. 47ff.; F. E. Brown, 'La protostoria della Regia', *RPAA*, 15, 1974–5, pp. 15ff.; lastly, R. T. Scott, *LTUR*, IV, 1999, pp. 189ff.; see in general P. Carafa, 'La cronologia dei contesti. L'età orientalizzante e arcaica', in Carandini 1997, pp. 599–601; P. C. Carafa, 'I contesti archeo-logici dell'età romulea e della prima età regia Roma', in Carandini and Cappelli 2000, pp. 68ff. On 'equus October' after H. H. Scullard, *Festivals and Ceremonies of the Roman Republic* (London: 1981), pp. 193–4, C. Ampolo, 'La città arcaica e le sue feste: due ricerche sul Septimontium e sull'*equus October*', *Archeologia Laziale* IV (Rome: 1981), pp. 233ff.

46. On the different phases of the Comitium see F. Coarelli, *LTUR*, I, 1993, pp. 309ff. (with bibliography cited therein); P. Carafa, 'Il comizio di Roma dalle origini all'età di Augusto', *BCAR*, suppl. 5 (Rome: 1988), pp. 105ff., in which it can be seen that a 'frequenting' of the Comitium between the middle and the end of the eighth century evidently cannot be considered an indication of its later purpose. Note besides that the idea that the 'hearth . . . later covered by two successive pavements' could have belonged to a 'local curia' was later rejected, since it was known that the *curiae*, both 'old' and 'new', arose in different locations (see lastly M. Torelli, *LTUR*, I, 1993, pp. 336–7). Had it been, more simply, the hearth of a hut, that would clearly indicate that the area, which was evidently still inhabited, had a dif-ferent purpose.

47. See C. Barbagallo, *Il problema delle origini di Roma da Vico a noi* (Milan: 1926); for a noticeably earlier period, H. J. Erasmus, *The Origins of Rome in Historiography from Petrarca to Perizonius* (Assen: 1962). On the various stances of criticism and hypercriticism from Vico to Niebuhr down to Gaetano De Sanctis and Ettore Pais, S. Mazzarino, *Vico, l'annalistica e il diritto* (Naples: 1971), *passim*.

48. E. Gjerstad, *Early Rome*, vols I–V (Lund: 1953–73); see, however, G. Colonna, 'Aspetti culturali della Roma primitiva: il periodo orientalizzante recente', *ArcClass*, 16, 1969, pp. 1ff.

49. M. Pallottino, 'Le origini di Roma: considerazioni critiche sulle scoperte e sulle discussioni più recenti', *ANRW*, I.1, 1971, pp. 22ff.

50. See lastly Cornell 1995, pp. 121ff., who for his part – so that Rome would assume the characteristics of a city-state only after 625 – tends to date all the seven kings 'in the period between *c.*625 and *c.*500' (with very notice-able corrections in Cornell, 'La leggenda della nascita di Roma', in Carandini and Cappelli 2000, pp. 45ff.); and for a similar chronology see also the observations of Carandini 1997, pp. 629–30.

51. H. Müller-Karpe, *Vom Anfang Roms* (Heidelberg: 1959); then H. Müller-Karpe, *Zur Stadtwerdung Roms* (Heidelberg: 1962), in which detailed

objections are put forward to Guidi, 'Sulle prime fasi', pp. 279ff., and the reply by Ampolo, 'Sulla formazione dela città di Roma'.

52. See p. 20ff.

53. On the position of the Porta Mugonia see G. Saflund, 'Porta Mugonia und via Sacra', *Corolla Archaelogica, Principi Hereditario Regni Sueciae Gustavo Adolfo Dedicata* (1932), pp. 64ff.; H. B. Evans, 'The "Romulean" Gates of the Palatine', *AJA*, 84, 1980, pp. 93ff.; Coarelli 1983, pp. 35ff.; F. Coarelli, *LTUR*, III, 1996, p. 318. On the original meaning of *via* see A. Walde and B. J. Hofmann, *Lateinisches Etymologisches Wörterbuch* (Heidelberg: 1954), vol. II, pp. 778–9; A. Ernout and A. Meillet, *Dictionnaire étymologique de la langue latine* (Paris: 1985), 4th edn, p. 731.

54. See Antistius Labeo in Festus, pp. 474–6 Lindsay: 'Septimontio ut ait Antistius Labeo, hisce montibus feriae: Palatio, cui sacrificium quod fit Palatuar dicitur; Veliae, cui item sacrificium; Fagu<t>ali, Suburae, Cermalo, Oppio, Caelio monti, Cispio monti'; compare Varro, *Ling.* VI.24: 'dies Septimontium [. . .] feriae non populi sed montanorum modo, ut Paganalibus qui sunt alicuius pagi'. On this see A. Fraschetti, 'Feste dei monti, festa della città', *StStor*, 25, 1984, pp. 46ff.; Fraschetti 1990, pp. 134ff.; see above all Ampolo, 'La città arcaica e le sue feste', pp. 233ff.; later, Carandini 1997, pp. 267ff., where it is observed that an earlier 'Trimontium' and a later 'Quinquemontium' are simply never documented in the literary tradition, nor are there positive indications in archaeological sources.

55. On the pomerium of Romulus see A. Basanoff, 'Pomerium Palatinum', *MAL*, 9, 1939, pp. 5ff. On the pomerium attributed to Servius Tullius documentary evidence has been gathered by R. Thomsen, *King Servius Tullius. A Historical Synthesis* (Copenhagen: 1980), pp. 213ff.; M. Andreussi, 'Roma: il pomerio', *AION Arc-StAnt*, 2, 1988, pp. 219ff.; M. Andreussi, *LTUR*, IV, 1999, p. 101; A. Giardina, 'Perimetri', in A. Giardina (ed.), *L'uomo romano* (Rome, Bari: 1989), pp. 23ff.

56. Pliny, *Nat. Hist.* III.69.

57. For the houses of Ancus Marcius, Tullus Hostilius and Tarquinius Priscus see F. Coarelli, 'Topographie antique et idéologie moderne: le Forum romain revisité', *Annales (ESC)*, 37, 1982, pp. 724ff.; Coarelli 1983, pp. 34ff.; and respectively D. Palombi, *LTUR*, II, 1995, pp. 30–1; F. Coarelli, *LTUR*, II, 1995, pp. 185, 204.

58. On the Subura see Varro, *Ling.* V.48: 'Subura<m> Iunius scribit ab eo, quod fuerit sub antiqua urbe; cui testimonium potest esse, quod subest ei loco qui terreus murus vocatur'; on the 'murus terreus Carinarum' see Coarelli 1983, pp. 111–13; and F. Coarelli, *LTUR*, III, 1996, pp. 334ff. For the two ancient etymologies see pp. 59–60 [Ital 61] with n. 63. For the two altars of Janus Curiatus and Juno Sororia, see Palombi 1997, pp. 44ff. (with additional bibliography); and E. Simon, '*Ianus Curiatius* und *Ianus Geminus* im frühen Rom', *Beiträge zur altitalischen Geistesgeschichte* (Münster: 1986), pp. 257ff. On the etymology of *Esquiliae* 'outside the settlement', Walde and Hofmann, *Lateinisches Etymologisches*

Wörterbuch, vol. I, p. 247; lastly see the debate in C. Buzzetti, *LTUR*, II, 1995, p. 234.

59. See, on Juno Sororia, H. J. Rose, 'De religionibus antiquis quaestiunculae tres', *Mnemosyne*, 53, 1925, pp. 406ff.; H. J. Rose, '*Mana* in Greece and Rome', *HThR*, 42, 1949, pp. 165ff.; J. Gagé, *Matronalia, Essai sur les dévotions et les organisations des femmes dans l'ancienne Rome* (Brussels: 1963), pp. 89ff.; Brelich 1976, p. 98; D. Visca, 'Le iniziazioni femminili: un problema da riconsiderare', *SMSR*, 42, 1973–6, pp. 241ff.; Coarelli 1983, pp. 111ff. See for a different interpretation G. Dumézil, *Mythe et épopée*, vol. III (Paris: 1981), 3rd edn, pp. 311ff.

60. On the sacrifices of atonement of Horatius the Elder see Livy I.26.13. On the *crimen perduellionis* and the creation under those circumstances of the *duumviri perduellionis*, L. Garofalo, 'In tema di provocatio ad populum', *SDHI*, 53, 1987, pp. 355ff.; B. Santalucia, 'Osservazioni sulla repressione criminale romana in età regia', in *Le délit religieux dans la cité antique* (Rome: 1981), pp. 42ff.; B. Santalucia, *Diritto e processo penale nella Roma antica* (Milan: 1998), pp. 19 and 28. See J. B. Solodow, 'Livy and the Story of Horatius, I.24–6', *TAPhA*, 109, 1979, pp. 251ff.; J. Poucet, 'Sur certains silences curieux dans le premier livre de Tite-Live', *Beiträge zur Altitalischen Geistesgeschichte*, pp. 212ff.

61. See the documents in A. Degrassi, I. *It*. XIII, 2, p. 215.

62. E. Pais I 2, 1913, pp. 453ff.; G. Dumézil, *Horace et les Curiaces* (Paris: 1942), pp. 79ff.

63. On the house of Tullus Hostilius see pp. 57–8 with n. 57. For the two etymologies of *Esquiliae* Varro, *Ling*. V.49: 'Alii has scripserunt ex excubiis regis dictas, alii ab eo quod <aesculis> excultae a rege Tullio essent'. On Opiter Oppius and Laevius Cispius, see Varro in Festo, p. 476 Lindsay: '[. . .] ab Opitre Oppius Tusculano qui [. . .], dum Tullus Hostilius Veios oppugnaret, consederat in Carinis, et ibi castra habuerat', while Laevius Cispius would have protected the part of the *Esquiliae* 'quae iacet ad vicum Patricium versus, in qua regione est aedis Mefitis', and see also the observations of Palombi 1997, pp. 15ff.

64. See G. Bartoloni and M. Cataldi Dini, 'Periodo IV A (730/20 to 640/30 BC)', *DdA*, 2, 1980, pp. 125ff. For the centrality of the Forum in the reign of Tullus Hostilius see, finally, also G. Tagliamonte, *LTUR*, II, 1995, p. 320; for the Esquiliae as a zone of cemeteries see Platner and Ashby 1929, pp. 202–3; also F. Coarelli, *LTUR*, I, 1993, pp. 218–19.

65. See A. Fraschetti, 'Il mondo romano' in G. Levi and J.-C. Schmitt (eds), *Storia dei giovani*, vol. 1, *Dall'antichità all'età moderna* (Rome, Bari: 1993), pp. 61ff. On Janus Curiatius, G. Capdeville, 'Les épithètes culturelles de Janus', *MEFR(A)*, 85, 1973, pp. 428ff.; for Juno Sororia see Dumézil, *Horace*, pp. 89ff.; and for a different slant Rose, 'Mana', pp. 165; and Coarelli 1983, pp. 113ff.

66. See p. 125ff.

NOTES TO CHAPTER 3

1. Livy I.8 and 13–14.
2. On Dionysius and Polybius see S. Gozzoli, 'Polibio e Dionigi d'Alicarnasso', *SCO*, 25, 1975, pp. 149ff.; E. Gabba, *Dionysius and the History of Archaic Rome* (Berkeley, Los Angeles, Oxford: 1991), p. 73.
3. See S. Mazzarino, 'Migrazioni "unniche": confronto tra due crisi', [1952], *Antico, tardoantico ed èra costantiniana* (Bari: 1974–80), vol. II, pp. 7ff., regarding the war of Antiochus III against the Greek Eudemus of Bactria. More generally see N. Loraux, '"Oikeios polemos". La guerre dans la famille', *StStor*, 28, 1987, pp. 3ff.; N. Loraux, 'Le 2 Boedremion. A propos d'un jour interdit du calendrier d'Athènes', in *La Commémoration. Colloque du centenaire de la section des sciences religieuses de l'EPHE* (Paris: 1988), pp. 59ff. (see also N. Loraux, *La cité divisée* (Paris: 1997), pp. 173ff.). For the discussion between Augustus and his friends Agrippa and Maecenas on the form of government which developed after the end of the civil wars, see E. Gabba, 'Progetti di riforme economiche e fiscali in uno storico dell'età dei Severi', in *Studi in onore di A. Fanfani* (Milan: 1962), vol. I, pp. 5ff.; F. Millar, *A Study of Cassius Dio* (Oxford: 1964), pp. 102ff.; U. Espinoza Ruiz, *Debate Agrippa–Mecenas en Dion Cassio. Respuesta senatorial a la crisis del Imperio Romano en época severiana* (Madrid: 1992); see also U. Espinoza Ruiz, 'El problema de la historicidad en el debate Agrippa–Mecenas en Dion Cassio', *Gerion*, 5, 1987, pp. 289ff.
4. See E. Gabba, 'Per la tradizione dell'"heredium" romuleo', *RIL*, 112, 1978, pp. 250ff.; also, more generally, L. Capogrossi Colognesi, *La terra in Roma antica: Forme di proprietà e rapporti produttivi*, vol. I (età arcaica) (Rome: 1981), *passim*.
5. Dionysius of Halicarnassus II.15. On the Romulean Asylum see p. 127ff.
6. See M. Pohlenz, 'Eine politische Tendenzschrift aus Caesars Zeit', *Hermes*, 59, 1924, pp. 157ff.; A. von Premerstein, *Von Werden und Wesen des Prinzipats* (Munich: 1937), pp. 9ff.; also K. Scott, 'The Identification of Augustus with Romulus-Quirinus', *TAPhA*, 56, 1925, pp. 82–4; E. Gabba, 'Studi su Dionigi d'Alicarnasso: I. La costituzione di Romolo', *Athenaeum*, 38, 1960, pp. 175ff.
7. On Romulus' religious institutions see Dionysius of Halicarnassus II.18–22. On Romulus and Augustus, in what is evidently quite a vast literature, see R. Merkelbach, 'Augustus und Romulus (Erklärung zur Horaz carm. I.12.37–40)', *Philologus*, 104, 1960, pp. 149ff.
8. See J. P. V. D. Balsdon, 'Dionysius on Romulus: A Political Pamphlet?', *JRS*, 61, 1971, pp. 18ff.; L. Fascione, *Il mondo nuovo. La costituzione romana nella 'Storia di Roma arcaica' di Dionisio d'Alicarnasso* (Naples: 1988), vol. I, pp. 28ff.
9. See pp. 39–40.
10. See p. 38ff. For the raising of an altar to Vesta by Titus Tatius see Varro, *Ling.* V.74. On the institution of the urban prefecture in the age of kings,

Tacitus, *Ann.* VI.11.1: 'Namque antea, profectis domo regibus ac mox magistratibus, ne urbs sine imperio foret, in tempus deligebatur qui ius redderet ac subitis moderetur; ferunt ab Romulo Dentrem Romulium'. On the centuriate system of Servius Tullius and its at least partial objective of surpassing the curiate system see pp. 42–4.

11. Dionysius of Halicarnassus II.18.2.

12. See respectively Varro, *Ling.* VI.33 ('nam primus a Marte'); Plutarch, *Num.* 18.2; Aulus Gellius III 16.16; Censorinus, *De die natali* 20; Solon, I.35; Servius, *ad Georg.* I.45; Macrobius, *Sat.* I. 11.5ff.; Johannes Lydus, *Mens.* I.16.9 Wuensch (ed.).

13. On the 'divinitas post mortem' promised to Caesar see Ovid, *Met.* XV. 843ff.; *Fast.* III.701–2; *Cons. ad Liviam* 241–6, with comments by A. Fraschetti, 'Come elogiare "trasversalmente" il principe', in F. E. Consolino (ed.), *Letteratura e propaganda nell'Occidente latino da Augusto ai regni romanobarbarici* (Rome: 2000), pp. 38–9.

14. On the problems connected with the ancient Roman calendar see above all A. Kirsopp Michels, *The Calendar of the Roman Republic* (Princeton, NJ: 1967), pp. 119ff.; also P. Brind'amour, *Le calendrier romain. Recherches chronologiques* (Ottawa: 1983); J. Rüpke, *Kalender und Öffentlichkeit. Die Geschichte der Representation und religiösen Qualifikation von Zeit in Rom* (Berlin, New York: 1995), *passim*.

15. De Sanctis I, 1980, pp. 370–1.

16. On the 'tempus lugendi' see M. Humbert, *Le remariage à Rome* (Milan: 1972), pp. 113ff.; A. García Sanchez, 'Algunas consideraciones sobre el "tempus lugendi"', *RIDA*, 23, 1976, pp. 141ff.

17. See for the institution of the Matronalia and the Carmentalia Plutarch, *Rom.* XXII.1; Ovid, *Fast.* III.239ff. For the Matronalia see J. Gagé, *'Matronalia. Essai sur les dévotions et les organisations des femmes dans l'ancienne Rome* (Brussels: 1963)'; for the Carmentalia, H. H. Scullard, *Festivals and Ceremonies of the Roman Republic* (London: 1981), pp. 62–3. On the *parricidium* see in particular Y. Thomas, 'Parricidium', *MEFR(A)*, 93, 1981, pp. 643ff.; A. Magdelain, 'Parricidas', in *Du châtiment dans la cité. Supplices corporels et peine de mort dans le monde antique* (Rome: 1884), pp. 549ff.; Magdelain 1990, pp. 519ff.

18. Livy, I.14.3; in this situation, 'ut tamen expiarentur legatorum iniuriae et regisque caedes, foedus inter Romam Laviniumque urbem renovatum'. On this presumed 'treaty', which it must be supposed already existed in the time of Romulus, see De Sanctis II, 1960, p. 267, n. 131.

19. Plutarch, *Rom.* 23.1–4. See commentary by C. Ampolo in Ampolo and Manfredini 1988, pp. 330–1.

20. Plutarch, *Rom.* 24.4. The problem lies in determining where Romulus conducted the expiatory rites. The manuscript tradition of Plutarch agrees: 'epi tes Pherentines pyles' ('near the Ferentine Gate'). Since there seems never to have been a 'Ferentine Gate' in Rome, *pyles* is usually corrected to *hyles* (see Ampolo and Manfredini 1988). See Poucet 1967, p. 288. On the loca-

tion of the Ferentine Woods, C. Ampolo, 'Ricerche sulla lega Latina, I, "Caput aquae Ferentinae" e "lacus Turni"', *PdP*, 36, 1981, pp. 219ff.

21. See pp. 48–9.

22. Licinius Macer, *HRR* I, 2nd edn, fr. 5.

23. On stoning as a form of spontaneous collective punishment see E. Cantarella, 'La lapidazione tra rito, vendetta e diritto', in *Mélanges P. Lévêque* (Paris: 1988), vol. I, pp. 83ff.; E. Cantarella, *I supplizi capitali in Grecia e a Roma* (Milan: 1991), pp. 326ff. For the Greek world, M. Gras, 'Cité grecque et lapidation', in *Du châtiment*, pp. 75ff.

24. J. Scheid, 'La mort du tyran. Chronique de quelques morts programmées', in *Du châtiment*, pp. 177ff., particularly p. 185; see also J. Gagé, 'Les autels de Titus Tatius. Une variante sabine des rites d'intégration dans les curies?', in *Mélanges J. Heurgon. L'Italie préromaine et la Rome républicaine*, vol. I (Rome: 1976) I, pp. 309ff.

25. Ennius, I, 2nd edn, fr. 109 Vahlen = 1 fr. 60 Skutsch, with commentary pp. 253ff.

26. *CIL* X 797 = *ILS* 5004, with notes by Y. Thomas, 'L'institution de l'origine. "Sacra principiorum populi Romani"', in M. Detienne (ed.), *Tracés de fondation* (Louvain, Paris: 1990), pp. 143ff.

27. On the *parentationes* to honour Titus Tatius after his death, like Acca Larentia and Tarpeia, see Dionysius of Halicarnassus II.52.5; A. Fraschetti, 'L'eroizzazione di Germanico', in A. Fraschetti (ed.), *La commemorazione di Germanico nella documentaria epigrafica: 'Tabula Hebana' & 'Tabula Siarensis'* (Rome: 2000), p. 158 with n. 34. For his burial near the Lauretum (Varro, *Ling.* V.152; Festus, p. 496 Lindsay) or the Armilustrium (Plutarch, *Rom.* 23.3), see Poucet 1967, pp. 287ff. On both places see M. Andreussi, *LTUR*, III, 1996, pp. 190–1; M. Andreussi, *LTUR*, I, 1993, pp. 126–7.

28. For Lucius and Gaius Caesar see respectively *CIL*, XI.1421 = *ILS*, 140 = *I.It.* VII.6, II. 27–30; *CIL* XI 1422 = *ILS*, 139 = *I.It.* VII.7, II.19–22. For *inferiae* and *parentationes* in this context see J. Scheid, 'Die Parentalien für die verstorbenen Caesaren als Modell für den römischen Totenkult', *Klio*, 75, 1993, pp. 188ff.; J. Scheid, 'Les décrets de Pise et le culte des morts', in *La commemorazione di Germanico*, pp. 129ff. For Germanicus and Drusus Caesar see Fraschetti, 'L'eroizzazione di Germanico', pp. 141ff.

29. See Plutarch, *Rom.* 24.4–5; Dionysius of Halicarnassus II.54.1–2.

30. On these traditions see Pais I.2, 1899, pp. 237ff.; Coarelli 1983, pp. 119ff.; especially C. Ampolo, 'La storiografia su Roma arcaica e i documenti', in E. Gabba (ed.), *Tria Corda. Studi in onore di A. Momigliano* (Como: 1983), pp. 19ff.

31. See Plutarch, *Rom.* 17.1 with 23.4; Livy I.14.4–11; Dionysius of Halicarnassus II.2–3.

32. Livy I.15.1ff.; Dionysius of Halicarnassus II.54.3; Plutarch, *Rom.* 2ff.

33. See De Sanctis I 1980, p. 387; Pais I.2, 1913, p. 437; Cornell 1995, pp. 399ff.

34. Briquel 1980, pp. 320ff.; D. Briquel in F. Hinard (ed.), *Histoire romaine*, vol. I, *Des origines à Auguste* (Paris: 2000), pp. 36–7.

35. Plutarch, *Rom.* 16.4ff.; 24.5; 25.6; Dionysius II.34.3 regarding Caenina. For Tarquinius Priscus' introduction of the triumph after his capture of Collatia see Livy I.38.3. Also D. Musti, *Tendenze nella storiografia romana e greca su Roma arcaica. Studi su Livio e Dionigi d'Alicarnasso* (Rome: 1970), pp. 34ff.; L. Bonfante Warren, 'Roman Triumphs and Etruscan Kings: The Changing Face of the Triumph', *JRS*, 60, 1970, pp. 49ff.; H. S. Versnel, *"Triumphus". An Inquiry into the Origin, Development and Meaning of the Roman Triumph* (Leiden: 1971), pp. 5ff.

36. See, for example, A. Fraschetti, 'A proposito di ex-schiavi e della loro integrazione in ambito cittadino a Roma', *Opus*, 1, 1982, pp. 97ff.; P. Gauthier, '"Générosité" romaine et "avarice" grecque: sur l'octroi du droit de cité', in *Mélanges W. Seston* (Paris: 1974), pp. 207ff.; A. Giardina, 'L'uomo romano', in A. Giardina (ed.), *L'uomo romano* (Rome, Bari: 1989), pp. xvii–xviii.

37. Pais I.2, 1913, p. 437.

NOTES TO CHAPTER 4

1. Dionysius of Halicarnassus II.56.

2. Livy I.16 (more particularly for the dismemberment of the body, 16.4: 'Fuisse credo tum quoque aliquos qui discerptum regem patrum manibus taciti arguerent; manavit enim haec quoque perobscura fama'). On the Goat's Marsh see F. Coarelli, "Il Pantheon, l'apoteosi di Augusto e l'apoteosi di Romolo", in 'Città e architettura nella Roma imperiale', in *ARID*, suppl. X, 1983, pp. 41ff.; also F. Coarelli, *LTUR*, I, p. 234.

3. On the testimony of Numerius Atticus, Suetonius, *Aug.* 100.7; Cassius Dio LVI.46.2.

4. Plutarch, *Rom.* 27–9. In 29.2 Plutarch merges the Poplifugia of 5 July with the 'Nonae Caprotinae' of 7 July. On the Poplifugia see H. H. Scullard, *Festivals and Ceremonies of the Roman Republic* (London: 1981), p. 159; on the 'Nonae Caprotinae' see J. N. Bremmer, 'Myth and Ritual in Ancient Rome: the Nonae Caprotinae', in Bremmer and Horsfall 1987, pp. 84–5. On the Vulcanale, in Plutarch the meeting place of the senate, see explicitly *Q. R.* 47, to be compared implicitly with *Rom.* 27.6. On the testimony of Ennius see below, n. 7; on the temple of Quirinus see below, n. 10.

5. See Appian, *B.c.* II.114; for Romulus the 'tyrant', Dionysius of Halicarnassus II.53.6; Plutarch, *Rom.* 27.1–3.

6. See John of Antioch, *HGF* IV fr. 32 Müller.

7. Ennius I² fr. 61 Vahlen = I fr. 61 Skutsch ('O Romule, Romule die, [. . .]') with I² fr. 117 Vahlen = I fr. 56 Skutsch ('<Teque> Quirine pater venoror Horamque Quirini'). See on this I. Cazzaniga, 'Il frammento 61 degli Annali di Ennio: "Quirinus Indiges"', *PdP*, 29, 1974, pp. 362ff.

8. See K. Latte, *Römische Religionsgeschichte* (Munich: 1960), p. 113; K. Latte, 'Quirinus. Eine kritische Überprüfung der Überlieferung und ein Versuch', *ANRW*, II, 17.1, 1981, p. 293; Wissowa 1912, p. 141; C. J. Classen,

'Gottmenschentum in der römischen Republik', *Philologus*, 106, 1962, p. 196.

9. See Cicero, *Leg.* I.3–4: 'Respondebo tibi equidem, sed non ante quam mihi tu ipse responderis, Attice, certene non longe a tuis aedibus inambulans post excessum suum Romulus Proculo Iulio dixerit se deum esse et Quirinum vocari templumque sibi dedicari in eo loco iusserit, et verumne sit, ut Athenis non longe item a tua illa antiqua domo Orithyiam Aquilo sustulerit; sic enim est traditum', with the reply 'Nihil sane, nisi ne nimis diligenter inquiras in ea, quae isto modo memoriae sint prodita'. See also Cicero, *Off.* III.41 ('pace vel Quirini vel Romuli dixerim'); *Nat. deor.* II.62 ('hinc etiam Romulus, quem quidem eundem esse Quirinum putant'); *Att.* XII.45.3 ('De Caesare vicino scripseram ad te quia cognaram ex litteris. Eum *synnaon* Quirini malo quam Salutis'). With reference to the house of Atticus being located on the Quirinal, see W. Eck, *LTUR*, II, 1995, pp. 161–2.

10. On the temple of Quirinus, see Ziolkowski 1992, pp. 139–44; P. Carafa, 'Il tempio di Quirino. Considerazioni sulla topografia arcaica del Quirinale', *ArcClass*, 45, 1993, pp. 119–43; R. Paris, 'Il tempio di Quirino', in *Dono Hartwig. Originali ricongiunti e copie tra Roma e Ann Arbor*, "Catalogo della mostra" (Rome: 1994), pp. 29ff.; F. Coarelli, *LTUR*, IV, 1999, pp. 185–7. On the temple of Salus 'on the hill', Ziolkowski 1992, pp. 144–8; F. Coarelli, *LTUR*, IV, 1999, pp. 229–30.

11. The calendar of Polemius Silvius, while it stated that Romulus had been 'occisus a suis', recorded the event on the day of the Quirinalia (*I.It.* XIII.2, p. 265), as did Ovid in *Fast.* II.475ff.; he dwells on Romulus' ascension to heaven on that date, noting the 'false' accusations against the senators (II.497: 'Luctus erat falsaeque patres in crimine caedis [. . .]').

12. On Jupiter Latiaris see Festus, p. 212 Lindsay; on Aeneas Jupiter Indiges or Pater Indiges, see Fraschetti, 'L'eroizzazione di Germanico', pp. 155ff. (with further reading).

13. See Horace, *Epod.* XVI.13–14 ('quaeque carent ventis et solibus ossa Quirini, / nefas videre! dissipabit insolens') with comments by Pseudo-Acron, *ad. l.* ('plerique aiunt in rostris Romulum sepultum esse et in memoriam huius rei leones duos ibi fuisse, sicut hodieque in sepulchris videmus, atque inde esse ut pro rostris mortui lauderentur'); also 'nam et Varro pro rostris fuisse sepulchrum Romuli dicit'; Porfirius, *ad. l.*: 'hoc sic dicitur, quasi Romulus sepultus sit, non ad caelum raptus aut discerptus. Nam Varro post rostra fuisse sepultum Romulum dicit'.

14. On the *imago* of Romulus at the funeral of Augustus, Cassius Dio LVI.34.2; on the *imagines* of Aeneas and Romulus at the funeral of Drusus Caesar, Tacitus IV.9.2; also see J.-C. Richard, 'Enée, Romulus, César et les funérailles impériales', *MEFR*, 78, 1966, pp. 67ff.

15. See Fraschetti 1990, pp. 72ff., for the funeral cortège of Augustus from Nola to Rome.

16. Following the excavations of G. Boni, 'Esplorazioni nel Comizio', *NSA*,

1900, pp. 295ff., see Pais, I.2, 1899, p. 741, with the comments by G. De Sanctis, 'Il "lapis niger" e la iscrizione arcaica del Foro romano', *RFIC*, 28, 1906, pp. 412ff.; also Coarelli 1983, pp. 161ff., with notes above all by F. Castagnoli, 'Il "niger lapis" nel Foro romano e gli scavi del 1955', *PdP*, 39, 1984, pp. 6ff.; then Castagnoli 1993, pp. 335ff.; and after this, although his argument is philologically unsound, P. Carafa, 'Il comizio di Roma della origini all'età di Augusto', *BCAR*, suppl. 5 (Rome: 1988), pp. 111ff. For a more comprehensive evaluation of this question, see C. Ampolo, 'La storiografia su Roma arcaica e i documenti', in E. Gabba (ed.), *Tria Corda. Studi in onore di A. Momigliano* (Como: 1983), pp. 9ff.

17. See Festus, p. 184 Lindsay, and Festus, p. 370 Lindsay: 'Statua est ludi eius, qui quondam fulmine ictus in Circo, sepultus est in Ianiculo. Cuius ossa postea ex prodigis, oraculorumque responsis senatus decreto intra Urbem relata in Volcanali, quod est supra Comitium, obruta sunt; superque ea columna, cum ipsius effigie, posita est.'

18. See Plutarch, *Q. R.* 47.

19. Pliny, *Nat. Hist.* XVI.236: 'Verum altera lotos in Volcanali quod Romulus constituit ex victoria de decumis, aequaeva urbi intellegitur, ut auctor est Masurius. Radices eius in forum usque Caesaris per stationes municipiorum penetrant. Fuit cum ea cupressus aequalis, circa suprema Neronis principis prolapsa atque neglecta.'

20. As is clear above all from Dionysius of Halicarnassus VI.67.2 (on 493 BC); VII.17.2 (on 492 BC); XI.39.1 (on 449, when Appius Claudius 'climbed up to the temple of Vulcan and called the people together'). That the temple of Vulcan stood 'a little above the Forum' ('mikron huperanestekoti tes agoras') is also clear from Dionysius of Halicarnassus II.50.2.

21. Festus, p. 184 Lindsay. For this very corrupt extract we usually welcome the insertions of O. Detlefsen, 'De Comitio Romano', *AnnInst*, 59, 1860, pp. 128f.: 'Niger lapis in Comitio locum funestim significat, ut ali Romuli morti destinatum, sed non usu ob in . . . <Fau>ustulum nutri<cium eius, ut alii Hostum Host>ilium avum Tu<lii Hostilii, Romanum regis>, cuius familia <e Medullia Romam venit post destruc>tionem eius'. De Sanctis, 'Il "lapis niger"', pp. 409–10, noted all the difficulties attached to the expression 'Romuli morti destinatum'. According to De Sanctis this expression is 'not Latin'.

22. See for Athens, and, more generally, for the entire Greek world, I. Malkin, *Religion and Colonisation in Ancient Greece* (Leiden, New York, Copenhagen, Cologne: 1987), pp. 200–3.

23. On Tarpeia, already a Vestal according to Varro, see p. 121ff.

24. See Varro, *Ling.* V.74: 'Feronia, Minerva, Novensides a Sabinis. Paulo aliter ab eisdem dicimus haec: Palem, Vestam, Salutem, Fortunam, Fontem, Fidem. Et arae Sabinum linguam olent, quae Tati regis voto sunt Romae dedicatae: nam, ut annales dicunt, vovit Opi, Florae, Vediovi Saturnoque, Soli, Lunae, Volcano et Summano, itemque Larundae, Termino, Quirino, Vortumno, Laribus, Dianae Lucinaeque'. See also Poucet 1967, pp. 46ff.; D.

Porte, 'Romulus-Quirinus, prince et dieu, dieu des princes. Étude sur le personnage de Quirinus et sur son évolution, des origines à Auguste', *ANRW*, II, 17.1, 1981, pp. 513–14.

25. On the temple of Quirinus see above, p. 91 with n. 10; on 'Quirini sacellum' Festus, p. 303 Lindsay; Pliny, *Nat. Hist.* XV.120: 'inter antiquissima namque delubra habetur Quirini, hoc est ipsius Romuli'. On 'Quirini sacellum' see F. Coarelli, *LTUR*, IV, 1999, p. 187.

26. A. Magdelain, 'Quirinus et le droit ("spolia opima", "ius fetiale", "ius Quiritium")', *MEFR(A)*, 96, 1984, pp. 195ff.; then in Magdelain 1990, pp. 241ff., in response to Dumézil 1974, especially pp. 167ff. See also Porte, 'Romulus-Quirinus', pp. 315ff., also in debate with G. Dumézil, *Jupiter, Mars, Quirinus. Essai sur la conception indo-européenne de la société et sur les origines de Rome* (Paris: 1941). Still a fundamental work on the etymology that incontestably links Quirinus to the *curiae* is P. Kretschmer, 'Lat. "quirites" und "quiritare"', *Glotta*, 10, 1920, pp. 147ff., whose conclusions are generally accepted, notwithstanding the reservations of C. Koch, 'Bemerkungen zum römischen Quirinus-Kult', in *Religio. Studien zu Kult und Glaube der Römer* (Nuremberg: 1960), p. 27. Lastly see A. L. Prosdocimi, 'Populus Quiritium Quirites', in *'Nomen Latinum'. Latini e Romani prima di Annibale* (Atti Congr. Int., Rome 24–6 Oct. 1995), *Eutopia*, 4, 1995, pp. 15ff.; also A. L. Prosdocimi, '"Curia", "Quirites" e il "sistema di Quirino"', *Ostraka*, 5, 1996, pp. 233ff.; D. Briquel, 'Remarques sur le dieu Quirinus', *RBPhH*, 17, 1996, pp. 99ff.

27. Magdelain, 'Quirinus et le droit', p. 200; then in Magdelain 1990, p. 232. On the 'feriae stultorum' see D. Baudes, 'Der dumme Teil des Volks (Ovid, *Fast.* 2.531). Zur Beziehung zwischen Quirinalia, Fornacalia und "Stultorum feriae"', *Museum Helveticum*, 58, 2001, pp. 32–9.

28. Ennius I² fr. 113 Vahlen = I fr. 61 Skutsch ('O pater, o genitor, o sanguen dis oriundum! Tu produxisti nos intra luminis oras'); see generally, E. Tiffou, 'Le thème de la lumière dans la fondation de Rome', *Latomus*, 57, 1998, pp. 316–17.

29. On Quirinus as a Mars 'qui praeest paci', 'Mars tranquillus', see Servius, *ad Aen.* VI.859 and I.292. For *Vofonio-* see H. Rix, 'Rapporti onomatistici tra il pantheon etrusco e quello romano', in *Gli Etruschi e Roma. Incontro di studi in onore di M. Pallottino* (Rome: 1981), p. 123; E. Benveniste, 'Symbolisme sociale dans les cultes gréco-italiques', *RHR*, 119, 1945, pp. 15–16; see also G. Dumézil, *L'héritage indoeuropéen à Rome* (Paris: 1949), p. 225. Brelich 1960, p. 114, calls attention to the 'unusual Gallic "divine" name of Teutanes, on whose etymology everyone now agrees that the name comes from the Celtic *teut (people, tribe)'.

30. John of Antioch, *FHG* IV fr. 32 Müller (the breaking storm and an eclipse of the sun favoured the work of the senators). On the role of the urban plebeians and the veterans during the funeral of Caesar, see Fraschetti 1990, pp. 55ff.

31. See Burkert 1962, pp. 367–9. On the banquet for the *feriae Latinae* see

C. Ampolo, 'L'organizzazione politica dei Latini e il problema degli "Albenses"', in A. Pasqualini (ed.), *Alba Longa. Mito, storia, archeologia* (Rome: 1996), pp. 135ff. For the list of the peoples who 'were accustomed to "receive flesh"' see Pliny, *Nat. Hist.* III.69.

32. See M. Delcourt, 'Romulus et Mettius Fufetius', in *Hommages à G. Dumézil* (Brussels: 1960), pp. 77ff.; M. Delcourt, 'Le partage du corps royal', *SMSR*, 34, 1963, pp. 3ff.; I. E. M. Edlund, 'Must a King Die? The Death and Disappearance of Romulus', *PdP*, 39, 1984, pp. 401ff. On the torture of Mettius Fufetius see Livy 1.28; Dionysius of Halicarnassus III.30.5–7. On the death of Tullus Hostilius, Livy I.31.8; Dionysius of Halicarnassus III.35.1–2.

33. On the *crimen* of *perfidia* see in general G. Piccaluga, 'La "colpa" di "perfidia" sullo sfondo della prima secessione della plebe', in *Le délit religieux dans la cité antique* (Rome: 1981), pp. 21ff.

34. See D. Briquel, 'Perspectives comparatives sur la tradition relative à la disparition de Romulus', *Latomus*, 36, 1977, pp. 253ff. The author is almost forced to admit more generally (p. 257) 'On aurait donc, dans le cas des fils de Rhéa Silvia, dans la mesure où on cherche à les rattacher à la tradition indo-européenne des jumeaux, une situation diamétralement opposée à ce que l'on serait en droit de s'attendre en se fondant sur le parallèle indo-européen' (p. 258); and again, 'Ainsi donc, le cas des jumeaux romains constitue une anomalie.'

35. On the bull and the cow at the time of the foundation, see p. 35; on the role of Romulus and his companions in recapturing the beasts, see p. 16ff.

36. See Dionysius of Halicarnassus II.51.1. Livy 1.14.1. and Plutarch, *Rom.* 23.1, completely ignore the theft of the animals. Therefore it seems largely useless to discuss the 'relative' antiquity of the two traditions (Briquel differs in 'Perspectives comparatives', pp. 275ff.). On the murder of Titus Tatius at Lavinium see pp. 74–80.

37. See Brelich 1960, pp. 63ff., with cross-references to figures of the type *dema* in A. E. Jensen, 'Das religiöse Wortbild einer frühen Kultur', in *Studien zur Kulturkunde*, vol. IX (Stuttgart, 1948); A. E. Jensen, *Mythos und Kult bei Naturvölkern* (Wiesbaden: 1951), pp. 113ff. See also J. Frazer, *The Golden Bough*, vol. VI (London: 1917), p. 462, which in turn refers to A. B. Cook, 'The European Sky-God', *Folklore*, 16, 1905, pp. 324ff.

38. See C. Ampolo, 'La formazione della città nel Lazio, Periodo IVB (640/630–580 a.C.)', *Dda*, 2, 1980, pp. 165–92. On the connection between the Quirinalia and the 'festival of fools' see p. 95ff.

39. M. Sahlins, *Islands of History* (Chicago, London: 1985), pp. 91ff.

40. See F. Coarelli, 'La doppia traduzione sulla morte di Romolo e gli "auguracula" dell'Arx e del Quirinale', in *Gli Etruschi e Roma*, pp. 173ff. (especially p. 177); and Coarelli, 1983, pp. 188ff.

41. See pp. 92–3.

42. On the institution of the *comitia centuriata* by Servius Tullius, see A. Fraschetti, 'Servio Tullio e la partizione del corpo civico', *Metis*, 9–10,

1984–5, pp. 1229ff. (with additional bibliography). On the Temple of Vulcan as the seat of the senate see p. 74.

43. Livy I.17.5–6: 'Ita rem inter se centum patres, decem decuriis factis singulisque in singulas decurias creatis qui summae rerum praeessent, consociant. Decem imperitabant: unus cum insignibus imperii et lictoribus erat: quinque dierum spatio finiebatur imperium ac per omnes in orbem ibat; annuumque intervallum regni fuit.'

44. For the period after the death of Numa, see Livy I.22.1; Dionysius of Halicarnassus III.1.1; after the death of Tullus Hostilius, Livy 1.32.1; Dionysius of Halicarnassus III.36.1. After the death of Ancus Marcius the case of the two Tarquins is evidently more complex (respectively Livy I.35.1–6; Dionysius of Halicarnassus III.46.1; Livy I.49.1); and that of Servius Tullius is rather confused: see Fraschetti, 'Servio Tullio', pp. 132ff.

45. Plutarch, *Num.* 2.10; see also Livy, cited above, n. 43; Dionysius of Halicarnussus II.57.1, according to which there were two hundred senators, yet previously (II.47.1–2) it was stated that there were a hundred and fifty. The ancient documents on the number of senators in Romulus' time have been collected by O. Briens-Moore, *RE*, suppl. VI, 1935, cols 663–6.

46. See Cicero, *Brut.* I.5.3 and *Leg.* III.9; above all see A. Magdelain, 'Auspicia ad patres redeunt', in *Hommages à J. Bayet* (Brussels: 1964), pp. 427ff.; also in Magdelain 1990, pp. 341ff.

47. S. Mazzarino, *Dalla monarchia allo stato repubblicano* (Milan: 1992), 2nd edn, pp. 46ff., especially p. 51.

48. Plutarch, *Rom.* 27.6 with *Num.* 2.9–10. For Romulus' burial as a precaution, 'furtively', by the senator suspects, see Dionysius of Halicarnassus II.56.4.

49. Ennius I² Vahlen, fr. 78 = fr. 47 Skutsch, with reference to both twins when the founder is chosen: 'Regni dant operam simul auspicio augurioque'; and I² Vahlen, fr. 95 = fr. 97 Skutsch 90–1 after the appointment of Romulus: 'Conspicit inde sibi data Romulus esse propritim / Auspicio regni stabilita scamna solumque.'

50. See Livy 1.17.5–9; Dionysius of Halicarnassus II.57; Plutarch, *Num.* 2.9–10; Cicero, *Rep.* II.23 and, at II.25, the note on the 'lex curiata' presented by Numa concerning his investiture ('qui, ut huc venit, quamquam populus curiatis eum comitiis regem iusserat, tamen ipse de suo imperio curiatam legem tulit'). We observe – and in such a context the note must appear very significant – that Cicero in *Rep.* II.26 attributes to Numa the institution of the 'auspicia maxima', corresponding – it is clear – to the king's 'imperium maius'. On this it suffices to see Mommsen I, 1887, pp. 104–5, and P. Catalano, *Contributi alla storia del diritto augurale* (Turin: 1960), vol. 1, pp. 444–50.

51. Cicero, *Rep.* II.17: 'et haec egregia duo firmamenta rei publicae peperisset, auspicia et senatum'.

52. See Livy, IV.2.2–5 (the consuls Marcus Genucius and Gaius Curtius said

the bill proposed by Gaius Canuleius would cause 'Conluvionem gentium, perturbationem auspiciorum publicorum privatorumque . . ., ne quid sinceri, ne quid incontaminati sit, ut discrimine omni sublato nec se quisquam nec suos noverit').

53. For the text of the disposition see Tab. III.1, *FIRA* I, 2nd edn, p. 53; and *Roman Statutes*, vol. II, ed. M. Crawford (London: 1996), p. 627: 'tertiis nundinis partis secanto. Si plus minusve secuerunt, se fraude esto.' See above all Gellius, XX, 1.19 ('Nam de inmanitate illa secandi partiendique humani corporis, si unus ob pecuniam debitam iudicatus addictusque sit pluribus, non libet meminisse et piget dicere') and 42–52, in particular 47–8: 'Tertiis autem nundinis capite poenas dabant aut trans Tiberim peregre venum ibant. Sed eam capitis poenam sanciendae, sicuti dixi, fidei gratia horrificam atrocitatis ostentu novisque terroribus metuendam reddiderunt.'

54. For a reconnection of the punishment to the crime of 'perfidia' according to the evidence of Cecilius Africanus in Aulus Gellius, see F. Fratto, 'Nuove osservazioni su "partes secanto"', in *Sodalitas. Studi in onore di A. Guarino*, vol. V (Naples: 1984), pp. 2099ff. (with bibliography). See G. Franciosi, '"Partes secanto" tra magia e diritto', *Labeo*, 24, 1978, pp. 263ff.; Franciosi had in mind the burial of body parts by creditors in their own fields in order to make them more fertile. For different explanations, see above all H. Lévy-Bruhl, *Quelques problèmes du très ancien droit romain* (Paris: 1934), pp. 152ff.; A. Magdelain, 'La "manus iniectio" chez les Étrusques et chez Virgile', in *Studi in onore di C. Sanfilippo* (Milan: 1982), pp. 287ff.; and in Magdelain 1990, pp. 653ff.

55. For the 'lock-out of the patrician order' see De Sanctis I, 1980, pp. 10ff. For an exhaustive discussion and appraisal of the question of plebeians in the consular colleges, at least in the first fifty years of the republic, see J. Heurgon (ed.), *Il Mediterraneo occidentale dalla preistoria a Roma arcaica* (Bari: 1972), pp. 254ff; also Cornell 1995, pp. 252ff.

56. Plutarch, *Pomp.* 25.9; on this question see the articles in C. Nicolet (ed.), '*Insula sacra*'. *La loi Gabinia Calpurnia de Délos* (Rome: 1980).

57. See p. 90 and above, n. 9.

58. Appian, *B.c.* II.114.

59. Cassius Dio XLVI.19.4–7; on the relationship between Fufius Calenus and Antony refer to R. Syme, *The Roman Revolution* (Oxford: 1939), p. 135. For Cicero's judgement of Calenus after the Ides of March see *Phil.* VIII.19: 'Excogitare quae tua ratio sit, Calene, non possum. Antea deterrere te ne popularis esses non poteramus; exorare nunc ut sis popularis non possumus'; *Phil.* X.3–6.

60. Weinstock 1971, pp. 176ff.

61. See Sahlins, *Islands of History*, p. 104.

62. Cassius Dio, XLIV.3.1 with Suetonius, *Iul.* 80.8: 'facile tempus et locum praetulerunt'.

63. On the 'sacred and inviolable' body of Caesar, Appian, *B.c.* II.106, 601;

Cassius Dio XLIV.5, 3; Livy, *Per.* 106; Nicolaus Damascenus, *V. Caesaris* 80; see also Weinstock 1971, pp. 220ff. On the sacrosanctity of Caesar, Mommsen II, 1887, pp. 148ff; G. Dobesch, *Caesars Apotheose und sein Ringen um den Königstitel* (Vienna: 1966), pp. 29–30; R. A. Bauman, 'Tribunician Sacrosanctity in 44, 36 and 35 BC', *RhM*, 124, 1981, pp. 167ff. On the tomb within the pomerium, Cassius Dio XLIV.7.1. On the tomb of Romulus see p. 91 and n. 13. On burial of the Vestals, A. Fraschetti, 'La sepoltura delle vestali e la Città', in *Du châtiment dans la cité. Supplices corporales et peine de mort dans le monde antique* (Rome: 1984), pp. 108ff.

64. For Romulus see Plutarch, *Rom.* 26.2; for the parallel honours decreed for Caesar, Cassius Dio XLIV.3–6; for the *spolia opima* to be placed in the temple of Jupiter Feretrius, Cicero, *Deiot.* 34. See also Weinstock 1971, p. 213, n. 1, in debate with R. Syme, 'Livy and Augustus', *HSCPh*, 64, 1954, p. 80, n. 25 (S. Weinstock, in *Roman Papers*, vol. I (Oxford: 1979), p. 419, n. 1, which considers the evidence of Cassius Dio 'a patent anachronism', modelled on the future behaviour of Augustus).

65. On the *'praenomen' Imperator* see R. Syme, '"Imperator Caesar": A Study in Nomenclature', *Historia*, 7, 1958, pp. 172ff.; R. Syme, in *Roman Papers*, vol. I, pp. 361ff.; then above all Weinstock 1971, pp. 103ff. On the 'ceremonies of thanks to the gods . . . in honour of Caesar' for any victory, Cassius Dio XLIV.6.2; XLVII.18.4.

66. On Caesar 'father of the country' see A. Alföldi, *Der Vater des Vaterlandes im römischen Denken* (Darmstadt: 1978), pp. 85ff.; Weinstock 1971, pp. 200ff. For the note *parricidium* on calendars, see Cassius Dio XLVII.19.1; Suetonius, *Iul.* 88.3; Cicero, *Fam.* XII.3.1; Valerius Maximus, I.8.8: 'publicum parricidium'; *Floro*, II.17.1. As has been noted, Caesar was declared 'parens patriae' on the column erected to him in the Forum, where the temple of Divus Julius arose later, by Amatius and the 'dangerous elements' of the city; see Fraschetti 1990, pp. 60ff. (bibliography included). On Romulus 'the father', Ennius I² fr. 61 Vahlen = fr. 61 Skutsch; Livy, I.14.6.

67. See Cicero, *Phil.* II.88: 'sed ad auspicia redeamus, de quibus rebus idibus Martiis fuit in senatu Caesar acturus'; as has been pointed out, this refers to the *obnuntiatio* of Antony to the election of Dolabella as consul.

68. Cassius Dio XLIV.20.2–3.

NOTES TO EPILOGUE

1. See B. G. Niebuhr, *Römische Geschichte*, vol. 1, ed. by M. Isler (Berlin: 1973), pp. 180ff.; for Fea's reactions see A. Fraschetti, 'Bartolomeo Borghesi, Carlo Fea e la sovranità della Repubblica di San Marino', in *Bartolomeo Borghesi. Scienza e libertà* (Bologna: 1982), pp. 296–7.

2. See T. Mommsen, *The History of Rome*, vol. 1, new edn,) trans. William Purdie Dickson (London: 1908), pp. 57–8. For 'reactionary' historiography see J. J. Bachofen and F. D. Gerlach, *Geschichte der Römer* (Basel:

1951); in particular for the historicity of Romulus compare F. D. Gerlach, 'Die Zeiten der römischen Könige', in *Vorgeschichte, Gründung und Entwicklung des römischen Staats* (Basel: 1986), p. 193. For this see also S. Mazzarino, *Vico, l'annalistica e il diritto* (Naples: 1971), pp. 44ff.

3. G. De Sanctis, *Storia dei Romani I. Roma dalle origine alla monarchia*, new edn based on unpublished material, ed. by S. Accame (Florence: 1980), p. 212 (the first volume appeared originally in 1907); E. Pais, *Storia di Roma dalle origini all'inizio delle guerre puniche I* (Rome: 1926), pp. 313ff.; the explicit reference was to T. Mommsen, 'Die Remuslegende', *Hermes*, XVI, 1881, pp. 3ff.; also in T. Mommsen, *Kleine Schriften IV* (Berlin: 1906), pp. 7ff. In this context it is impossible to leave out A. Rosenberg, *RE*, I. A I., 1914, cols 1074 ff.; also unsurpassed for its subtle skill in the analysis of classical literary documents. For a typical discussion of the 'historical' existence of Romulus compare C. Barbagallo, *Il problema delle origini di Roma, da Vico a noi* (Milan: 1926).

4. Cornell 1995, p. 80.

5. See A. Carandini, *La nascita di Roma. Dèi, Lari, eroi e uomini all'alba di una civiltà* (Turin: 1997), *passim*; A. Carandini and P. Terrenato (eds), 'Palatium e Sacra via I', *Bolletino di Archeologia*, XXXI–XXXIV, 2000; compare in addition A. Carandini, 'Variazioni', in Carandini and Cappelli 2000, pp. 100ff. For a collection of similar hypotheses compare A. Grandazzi, *The Foundation of Rome*, trans. J. M. Todd (Ithaca, NY, London: 1997), pp. 177ff.

6. For Aeneas, founder of Rome, see Sallust, *Cat.* 6.1 ('Urbem Romam, sicut ego accepi, condidere atque habuere initio Troiani qui, Aenea duce profugi, sedibus incertis vagabantur, cumque is Aborigenes, genus hominum agreste, sine legibus, sine imperio, liberum atque solutum'); for Timaeus, Callias and Alcimus see the various datings of the foundation of Rome in J. Heurgon (ed.), *Il Mediterraneo occidentale dalla preistoria a Roma arcaica* (Bari: 1972), pp. 202–3.

7. See J. Poucet, 'Les rois de Rome', in *Histoire et Tradition* (Brussels: 2000), pp. 165ff; E. Gabba, 'Ancora sulle origini di Roma', *Athenaeum*, LXXXIX, 2001, pp. 589ff.; in general T. P. Wiseman, 'Reading Carandini', *JRS*, XCI, 2001, pp. 182ff. (especially p. 183).

8. On the marginal space reserved for the youths at the moment of their initiation a fundamental study remains A. van Gennep, *I riti di passaggio* (Turin: 1981), pp. 95ff.; for Rome in particular see A. Fraschetti, 'Il mondo romano', in G. Levi and J.-C. Schmitt (eds.), *Storia dei giovani I. Dall'antichità all'età moderna* (Rome, Bari: 1993), pp. 61ff. Remus' lack of respect for the ritual sharing at the banquet following the sacrifice can be illustrated according to J. Scheid, 'La spartizione a Roma', *Studi storici*, XXV, 1984, pp. 945ff.; also J. Scheid, 'La spartizione sacrificale a Roma', in C. Grottanelli and N. Parise (eds), *Sacrificio e società nel mondo antico* (Rome, Bari: 1988), pp. 267ff.; also J. Scheid, *La religion des Romains* (Paris: 1998), pp. 65ff. The position of Remus is rendered more serious by the

detail that he eats the sacrificial meat half-raw: see P. Vidal-Naquet, 'Le crue, l'enfant grec et le cuit', in Vidal-Naquet 1981, pp. 177ff.

9. For the pomerium see A. Giardina, 'Perimetri', in A. Giardina (ed.), *L'uomo romano* (Rome, Bari: 1989); F. Marazzi, 'L'ultima Roma antica', in A. Giardina (ed.), *Storia di Roma dall'antichità a oggi* (Bari: 2000), pp. 23ff.

10. For the legends of Tarpeia, Mettius Fufetius and the death of Titus Tatius, see J. Poucet, *Recherches sur la légende sabine des origines de Rome* (Kinshasa: 1967), pp. 8ff., pp. 241ff., pp. 276ff. respectively.

11. De Sanctis, *Storia dei Romani I*, p. 387; Pais, *Storia di Roma I*, p. 437; Cornell 1995, pp. 399ff.; they date these conquests only to the end of the fifth century BC. For the foundation of colonies which at the same time created new citizens, A. Fraschetti, 'A proposito di ex-schiavi e della loro integrazione in ambito cittadino a Roma', *Opus*, I, 1982, pp. 97ff.; A. Giardina, 'L'uomo romano', in *L'uomo romano*, pp. xvii–xviii, regarding a letter from Philip V of Macedon to the inhabitants of Larissa. Philip took the Romans as an example of those who increased the number of their citizens (Dittenberger, *Syll.*² 239 = ILS 8763).

12. See A. Fraschetti, 'Il corpo del fondatore e le origini del patriziato romano', in P. Moreau (compiler), *Corps romains* (Grenoble: 2002), pp. 161ff.

13. On Romulus and Numa see G. Dumézil, *Mitra–Varuna. Essai sur deux représentations indo-européennes de la souveraineté* (Paris: 1948), pp. 5ff. For the more plausible version (assassination), see Dionysius of Halicarnassus II.65.2; compare Plutarch, *Rom.* 26.6.

NOTES TO APPENDIX I

1. See p. 47ff.
2. Propertius, IV.4; Plutarch, *Rom.* 22.1; *Chronographer of 354*, MGH, AA IX.1, p. 144.
3. J. A. Ambrosch, *Studien und Andeutungen im Gebiet des altrömischen Bodens und Kultus*, vol. I (Breslau: 1839), p. 148 with n. 86; A. Schwegler, *Römische Geschichte*, vol. I (Tübingen: 1853), pp. 485ff.; E. Pais, *Ancient Legends of Roman History* (New York: 1905), pp. 96ff.; and, from a different perspective, beginning with H. R. Sanders, *The Myth about Tarpeia*, Ann Arbor, University of Michigan, Humanistic Series 1 (New York: 1904).
4. See S. Reinach, 'Tarpeia', *RA*, 1908, pp. 42ff.; S. Reinach, *Cultes, mythes, et religions*, vol. III (Paris: 1913), 2nd edn, pp. 223ff.; Z. Gansiniec, 'Tarpeia. The Making of a Myth', *Acta societatis archaeologicae Polonorum*, I (Wratislaviae: 1949); G.-C. Picard, *Les Trophées romains* (Paris: 1957), pp. 110ff.; cf. B. Waden Boyd, 'Tarpeia's Tomb. A Note on Propertius 4.4', *AJPh*, 105, 1984, pp. 85–6.
5. See especially A. La Penna, 'Tarpeia, Titus Tatius, Lucomedius', *SCO*, 6, 1965, pp. 112ff.; with following discussion by G. Devoto, 'La leggenda di Tarpea e gli Etruschi', *SE*, 26, 1958, pp. 1ff.; later also U. Hetzner,

'Andromeda und Tarpeia', *Beiträge zur Klassischen Philologie*, part 8 (Meisenheim: 1963), pp. 52ff.; and J. Beaujeu, 'L'énigme de Tarpeia', *IL*, 21, 1969, pp. 163ff.

6. See H. Müller, 'Zu Plutarch: Romulus XVII.5 (= Simylos fr. 1.5 sq. *Anthol. Lyr. Gr.*, II 6 op. 102 D.)', *MH*, 20, 1963, pp. 114ff.; E. Brenk, 'Tarpeia among the Celts: Watery Romance from Simylos to Propertius', in C. Deroux (ed.), *Studies in Latin Literature and Roman History* (Brussels: 1979), pp. 166ff.

7. A different view was held by I. Santinelli, 'Tarpeia vestale', *RFIC*, 31, 1903, pp. 236ff., who thought the tradition was very late.

8. Livy, I.11.6.

9. Valerius Maximus, IX.6.1; Suetonius, *De viris illustribus*, II.5; Servius, *ad Aen.* VIII.348; in Florus, I.1.12, too, even though the detail of the water is missing, the girl is still referred to as *virgo*.

10. Plutarch, *Num.* 10.1.

11. M. C. Martini, *Due studi sulla riscrittura annalistica dell'età monarchica a Roma. I. Il fatto di Tarpea virgo Vestalis ante litteram. II. Servius Tullius, 'il re della fiamma'* (Brussels: 1998), pp. 9ff.

12. cf. also Plutarch, *Parall. Min.* 15; Appianus, *Reg. fr.* 4; Suida, p. 269 Adler.

13. See T. Cornell, 'Some Observations on the "crimen incesti"', in *Le délit religieux dans la cité antique* (Rome: 1981), pp. 27ff.; A. Fraschetti, 'La sepoltura delle vestali e la Città', in *Du châtiment dans la cité. Supplices corporales et peine de mort dans le monde antique* (Rome: 1984), pp. 98–9.

14. See J. P. Small, *LIMC*, VII, 1, 1994, pp. 846–7.

15. M. Crawford, *Roman Republic Coinage* I (Cambridge: 1974), p. 352, notes 2a, b, c, and discussion pp. 355–6; prior to this most notably J.-P. Morel, 'Thèmes sabins et thèmes numaiques dans le monnayage de la République romaine', *MEFR*, 74, 1962, pp. 32ff.

16. Fraschetti 1990, pp. 308ff.

17. The crescent and star are linked instead to the Punic goddess Tanit by Picard, *Les Trophées*, pp. 109–10.

18. *RIC*, I, 2nd edn, no. 299.

19. Small, *LIMC*, VII, 1, 1994, p. 846, with reference to J. D. Evans. The first to write on this was A. Bartoli, 'Il fregio figurato della basilica Emilia', *BdA*, 35, 1950, pp. 292 ff.; see also G.-C. Picard, 'Le châtiment de Tarpeia (?) et les frises historico-légendaires de la basilique Aemilia à Rome', *RA*, 49, 1957, pp. 181ff.; G. Carettoni, 'Il fregio figurato della basilica Emilia', *RIASA*, 19, 1961, pp. 5ff.; F. Albertson, 'The Basilica Aemilia Frieze: Religion and Politics in the Late Republic', *Latomus*, 49, 1990, pp. 801ff.; N. Kampen, 'Reliefs of the Basilica Aemilia: A Redating', *Klio*, 93, 1991, pp. 48ff.; most recently D. A. Arya in Carandini and Cappelli 2000, pp. 303ff.

NOTES TO APPENDIX II

1. A. Carandini and P. Carafa (eds), 'Palatium e Sacra via', I, 'Prima delle mura, l'età delle mura e le case arcaiche', *BA*, 31–3, 1995, but in fact 2000.

2. See A. Carandini, 'Le mura del Palatino, nuova fonte sulla Roma di età regia', *BA*, 16–18, 1992, pp. 1ff.

3. J. Poucet, 'La fondation de Rome: croyants et agnostiques' *Latomus*, 53, 1994, pp. 95ff.; Cornell 1995, pp. 70ff.; E. Gabba, *Athenaeum*, 87, 1999, pp. 324ff. Outstanding is A. M. Bietti Sestieri, 'L'archeologia processuale in Italia, o l'impossibilità di essere normali', in N. Terrenato (ed.), *Archeologia teoretica, X Ciclo di lezioni sulla ricerca applicata in archeologia*, (Certosa di Pontignano, Siena, 9–14 agosto 1999), pp. 216ff.; also T. P. Wiseman, *JRS*, 90, 2000, pp. 212–14; J. Martínez-Pinna, 'Los Reyes de Roma entre la leyenda y la historia', *Gerión*, 19, 2001, p. 700.

4. See A. Grandazzi, *The Foundation of Rome*, trans. J. M. Todd (Ithaca, NY, London: 1997) pp. 195ff. I shall not enter into the complex problems of ancient Roman history developed by A. Carandini (Carandini 1997), where grounds for cordial disagreement are clearly discernible, especially in chapter II and also generally throughout.

5. See p. 1.

6. For the various datings of the foundation of Rome see J. Heurgon, *Il Mediterraneo occidentale dalla preistoria a Roma arcaica* (Bari: 1972), pp. 202–3.

7. A. Carandini, 'Palatium', p. 63.

8. A. Gallone, 'Sepolture alle pendici settentrionali del Palatino', in Carandini and Cappelli 2000, pp. 291–2. For the five tombs as 'burials' of 'sacrificial remains' see Carandini 1997, pp. 507–8; Carandini, '"Res sanctae" e "res religiosae"', in Carandini and Cappelli 2000, p. 293.

9. Livy, XXII 7.6; Fraschetti 1981, pp. 51ff.

10. See p. 122.

11. C. Fea, *Delle lodi di Romolo e di Roma secondo l'idea di una nuova storia romana* (Rome: 1832), p. 5. On Carlo Fea see A. C[oppi], *Cenni Biografici di Carlo Fea* (Rome: no date, but 1836); P. Visconti, *Biografia dell'abate d. Carlo Fea* (Rome: 1836); J. Sandys, *History of Classical Scholarship*, vol. III (Cambridge: 1920), p. 219 and p. 244; E. Tea, 'Carlo Fea e gli scavi del Foro romano dal 1809 al 1935', *Atti del III Congr. Intern. Di Studi romani*, II (Rome: 1933), pp. 230ff.; C. De Angelis d'Ossat, 'Carlo Fea e lo studio dei monumenti romani', *Boll. Dep. Liguria-sez. Ingaunia e Intemelia*, 2, 1936, pp. 315ff.; P. Pelagatti, *EAA*, III, 1960, p. 611; O. Rossi Pinelli, 'Carlo Fea e il chirografo del 1802', *Ricerche di Storia dell'arte*, 7, 1978–9, pp. 27ff.; P. Bartoccini, *Roma nell'Ottocento* (Bologna: 1985), p. 323; R. T. Ridley, *DBI*, 45, 1995, pp. 518ff.; and R. T. Ridley, *The Pope's Archaeologist. The Life and Times of Carlo Fea* (Rome: 2000).

12. See A. Verri, 'Le notti romane', in *Al sepolcro degli Scipioni*, ed. by R. Negri (Bari: 1967), especially p. 149; P. Treves, *L'idea di Roma nella cultura italiana del secolo XIX* (Milan: 1962), pp. 55–6; for the place of the *Notti*

romane in contemporary culture E. Gabba, 'Considerazioni su taluni problemi di storia romana nella storiografia italiana dell'Ottocento' [1993],
Cultura classica e storiografia moderna (Bologna: 1995), pp. 106–7.

13. B. G. Niebuhr, *Römische Geschichte*, vol. I, pp. 180ff. For Niebuhrian 'criticism' see S. Mazzarino, *Storia antica e storiografia moderna* (Naples:
1954), pp. 31ff.; A. Momigliano, 'G. C. Lewis, Niebuhr e la critica delle
fonti [1953]', in *Contributo alla storia degli studi classici* (Rome: 1955), pp.
249ff. Niebuhr's sojourn in Rome is well documented in A. Campana,
'Niebuhr e Borghesi', 'Gibbon–Niebuhr–Ferrabino', *Enciclopedia 78–79*
(Rome: 1980), pp. 299ff.

14. J. Michelet, *Histoire romaine. République* (Paris: 1876), 4th edn, pp. 89ff.;
the first chapter of the first book is significantly titled 'Les rois. Epoque
mythique. Explications conjecturelles'. I infer the detail of the work's conception in Rome from G. Monod, *Jules Michelet. Etudes sur sa vie et ses
oeuvres avec fragments inédits* (Paris: 1905), p. 12. Michelet's *Principes de
philosophie de l'histoire traduits de la 'Science Nuova' de J.-B. Vico* (Paris:
1828) also attest to his profound admiration of Vico. Evidently the sojourn
in Rome had a very different effect on Michelet from that on J. J. Ampère,
L'Histoire romaine à Rome, vol. I (Paris: 1866), 3rd edn, p. vii: 'On peut
nier l'existence de Romulus dans une université d'Allemagne; c'est plus dif-
ficile quand on voit de ses yeux un mur qui n'a pu être que le mur de la
petite Rome du Palatin.'

15. See C. Fea, *Storia dei vasi fittili dipinti che da quattro anni si trovano nello
Stato Ecclesiastico in quella parte che è nell'antica Etruria colla relazione
della colonia Lidia che li fece per più secoli prima del dominio dei Romani*
(Rome: 1832). On p. vi there is a reference to Niebuhr, who doubted 'even
the origin of the City that is believed; and the existence of *Romulus*', and
on pp. vi–viii many of the arguments already advanced in the *Lodi* are
repeated. On Niebuhr's scepticism regarding the historicity of the immigration of the Lydians, see *Römische Geschichte*, vol. I, pp. 90ff.

16. Don Agostino Chigi, *Il tempo del papare* (Milan: 1966), p. 100.

17. A. Mai, *Ragionamento letto alla Pontificia Accademia Romana di
Archeologia nel dì solenne 21 di aprile 1837 anniversario della fondazione
di Roma*, printed originally at Bergamo in 1838 and reproduced in P.
Treves, *Lo studio dell'antichità classica nell'Ottocento*, vol. II, *La
Restaurazione* (Turin: 1978), p. 389; see also P. Treves, 'Ciceronianesimo e
anticiceronianesimo nella cultura italiana del secolo XIX', *RIL*, 92, 1958,
pp. 423–4.

18. Mai, *Ragionamento*, p. 396.

19. S. Timpanaro, 'Angelo Mai' [1956], in *Aspetti e figure della cultura
Ottocentesca* (Pisa: 1980), pp. 243ff., from which I draw my citations, and
whose overall reconstruction I share, despite the later paper by P. Treves,
in *Lo studio dell'antichità classica*, pp. 362–3.

20. See S. Mazzarino, *Vico, l'annalistica e il diritto* (Naples: 1971), pp. 44–6,
especially p. 45. See F. D. Gerlach, *Die Zeiten der römischen Könige*,

Vorgeschichte, Gründung und Entwicklung des römischen Staats (Basel: 1863), p. 193. As for the full historicity of Romulus, not only according to Gerlach but also according to Bachofen, and the profoundly anti-liberal values of such historiographical attitudes, see C. Ampolo, 'Bachofen, Gerlach e l'Italia arcaica', *ASNP*, 17, 1988, pp. 881ff.

Bibliography

Alföldi, A. (1974), *Die Struktur des voretruskischen Römerstaates*, Heidelberg.

Ampolo, C., and Manfredini, M. (eds) (1988), *Plutarco. Le vite di Teseo e di Romolo*, Milan.

Brelich, A. (1960), 'Quirinus. Una divinità romana alla luce della comparazione storica', *SMSR*, 31, 63–119.

Brelich, A. (2nd edn) (1976), *Tre variazioni romane sui tema della origini*, Rome.

Bremmer, J. N., and Horsfall, N. M. (1987), *Roman Myth and Mythography* (University of London; Institute of Classical Studies Bulletin Supplement 52), London.

Briquel, D. (1980), 'Trois études sur Romulus', in R. Bloch (ed.), *Recherches sur les religions dans l'antiquité classique*, Geneva, Paris, pp. 267–346.

Burkert, W. (1962), 'Caesar und Romulus-Quirinus', *Historia*, 11, 356–76.

Carandini, A. (1997), *La nascita di Roma. Dèi, Lari, eroi e uomini all'alba di una civiltà*, Turin.

Carandini, A., and Cappelli, R. (eds) (2000), *Roma. Romolo, Remo e la fondazione della città*, Catalogo della mostra, Rome.

Castagnoli, F. (1993), *Topografia antica: un metodo di studio*, vol. I, *Roma*, Rome.

Coarelli, F. (1983), *Il Foro Romano*, vol. I, *Periodo arcaico*, Rome.

Coarelli, F. (1988), *Il Foro Boario. Dalle origini alla fine della Repubblica*, Rome.

Cornell, T. (1995), *The Beginnings of Rome. Italy from the Bronze Age to the Punic Wars (1000 to 264 BC)*, London.

Dagron, G. (2nd edn) (1984), *Naissance d'une capitale: Constantinople et ses institutions de 330 à 451*, Paris.

De Sanctis, G. (1960, 1980), *Storia dei Romani*, vols I–II, Florence.

Dumézil, G. (2nd edn) (1974), *La religion romaine archaïque*, Paris. In English as *Archaic Roman Religion*, trans. by Philip Krapp, Chicago and London, 1966, 2 vols.

Fraschetti, A. (1981), 'Le sepolture rituali del Foro Boario', in J. Scheid (ed.), *Le délit religieux dans la cité antique*, Rome, pp. 51–115.

Fraschetti, A. (1990), *Roma e il principe*, Rome, Bari.

Magdelain, A. (1990), *'Jus, imperium, auctoritas'. Études de droit romain*, Rome.

Mazzarino, S. (1966), *Il pensiero storico classico*, vols I–II, Bari.

Mommsen, T. (1887), *Römisches Staatsrecht*, vols I–II, Leipzig.

Pais, E. (1898-9), *Storia di Roma*, vol. I, Turin.

Pais, E. (1913), *Storia critica di Roma durante i primi cinque secoli*, vol. I, Rome.

Palombi, D. (1997), 'Tra Palatino ed Esquilino: Velia, Carinae e Fagutal. Storia urbana di tre quartieri di Roma antica', *RIASA* I, Suppl. 1, Rome.

Platner, S. B., and Ashby, T. (1929), *A Topographical Dictionary of Ancient Rome*, Oxford.

Poucet, J. (1967), *Recherches sur la légende sabine des origines de Rome*, Louvain-Kinshasa.

Richard, J.-C. (1978), *Les origines de la plèbe romaine. Essai sur la formation du dualisme patricio-plébéien*, Rome.

Rosenberg, A. (1914), *Paulys Realencyclopädie der classischen Altertumswissenschaft* II 1, 1914, cols 1074–104.

Scheid, J. (1984), 'Contraria facere. Renversements et déplacements dans les rites funéraires romains', *AION ArchStAnt*, 6, 117–39.

Skutsch, O. (1985), *The Annals of Q. Ennius*, Oxford.

Ulf, C. (1982), *Das römische Lupercalienfest. Ein Modelfall für Methodenprobleme in der Altertumswissenschaft*, Darmstadt.

Vahlen, I. (2nd edn) (1903), *Ennianae Poesis Reliquiae*, rec. I. Vahlen, Leipzig.

Vidal-Naquet, P. (1981), *Le chasseur noir. Formes de pensée et formes de société dans le monde grecque*, Paris.

Weinstock, S. (1971), *Divus Julius*, Oxford.

Wiseman, T. P. (1995), *Remus. A Roman Myth*, Cambridge.

Wissowa, G. (2nd edn) (1912), *Religion und Kultus der Römer*, Munich.

Ziolkowski, A. (1992), *The Temples of Mid-Republican Rome and their Historical and Topographical Context*, Rome.

Index